IMAGES
of America

REMEMBERING BOONE

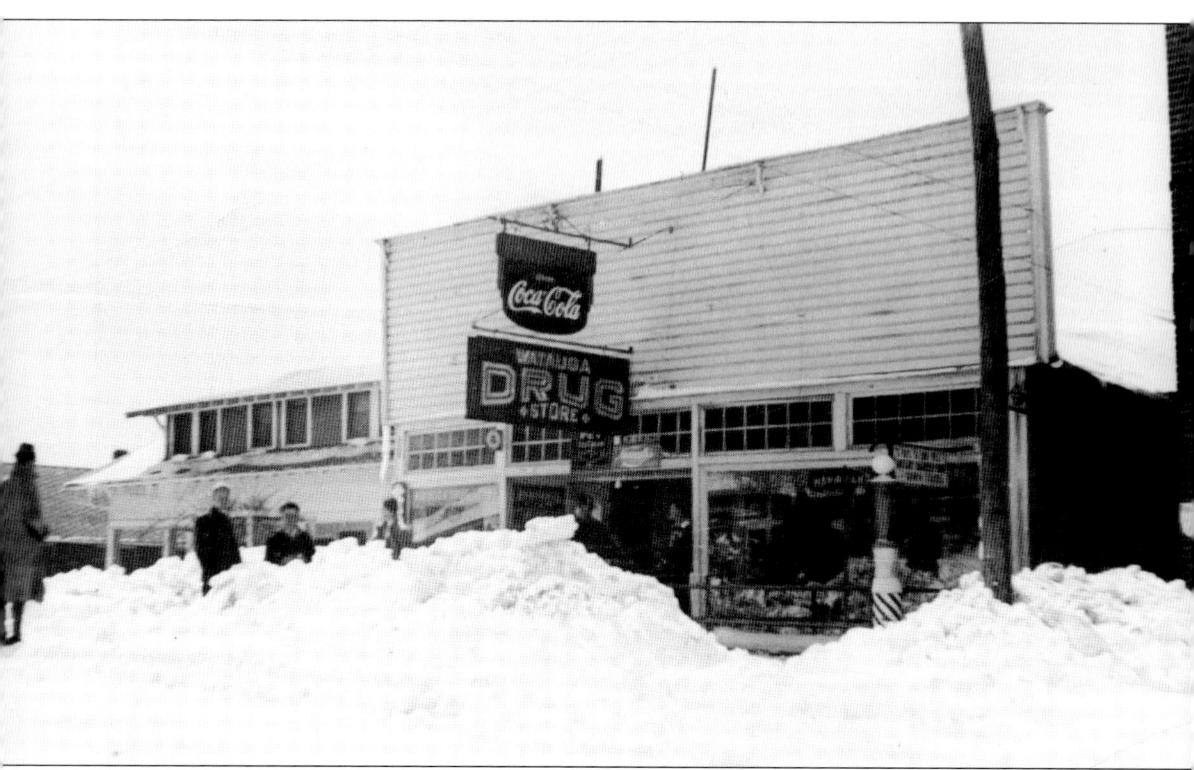

This mid-1930s image shows the David F. Greene bungalow (far left), the Greene Inn (center), and C.L. Rhyne's Watauga Drug Store. When it was first built, the Greene Inn incorporated a portion of the original Councill's Store building, which had been moved to the south side of King Street in the 1880s. All three buildings were demolished before 1960. (Historic Boone Collection.)

On the Cover: This 1923 image of the south side of King Street shows, from left to right, the Greene and Bingham building, the Qualls Block, W.R. Winkler's Garage (in a remnant of the Old Brick Row), the Boone Drug Company building, the Critcher Hotel, the Watauga County Bank building, the Farmer's Hardware block, and the W.L. Bryan residence. (Historic Boone Collection.)

IMAGES
of America

REMEMBERING BOONE

Dr. Eric W. Plaag

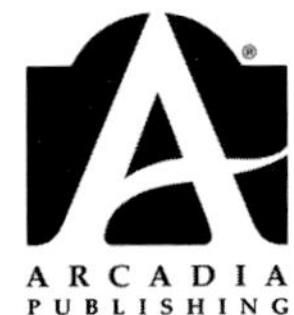

ISBN 978-1-4671-0734-1

Published by Arcadia Publishing
Charleston, South Carolina

Printed in the United States of America

Library of Congress Control Number: 2021943579

For all general information, please contact Arcadia Publishing:
Telephone 843-853-2070
Fax 843-853-0044
E-mail sales@arcadiapublishing.com
For customer service and orders:
Toll-Free 1-888-313-2665

Visit us on the Internet at www.arcadiapublishing.com

*To Palmer Blair, Paul and Ruby Weston, George Flowers,
and the many other Boone photographers whose images
of their present help us better understand our past.*

Contents

ACKNOWLEDGMENTS

This book would not have been possible without the generous donations of photographs and other materials to the Digital Watauga Project (digitalwatauga.org). Those donors include Sarah Lynn Blair Spencer and the children of Palmer Blair, Historic Boone, Bobby Brendell, J.P. Greene, Grace C. Dorsey, the Appalachian Theatre of the High Country, Sam Adams, Leroy Coffey, Roberta Jackson, Curtis Hubbard, Rosemary Virginia, Julie A. Richardson, Rejean Young, Becky Russell Roark Haney, Diane Blanks, Dave Barker, Emily and Andy Stallings, the Town of Boone, the Downtown Boone Development Association, Sai Estep, Lori Ledford Hill, Judy and Allan Wagner, Gary Edmisten, Kathy Blair, Eric Plaag, Carolina Historical Consulting LLC, the Cy Crumley Scrapbook, the Boone Area Chamber of Commerce, and the E.T. Glenn and Lorena Lawrence Glenn Trust. Stacia Bannerman at Arcadia Publishing was patient and understanding as I wrestled this bear into submission, for which I am deeply thankful.

This book also would not have been possible without the absolutely amazing team at Digital Watauga, including Sai Estep, Jennifer Woods, Tara Bradshaw, and Sophie Pillsbury, who worked hard—and mostly remotely—through a global pandemic to make the task of finding relevant materials so much easier than it once was. Thanks also to our principal volunteers, Shannon Russing and Ken Sheldon, who also did a lot of the work to organize these collections. The Digital Watauga team is, in turn, grateful for ongoing financial support from its key donors, a list of which can be found at www.wataugacountyhistoricalsociety.org/join-usdonate. Digital Watauga is a partnership with the Watauga County Public Library, and we are fortunate to work with their outstanding staff, particularly Jane Blackburn, Monica Caruso, Ingrid Hayes, and Kilby Spencer.

Finally, I am most grateful to Teresa, who endures my endless rantings about local history but loves me anyway, and Charley, who sat by my side for nearly every moment of the photograph-selecting, writing, and editing process.

All of the images in this book are from the collections of the Digital Watauga Project, which will be the sole recipient of all royalties and other author proceeds from the sale of this book.

INTRODUCTION

The town of Boone, North Carolina, serves as the county seat for Watauga County, which was created in 1849 from portions of Ashe, Wilkes, Caldwell, and Yancey Counties. Known as Councill's Store as early as 1823, when a post office was established there, the community changed names by 1850 to Boone in honor of Daniel Boone, who was believed to have hunted in the area. (The original map of the town was not reproducible for this book but can be viewed at digitalwatauga.org/items/show/931.) Formal incorporation of the Town of Boone did not occur until January 23, 1872, when the act was ratified by the state legislature. This book is intended to be part of the celebration of the 150th anniversary of Boone's official incorporation.

The Town of Boone sits near the center of the present-day boundary of Watauga County. Located in what is essentially a geographic bowl, Boone is surrounded by mountains on nearly all sides. Immediately to the north of town is the east portion of Rich Mountain and a popular local landmark, Howard's Knob, both of which have long served as barriers to northward movement. To the west is a valley divide that allows passage through Hodges Gap southwest of town, and a small notch northwest of town near the Oak Grove community. To the south, Pine Ridge, Deck Hill, and Yarnell Knob create another difficult barrier that leads to the more distant peaks of Flat Top Mountain and yet another Rich Mountain, which is near Blowing Rock. The area east of town, meanwhile, is dominated by a series of hills leading to Wilson Ridge to the southeast.

As a sleepy county seat for the second half of the 19th century and the early years of the 20th century, Boone primarily relied on local agrarian interests, timber harvesting, some attempts at mining, and court traffic to sustain its economy. However, two changes in the early 20th century dramatically altered Boone's economy and its settlement patterns.

The first was the growth of the Watauga Academy (founded in 1899) from a small teachers' school into the four-year college known as Appalachian State Teachers College. After the four-year college opened in 1929, enrollment continued to increase exponentially, and today, the school is known as Appalachian State University (ASU) and was home to 20,023 students as of 2021—surpassing the local population of 19,965 people that same year.

The second change was the extension of the Linville River Railway from Shulls Mill to Boone in October 1918. While the line served both freight and passenger traffic, its primary significance lay in the introduction of mass quantities of building materials—brick, concrete, limestone, lumber, and sand—into an area that was virtually unreachable by truck traffic in the first quarter of the 20th century. Not surprisingly, Boone's commercial center was transformed over the next 25 years from a near-equal mix of domestic architecture and frame commercial establishments into an impressive array of brick and steel-frame commercial block buildings. After the train stopped running in 1940 as a result of a major flood, improved highways into the area continued to bring new industry and diversity to the downtown area. By the 1950s, Boone was running out of space in its original downtown, partly because the growth of the university from the southeast was also beginning to crowd the area. While annexations of new land into the town's corporate limits had been happening since at least the early 20th century, this growth led to new annexations, particularly to the east, where the small "suburb" community of Perkinsville was located, and to the southeast, where demand for tourist lodging and services had already led to the nascent development of a business corridor. As a result, urban sprawl moved to the east and south of town along US Highways 321 and 421 in particular, where agricultural lands were ripe for development along the two principal roads leading to larger, distant population centers.

While the town is often reported to have an elevation of 3,333 feet, a geodetic benchmark in the heart of downtown near the corner of Depot and West King Streets reports the elevation as 3,323.602 feet. The original downtown area is primarily to the north of Boone (Kraut) Creek, which flows downstream to its intersection with Winkler's Creek on the southeast side of town. Winkler's Creek then merges with the East and Middle Forks of the New River to form the South Fork of the New River, which flows to the northeast on the east side of the current town boundaries. Because of the abundance of drainage from the hills and mountains surrounding Boone, both the original downtown and the lower areas to the southeast are prone to frequent flooding. This has been an increasing cause for concern in recent years, as floods now frequently inundate the floodplain areas that were rapidly developed in the 1960s, 1970s, and 1980s.

Downtown is dominated by its principal artery, West King Street, which runs southeast to northwest through the center of town, with Queen Street to the north and Howard Street to the south serving as important secondary routes. Another major thoroughfare, Rivers Street, dates to about 1968 and runs along the old Linville River Railway railbed; Rivers Street now serves as a major boundary (and occasional Maginot Line) between Boone's downtown and portions of ASU. The primary cross streets in the downtown area run southwest to northeast and are, from west to east, Water/Burrell Street, Depot Street, Appalachian Street, and College Street.

This book is organized chronologically, with chapters emphasizing key issues in Boone's development over time. While a comprehensive history of Boone would be impossible in this format, images have been carefully selected to emphasize issues and experiences for residents of and visitors to Boone during the period between the platting of the original town limits in 1850 and the present. Some of the issues addressed in this book remain a source of contention within the Boone community, but as we historians often say, if studying history always makes you feel proud, warm, and fuzzy, then you probably are not actually studying history. With any luck, the images in this book and the issues that surround them will help readers make connections with the past, allow them to better understand key historical figures and events in Boone, and perhaps trigger some new insights into how Boone can preserve and sustain the qualities that make it one of the most beloved and desirable communities in all of North Carolina.

[Note: Much of this introduction is based on Eric W. Plaag's *Comprehensive Architectural Survey of Downtown Boone, North Carolina*.]

One

Early Boone and the Lost Province

1850–1918

We know relatively little about the first non-Indigenous people who came to the Boone valley during the mid-1700s, but most of them were probably long hunters, trappers, or traders who stayed briefly, perhaps even seasonally, rather than for the entire year. One of the area's first colonial settlers was Benjamin Howard (1742–1828), a Loyalist farmer who kept cattle in the Boone valley and is reported to have hidden in a cave on Howard's Knob during the American Revolution. Howard also kept a cabin on what is now the Appalachian State University campus, where Daniel Boone (1734–1820) is said to have stayed when he hunted in the area.

By the 1820s, Jordan Councill Jr. (1799–1875) had a general store and a post office—Councill's Store—on what is now King Street in downtown Boone. When the North Carolina legislature carved out Watauga County from surrounding counties in January 1849, it selected Boone as the county seat. Officials laid out the streets of Boone in 1850, and by 1851, a courthouse had been built on the present site of the Frank A. Linney House.

The official incorporation of Boone occurred on January 23, 1872, and just a year later, the courthouse caught fire, destroying most of the county records. Boone officials erected a new brick courthouse at King and Water Streets in 1875. A brick jail followed on lower Water Street (now Burrell Street) in 1889, but most buildings remained frame or log, and the town's development was slow and haphazard. By the 1870s, the Coffey and Blair Hotels on King Street provided accommodations during court weeks. Boone's first newspapers did not begin printing until the 1880s. Other than the downtown area, Boone remained a remote and thinly settled hamlet.

Things changed in 1899, when the Dougherty brothers opened the Watauga Academy. Renamed Appalachian Training School for Teachers in 1903, it brought much-needed interaction with the outside world, given the area's reputation for being part of the Lost Provinces—five remote, mountainous counties that were geographically cut off from the rest of North Carolina because of poor roads and limited transportation infrastructure. These two forces—education and transportation—became the catalysts for Boone's development.

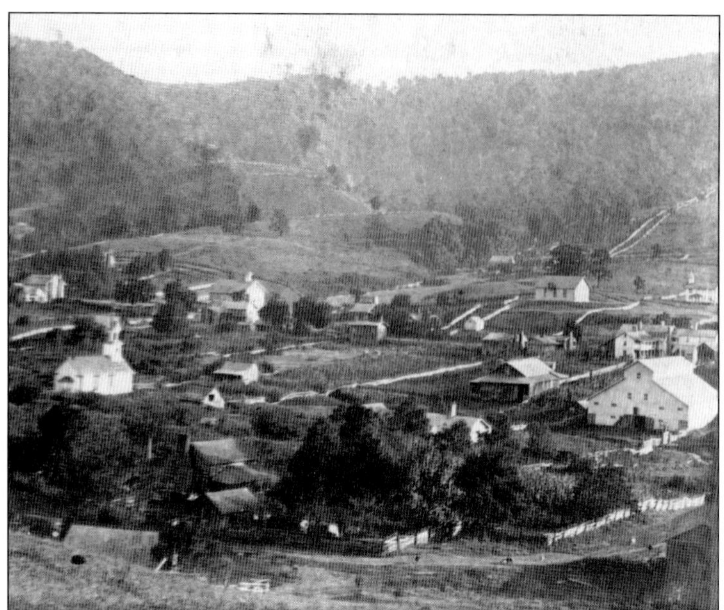

This c. 1885 photograph by L.A. Ramsour of Morganton, North Carolina, was taken from a point on the south side of Boone looking northwest. Notable landmarks include the first Boone Baptist Church at left, the 1875 Watauga County Courthouse at center left, and the steepled Masonic hall on the north side of Queen Street at upper right. (Historic Boone Collection.)

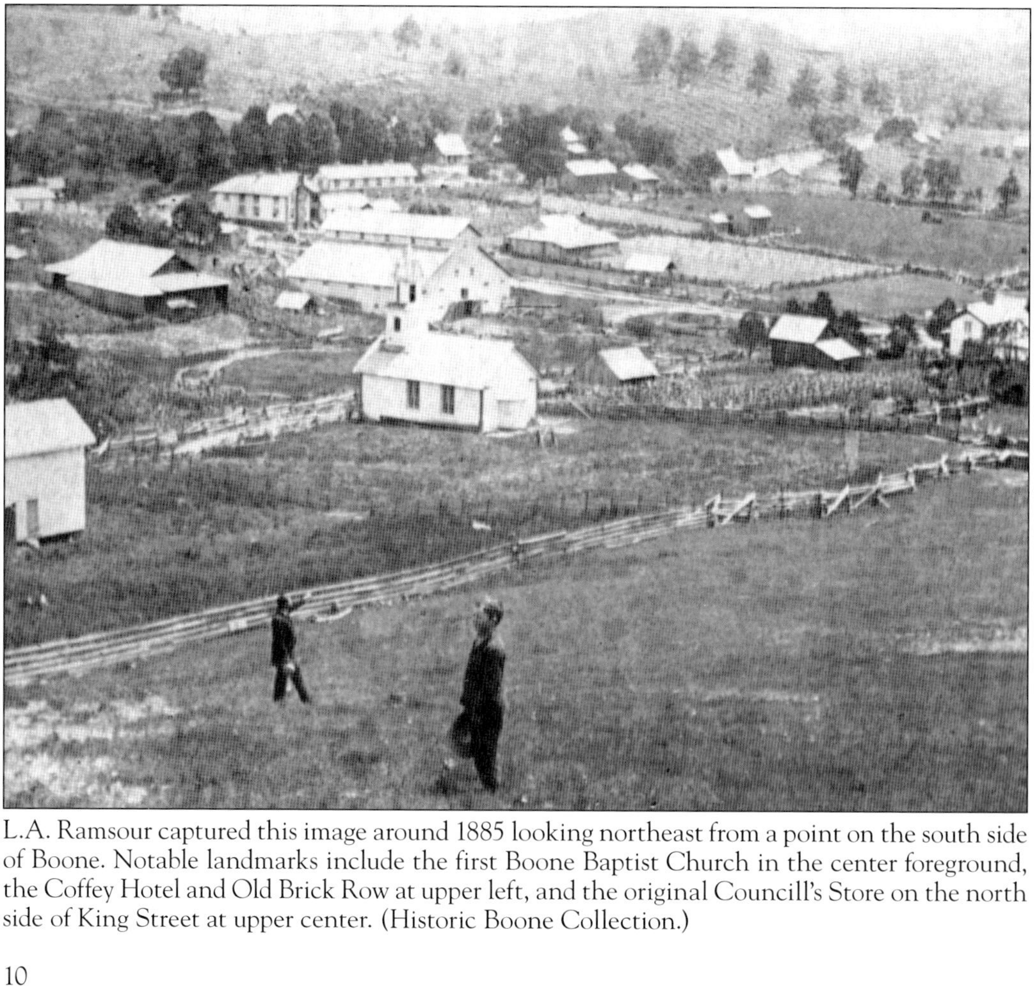

L.A. Ramsour captured this image around 1885 looking northeast from a point on the south side of Boone. Notable landmarks include the first Boone Baptist Church in the center foreground, the Coffey Hotel and Old Brick Row at upper left, and the original Councill's Store on the north side of King Street at upper center. (Historic Boone Collection.)

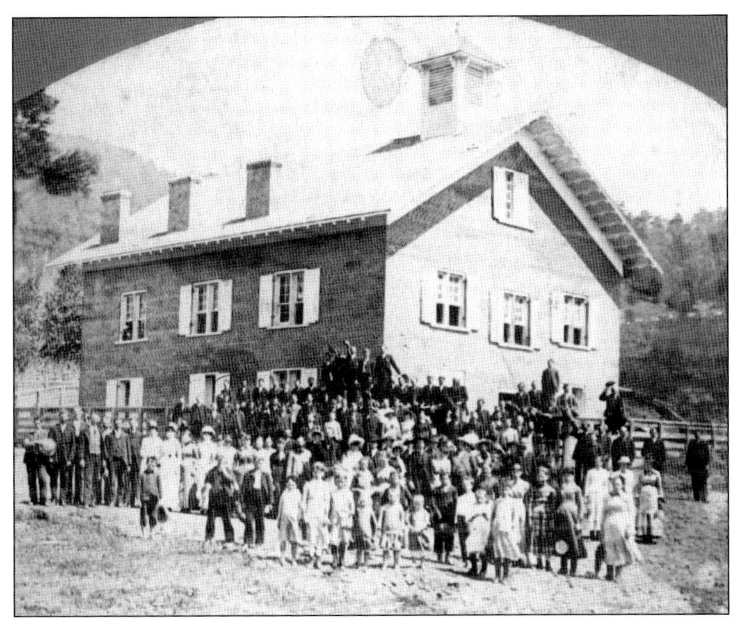

This c. 1885 image by L.A. Ramsour shows Boone residents gathered around the 1875 Watauga County Courthouse, frequently misidentified as a school, with its entrance facing North Water Street. The distinctive chimneys, belfry, and gabled roof were removed in 1906 when the building was converted into the first Watauga County Bank. A private owner renamed the old courtroom Ku Klux Klan Hall in the mid-1920s. (Historic Boone Collection.)

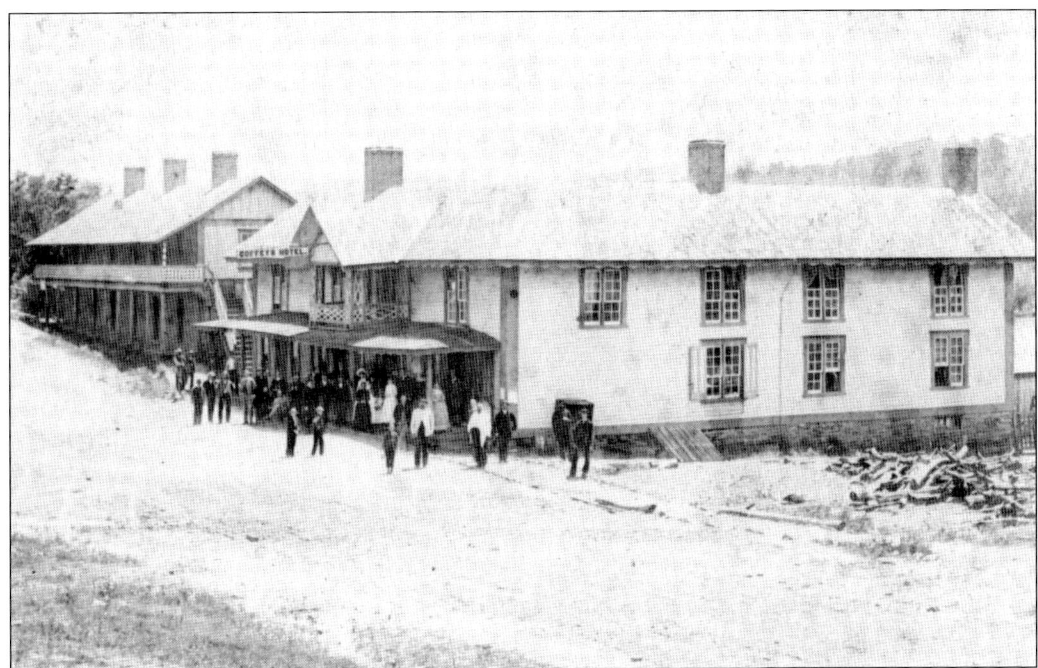

L.A. Ramsour's c. 1885 image of the Old Brick Row (left) and the Coffey Hotel illustrates the poor accommodations available to 19th-century travelers who found themselves in Boone. The Old Brick Row, which originally housed the Coffey brothers' saddle and harness operation, offered budget rooms. In 1888, writer Charles Dudley Warner called Boone "a God-forsaken place. . . . There is nothing special to be said about Boone." (Historic Boone Collection.)

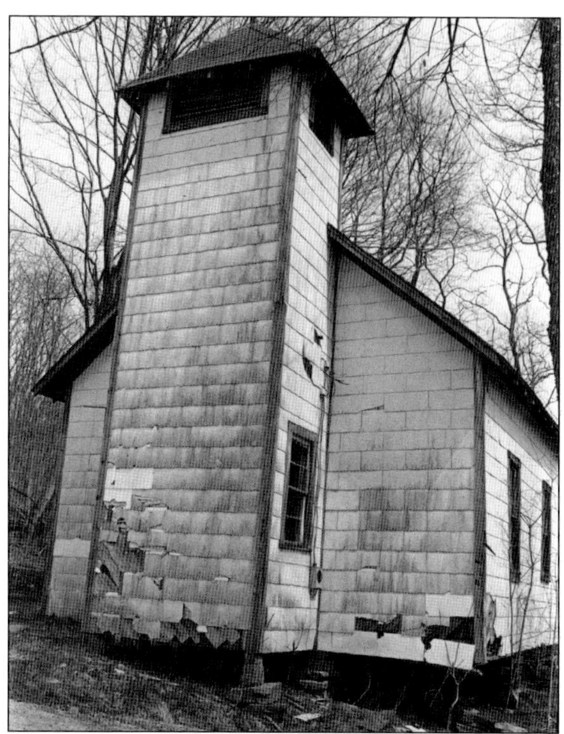

Early members of the Junaluska community, many of whom had been enslaved by Boone's prominent families before 1865, built homes and continued to work the land on the Junaluska hillside after the Civil War. In 1898, Junaluska residents built the Boone Chapel, a Methodist Episcopal (Colored) church. It served as Boone's principal Black church until 1918. After years of neglect, it was demolished in 1996. (George Flowers Collection.)

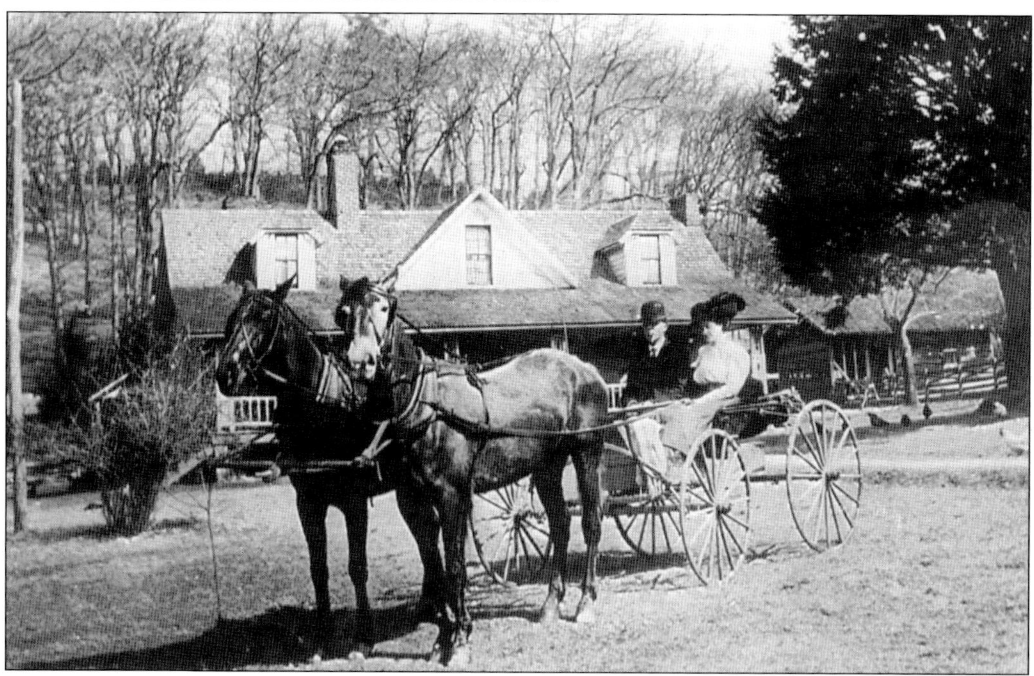

Henry Blair built the original Blair Farm house in 1844; several alterations by Henry and his son George came in the following decades. This image shows George Henry Blair and his wife, Mary Adelaide (Rousseau) Blair, in a horse-drawn carriage outside the home around 1900. Located on the south side of Boone, the Blair Farm was listed in the National Register of Historic Places in 2008. (Historic Boone Collection.)

From Boone's earliest days, heavy logging on the nearby mountainsides, particularly on Howard's Knob overlooking Boone, destabilized soils and led to devastating floods. This February 28, 1902, photograph shows damage and debris following a flood that the town paper described as the worst in a generation. At left is the original *Watauga Democrat* building, with the 1875 courthouse in the distance. (Historic Boone Collection.)

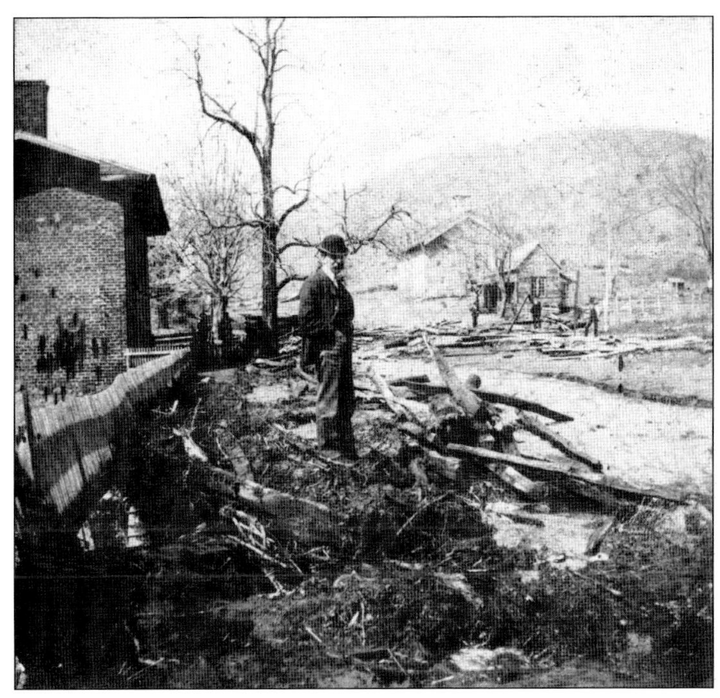

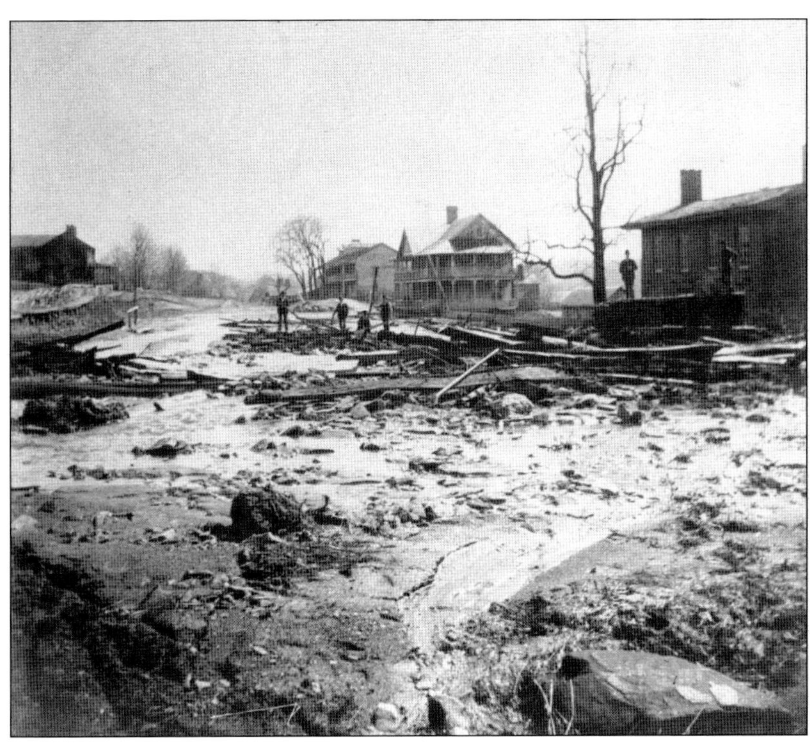

This photograph looks east on King Street and shows the aftermath of the February 1902 flood. From left to right are the J.D. "Crack" Councill House (on what is now the site of the post office); the Blair Hotel (on what is now the Farmer's Hardware site); the residence of William Lewis Bryan, Boone's first mayor (1837–1928); and the first *Watauga Democrat* building. (Palmer Blair Collection.)

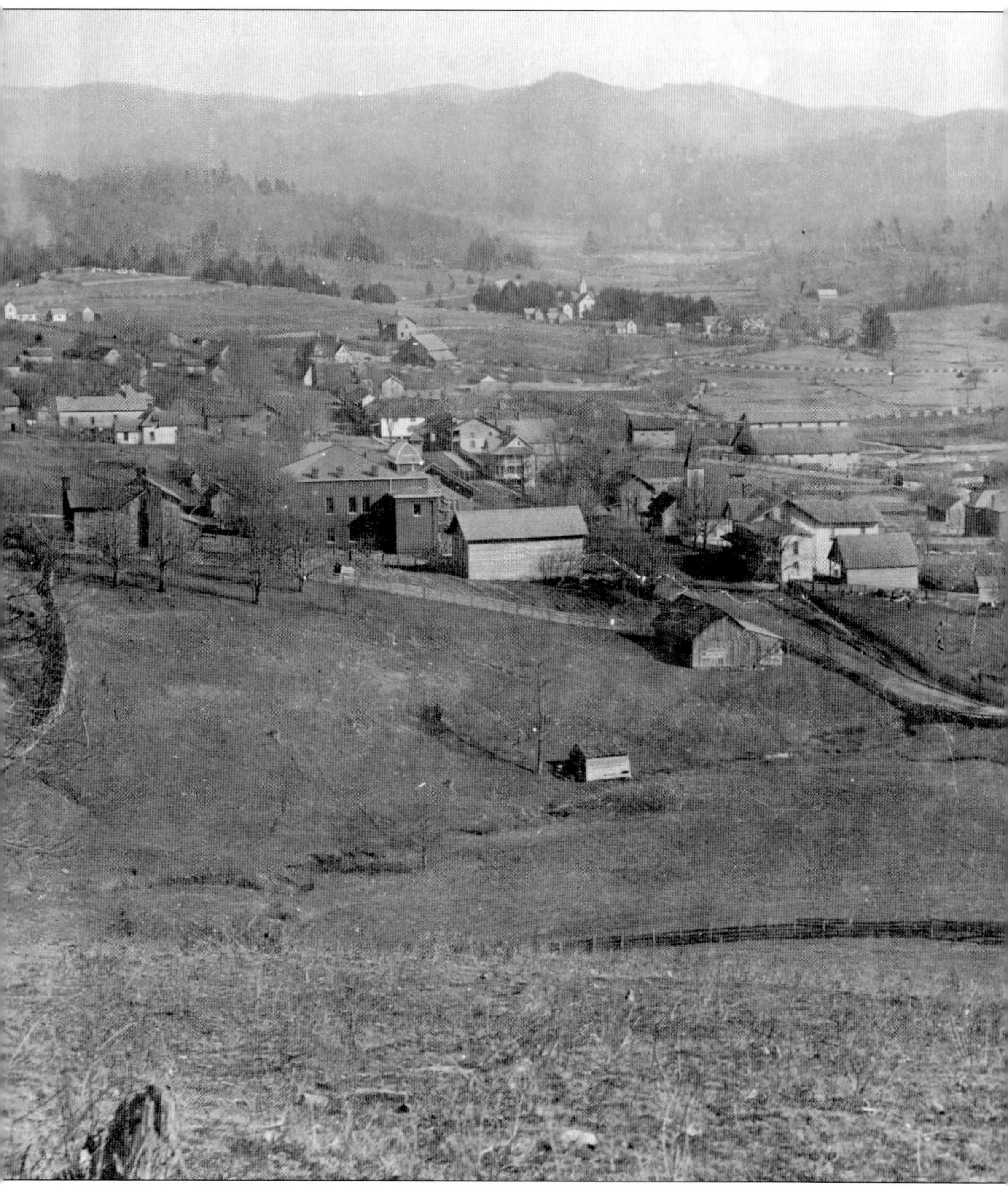

Taken around 1905 from the vicinity of Charles Street, this image offers an expansive view of Boone. The home of Judge Leonidas L. Greene (1845–1898) is at lower right, while the steeple of the first Boone Baptist Church is visible in the distance at center right. King Street runs to the east from the vicinity of Judge Greene's home toward the upper left. Notable buildings on the north side of King Street (in the left foreground) include the 1905 courthouse with its distinctive

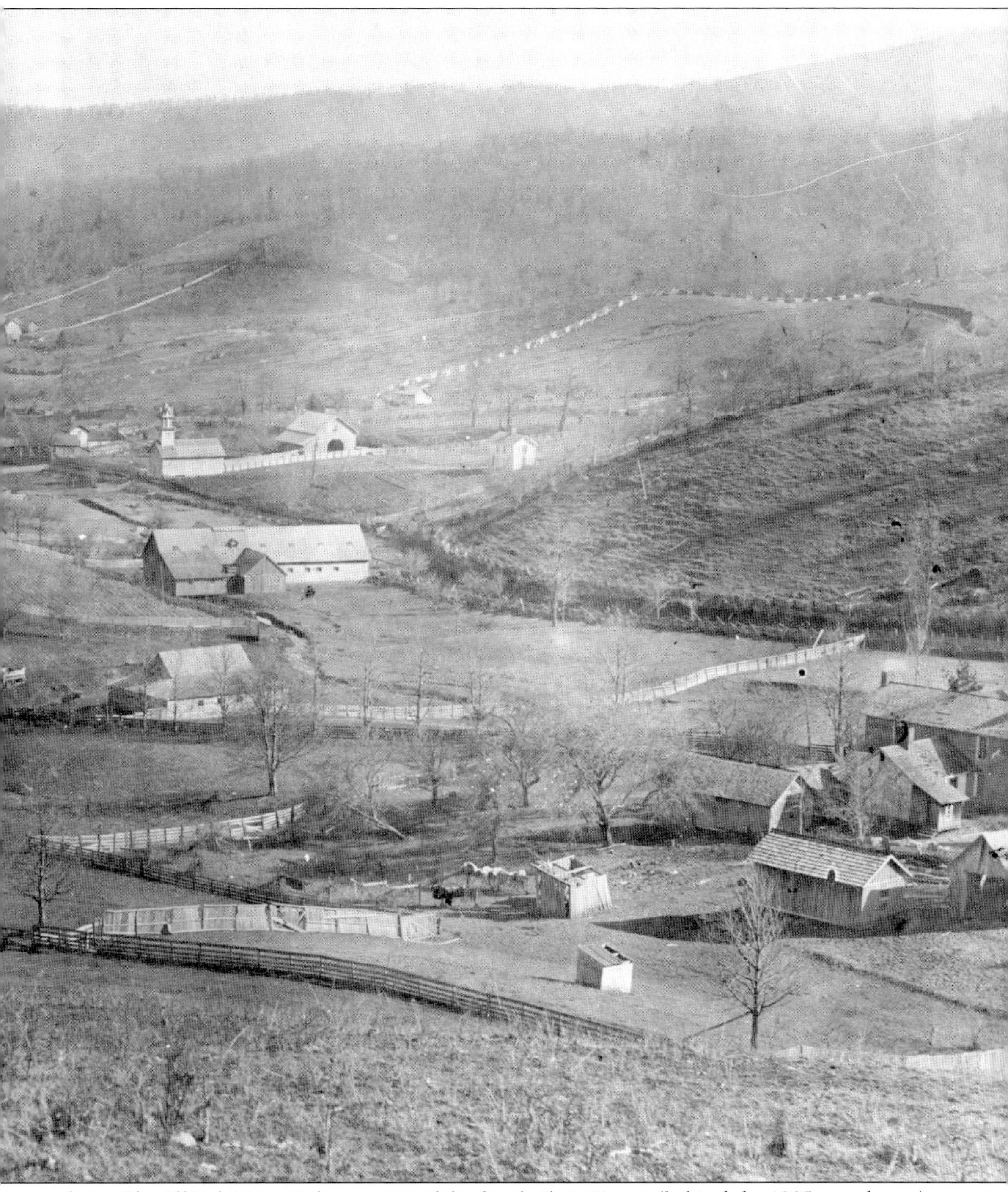

dome; Sheriff Jack Horton's house, one of the first built in Boone (behind the 1905 courthouse); and the 1875 courthouse. Notable buildings on the south side of King Street include the Blackburn Hotel, the old Boone Methodist Church, the Rivers Old Home Place, and the town well at the intersection of Water and King Streets. (Historic Boone Collection.)

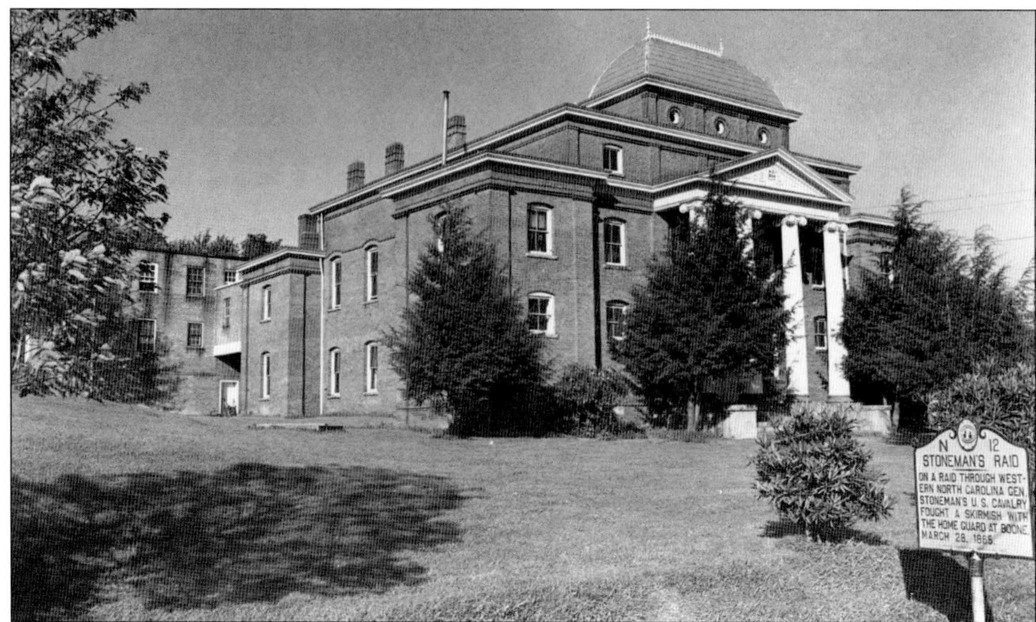

Built in 1905 from a Beaux Arts design by Wheeler and Runge, the 1905 Watauga County Courthouse was the county's third following the 1873 fire that destroyed the original courthouse and the abandonment of the 1875 courthouse. A jail was added to the rear in 1927 and is visible in this 1950s image, along with the historical marker commemorating George Stoneman's March 1865 Union raid on Boone. (Palmer Blair Collection.)

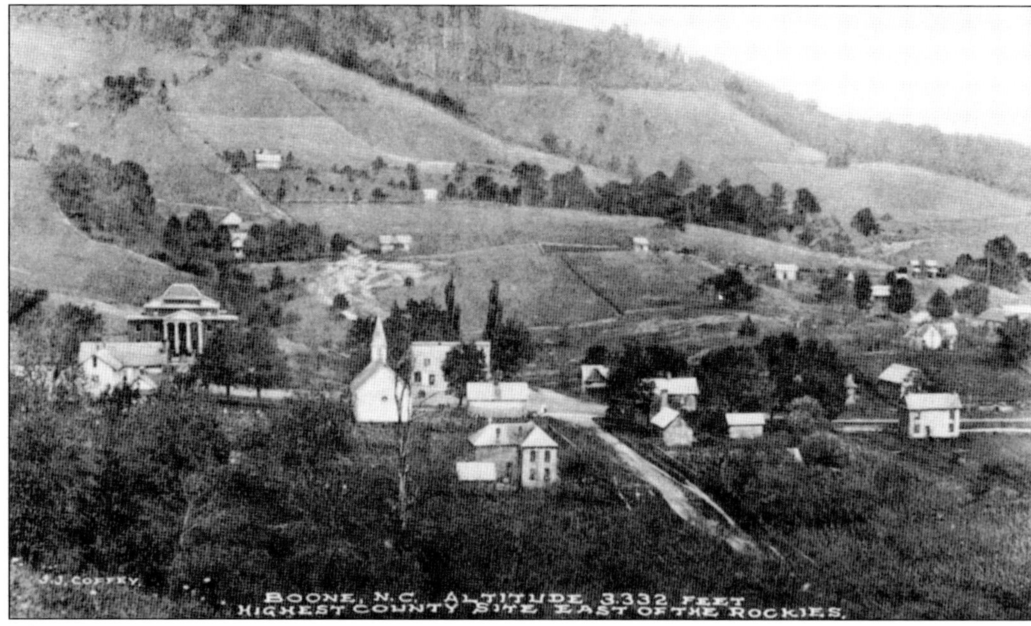

This c. 1905 postcard looks north toward Howard's Knob and shows the extent of logging up the hillside, with the Boone Chapel at upper left. Buildings in the foreground include (from left to right) the Blackburn Hotel, the 1905 courthouse, the old Methodist church, the 1875 courthouse, the Lovill Law Office, the 1889 Watauga County Jail, the Rivers Old Home Place, and the first *Watauga Democrat* building. (Bobby Brendell Postcard Collection.)

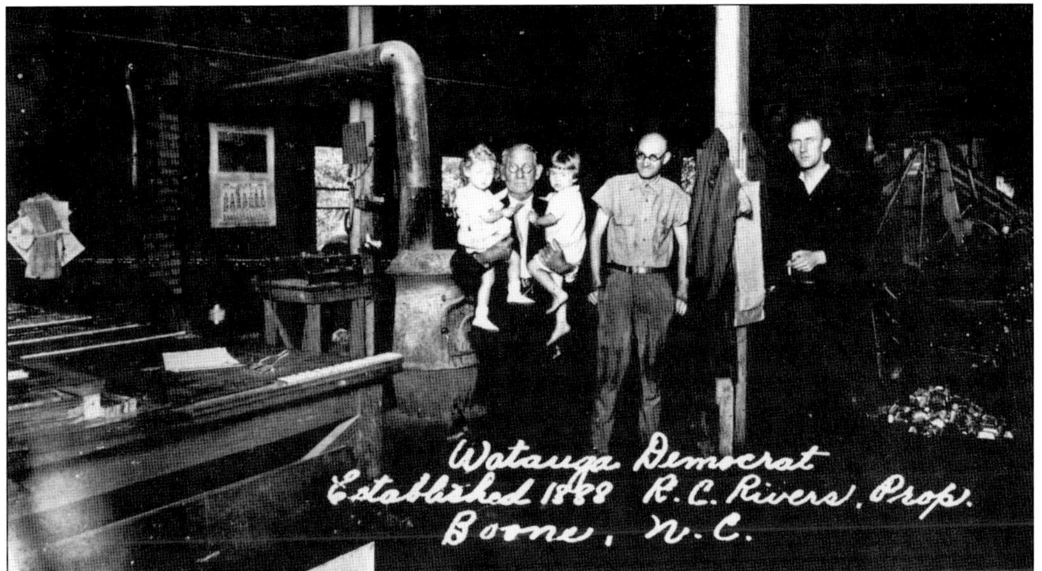

This c. 1902 image shows Robert Campbell Rivers Sr., editor of the *Watauga Democrat* (founded in 1888), holding two of his children—Rob and Velma—inside the newspaper's first building. After the death of his father in 1933, Robert Jr. served as editor of the paper until his death in 1975. Thereafter, his daughter Rachel Rivers-Coffey and her husband, Paul Armfield Coffey, ran the paper until it was sold in 1994. (Rosalea Dorsey Collection.)

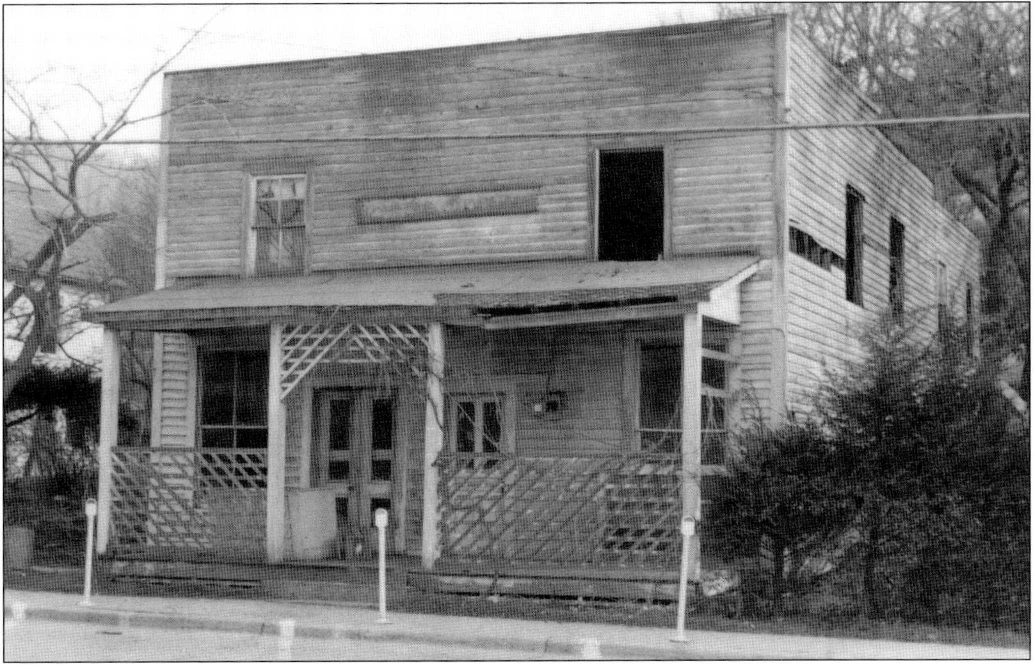

Pictured just before its demolition is the Jennie Coffey Store, on the north side of King Street and originally known as the Moretz and Farthing Store (built in 1899). Jennie Coffey (1852–1954) purchased the building in 1915 and ran a hat shop, school supply store, and variety store there for decades, despite her advanced age. The building was demolished to make way for the two-story brick Hodges Building that was completed in September 1956. (Historic Boone Collection.)

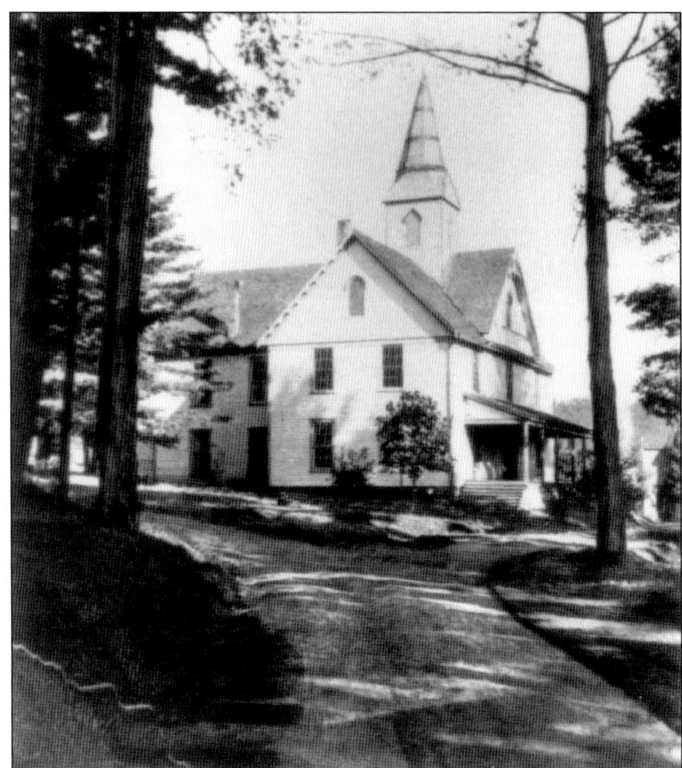

Dr. Blanford Barnard Dougherty and his brother Dauphin Disco Dougherty founded Watauga Academy in 1899 in order to improve education in the High Country. The school's first building was constructed on land donated by J.F. Hardin and Daniel Dougherty and cost about $1,000 to build using donations from the community. The academy became Appalachian Training School, offering a preparatory path for teachers, in 1903. (Historic Boone Collection.)

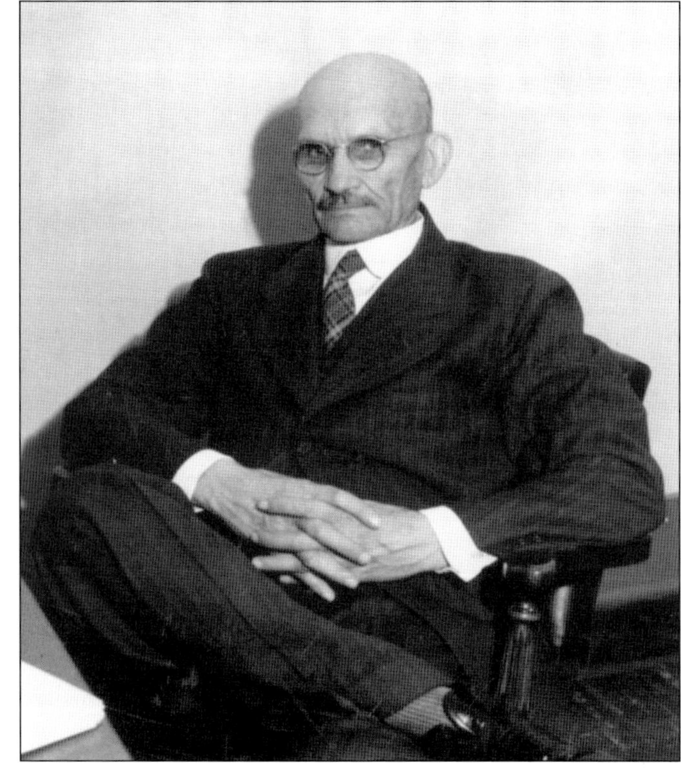

Dr. Blanford Barnard Dougherty (1870–1957), often referred to as Blan or B.B., served at Appalachian Training School and its later iterations in various capacities—including as president—for 55 years. He was also a powerful force in Boone politics and business well into the 1950s, ultimately linking the fortunes of Boone with those of the Appalachian State Teachers College. (Historic Boone Collection.)

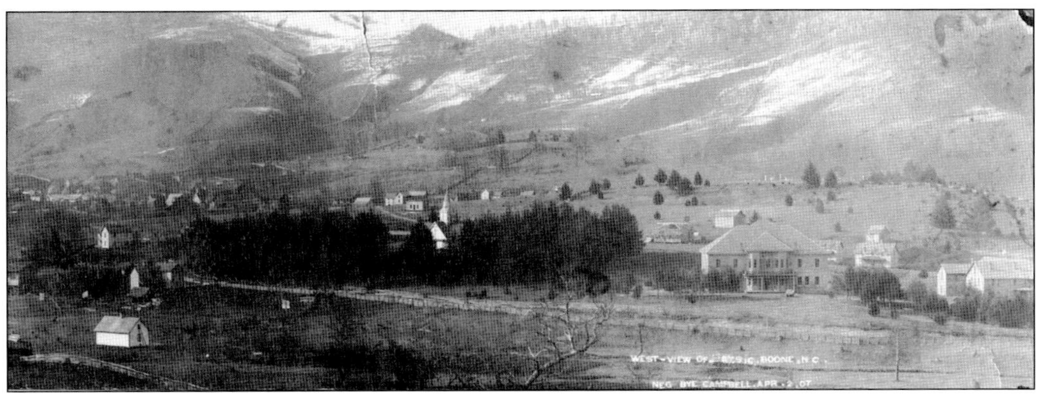

This April 1907 photograph of the Appalachian Training School campus illustrates the extent of logging to the ridgelines during this period. At center is the Watauga Academy building, with the first administration building just to the right. Headstones in the Boone Cemetery are visible on the low ridge above the administration building, while the buildings of downtown are at left in the far distance. (Historic Boone Collection.)

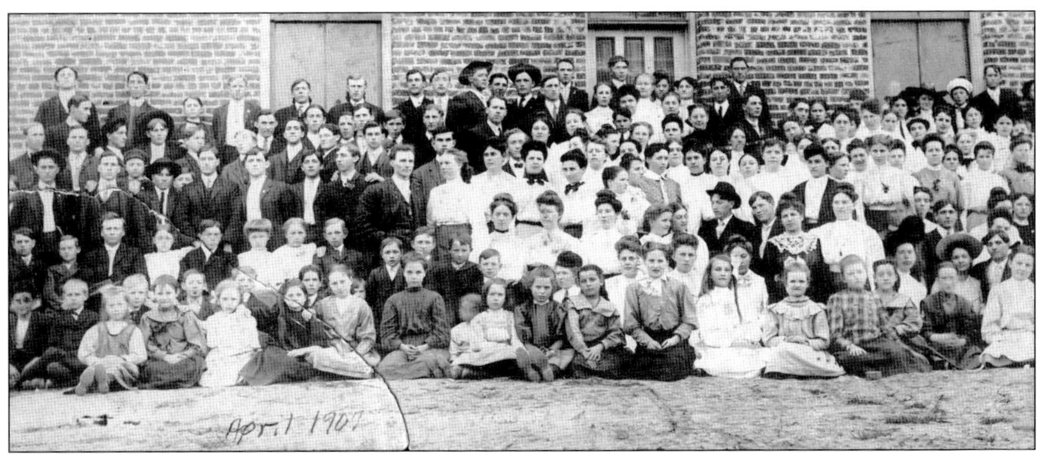

Students of all ages at the Appalachian Training School gathered for this photograph in front of an unidentified campus building in April 1907. While the school primarily functioned as a regional high school and catered to young adults (particularly those interested in teaching), in the early years, approximately 10 percent of the total number of enrolled students were children seeking basic education. (Historic Boone Collection.)

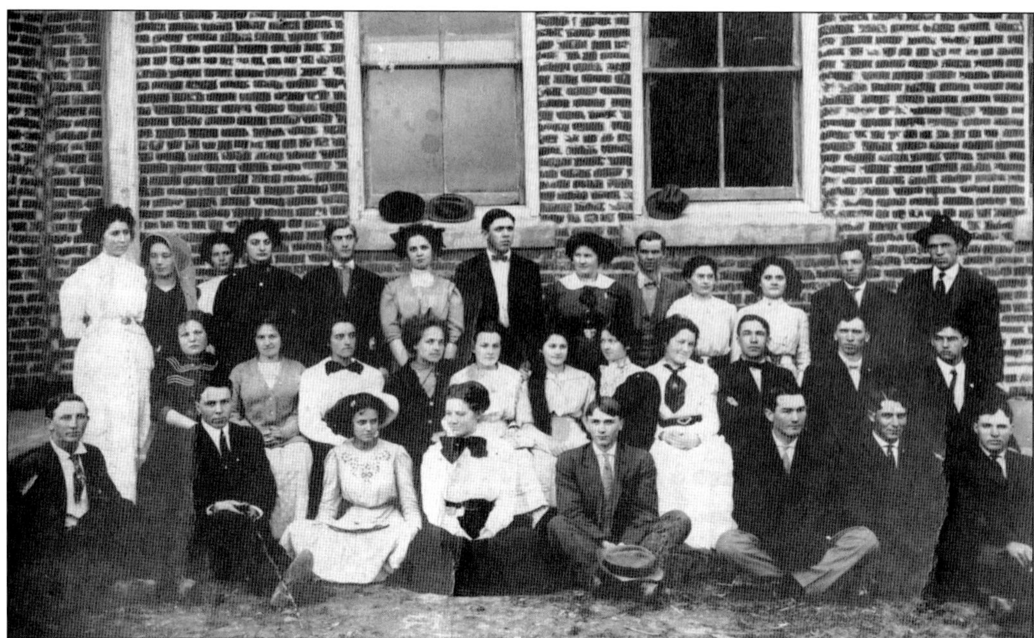

Educational programming at Appalachian Training School focused on the arts and music; Lillie Shull Dougherty (1874–1945) served as the school's first music teacher. She later served as business manager and treasurer of the school following the untimely death of her husband, Dauph. In this c. 1910 image, members of the Appalachian Training School Glee Club pose in front of the first administration building. (Bethel Collection.)

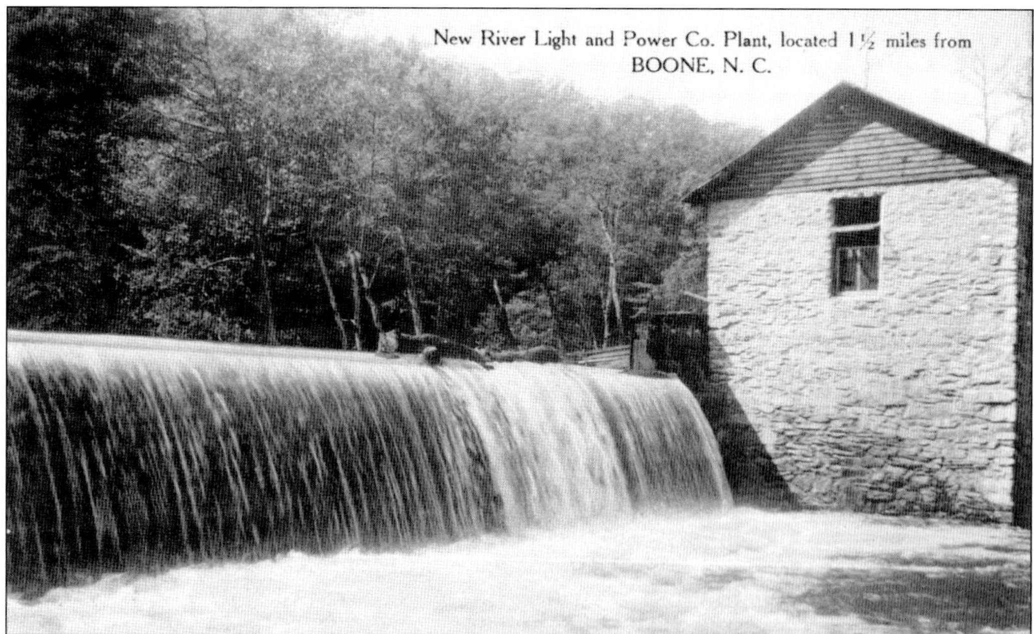

Boone's first electricity was generated beginning in 1915, when the Dougherty brothers established New River Light and Power Company to provide service to the community. This plant and dam on the South Fork of the New River burned in 1923, but ruins of the powerhouse and dam can still be seen from Boone's Greenway Trail. (Bobby Brendell Postcard Collection.)

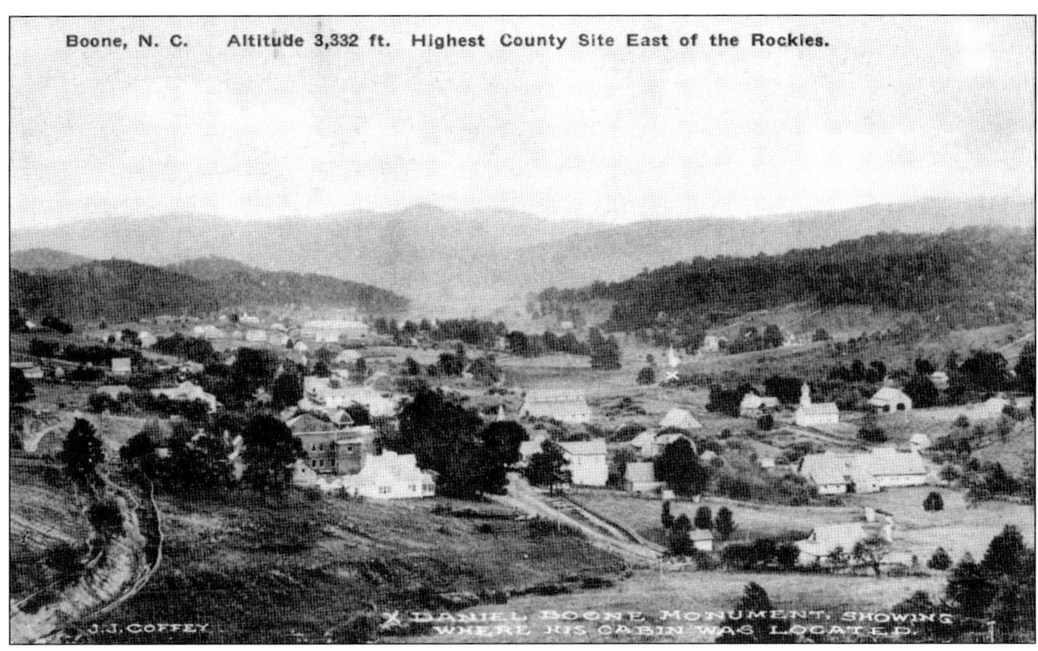

The white "X" at right center on this postcard marks the location of Benjamin Howard's cabin, which is where Daniel Boone allegedly stayed on his visits to the area. In reality, the Daniel Boone Monument, erected in 1912, was probably just a crafty tourism scheme created by Boone mayor William Lewis Bryan. In 1913, Bryan convinced the Daughters of the American Revolution to run their Daniel Boone Trail tourism route down King Street. (Bobby Brendell Postcard Collection.)

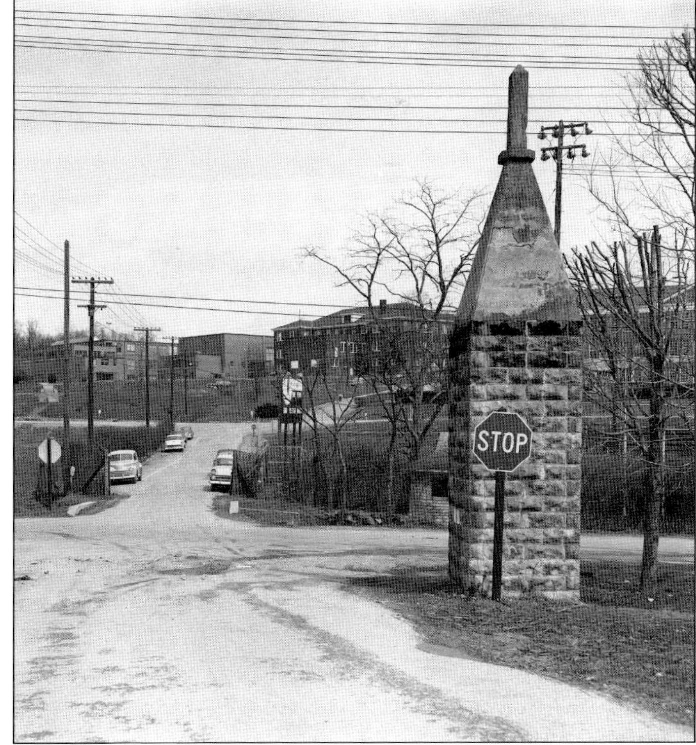

The original Daniel Boone Monument sits on the east side of Newland Drive at Faculty Street in this March 1957 view looking northeast toward the campus of Appalachian State Teachers College. This iteration of the monument sat just north of where the Duck Pond is today. Appalachian State University removed the monument in 1968 during the widening of Rivers Street. (Palmer Blair Collection.)

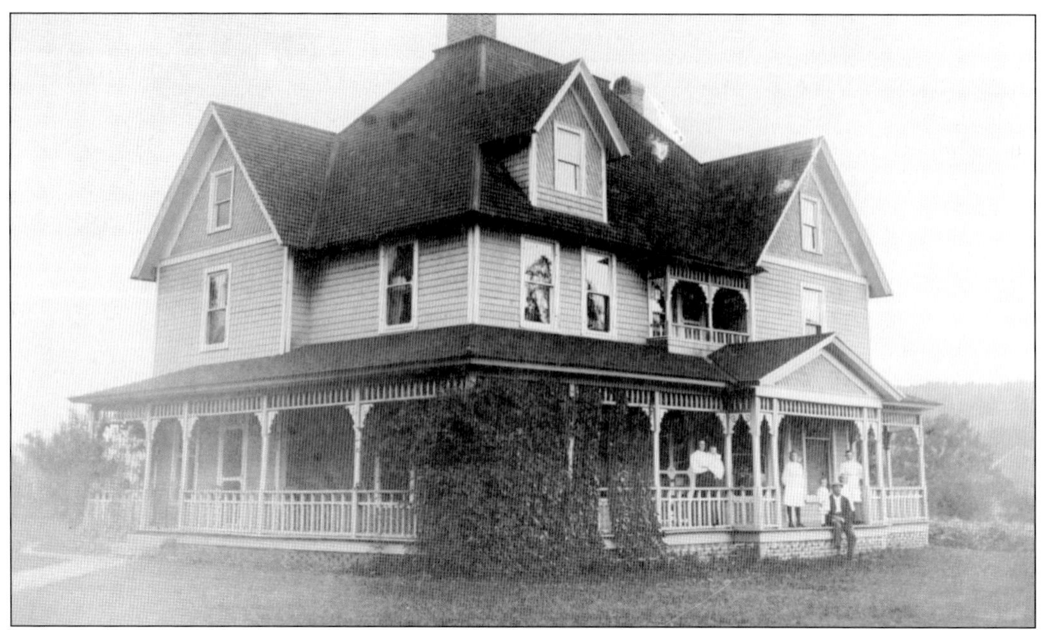

Edgar Stuart Coffey (1867–1925) built this handsome residence in 1900 near the southeast corner of King and Appalachian Streets. It was regarded as one of the most architecturally refined homes in town. Coffey, a law partner with Frank A. Linney and a one-time North Carolina state senator, was a significant early figure in Boone politics and business. This home was demolished in 1948. (Historic Boone Collection.)

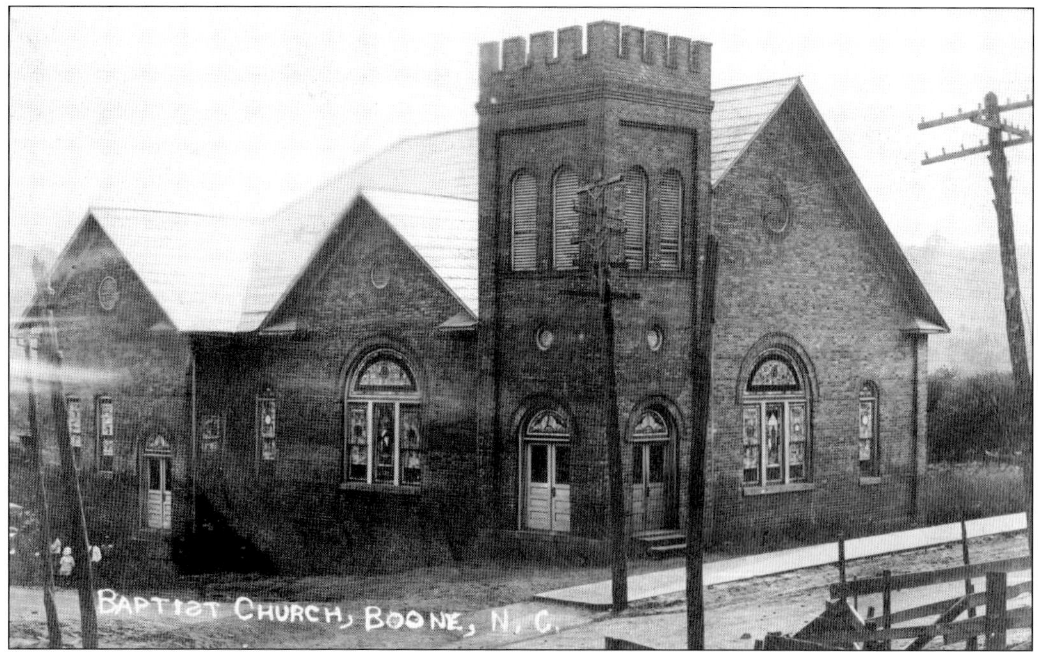

The second First Baptist Church of Boone was completed in 1916 at the southwest corner of present-day College and King Streets. The impressive brick structure and its crenellated tower, which were allegedly plagued by soft brick kilned locally, lasted just 20 years before the present auditorium was built on the site in 1937. (Bobby Brendell Postcard Collection.)

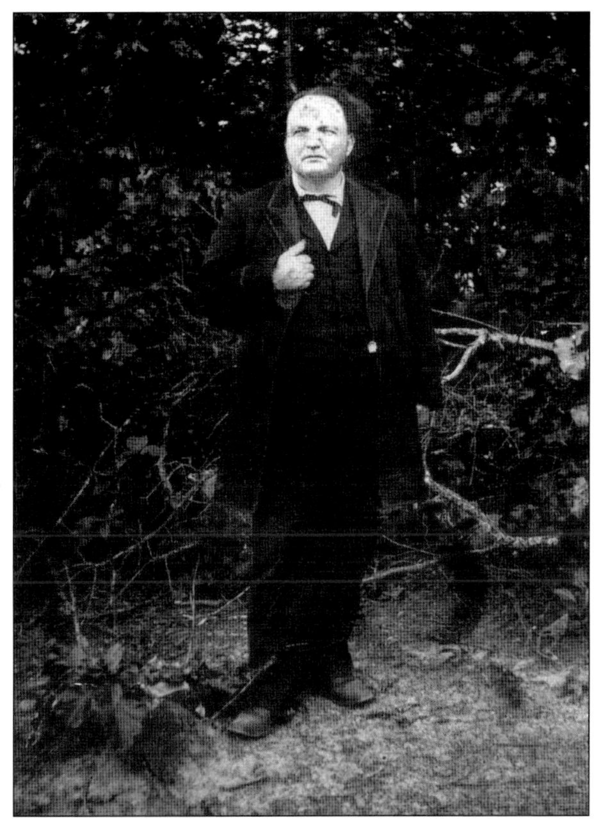

Romulus Zachariah Linney (1841–1910) was an attorney, statesman, and US representative (from 1895 to 1901) who lived in Taylorsville but summered near Boone. In 1902, Linney purchased Tater Hill and much of Rich Mountain north of Boone, building the Junaluska Turnpike from Boone to Silverstone in 1905. His son was Franklin Armfield Linney (1874–1928), and his great-great-granddaughter is actress Laura Linney (born 1964). (Historic Boone Collection.)

Frank Linney Coffey (1936–2017), grandson of Frank A. Linney, poses on the stoop of the Linney House springhouse in downtown Boone in the 1970s. The washhouse was built around 1902, and for many decades served as a gathering spot for Boone residents, whose signatures adorned the plaster ceiling of the interior until water damage caused the plaster to fail in 2020. (Historic Boone Collection.)

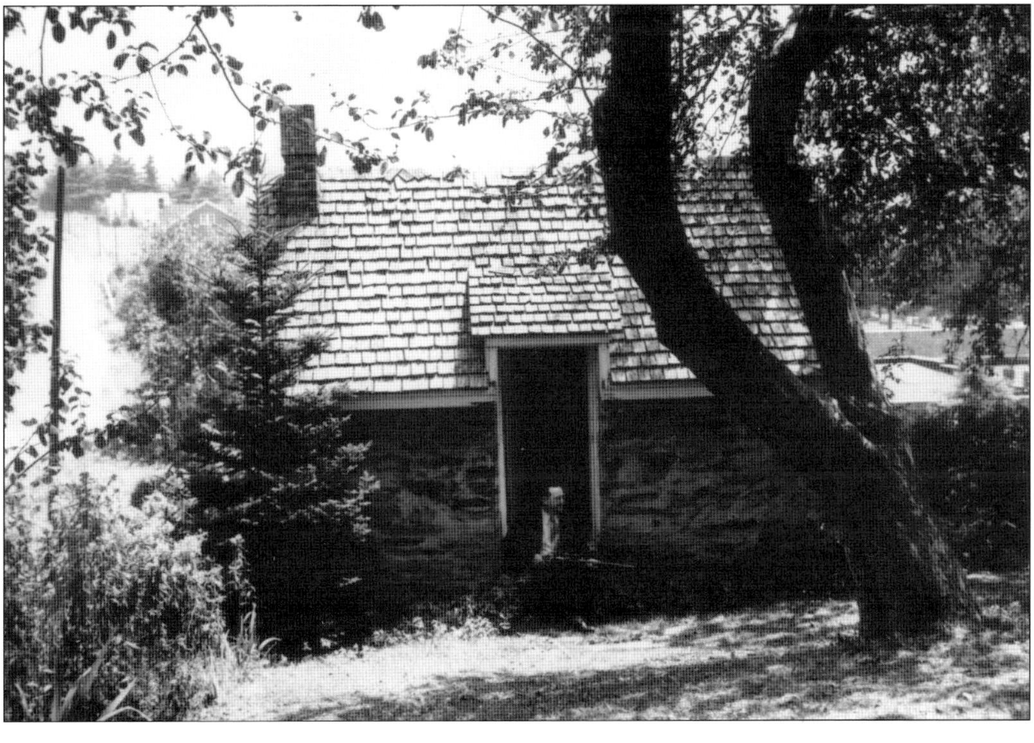

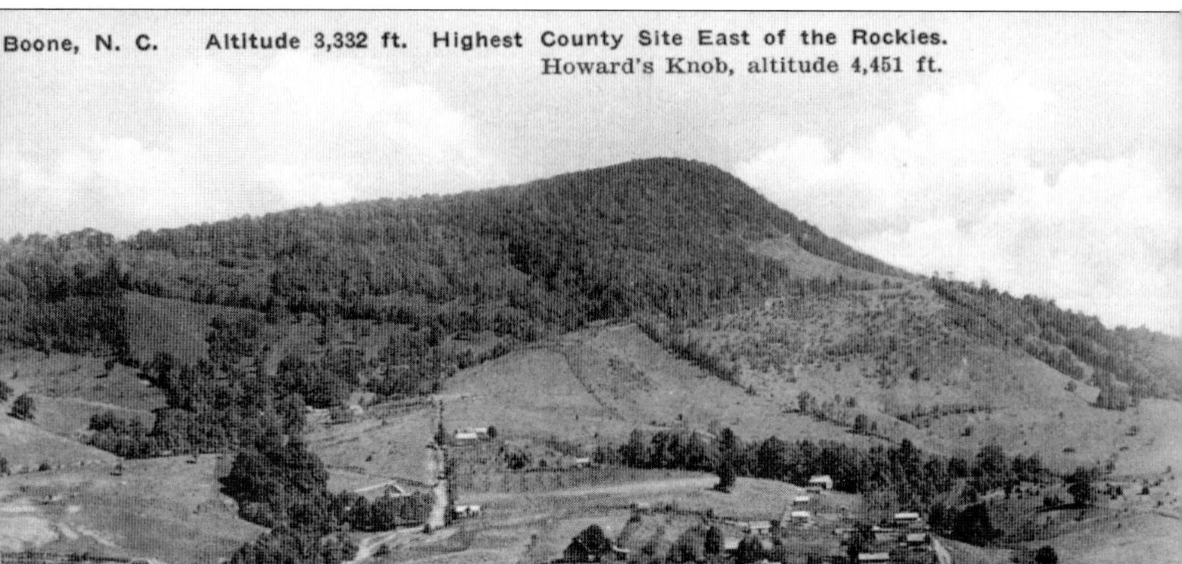

This c. 1915 postcard shows Howard's Knob, the Junaluska hillside, and the Town of Boone from the Dr. H. McDuffie Little residence at left to the Critcher Hotel at right. Other notable buildings on the south side of King Street include, from left to right, the Blackburn Hotel and General Store, the second Boone Methodist Church (with the Watauga County Jail immediately south of it), the Lovill Law Office, the Rivers Old Home Place, the new Boone post office, the first *Watauga Democrat* building, the W.L. Bryan House and cottage, the Blair Hotel, and the Yellow House (an early Boone tavern) with the large Critcher barn to its south. Buildings on the north side of King Street include, from left to right, the 1905 domed courthouse, the altered 1875 courthouse, the Nathan Horton House, the Jennie Coffey Store, the J.M. and Ida Moretz House, the Frank A. Linney House, and Dr. J. Walter Jones's new drugstore. Early Junaluska community homes and a public school for Black students are visible north of the Linney House. (Bobby Brendell Postcard Collection.)

Two

Watch Boone Grow
1919–1939

Following the end of World War I and the influenza pandemic of 1918–1920, Boone quickly transformed into a thriving economic and educational center. The Dougherty brothers had advocated for rail service to Boone since 1907, and they got their wish in 1918 when the Linville River Railway line was extended from Shulls Mill to Boone. The effect of this new railway on Boone was nearly immediate, since construction materials from distant markets were now readily available.

Local businessmen seized on the opportunity by launching a Watch Boone Grow campaign, which encouraged not only new commercial brick structures in the downtown area but also residential development on the fringes of Boone. Local developers encouraged officials to annex these areas into town, expanding Boone's footprint. These new residential subdivisions included Buena Vista, adjacent to the Junaluska Turnpike and an established Black community later known as Junaluska; Daniel Boone Park in the Grand Boulevard vicinity; Wardview Heights, including Hippie Hill and other areas east of Grand Boulevard; and Cherry Park on the old B.J. Councill land.

Just south of King Street, development also spiked as the demand for warehouse space surged near the depot. Between 1924 and 1928, several warehouses went up along Howard Street, a new thoroughfare between King Street and the railroad tracks. The party started winding down in the late 1920s, however, as glutted local tobacco markets meant less cash for development. The October 1929 stock market crash forced both local banks to close, and construction in Boone remained relatively limited until 1936. That year, foreclosures and cheap sales of land in Boone encouraged savvy investors to take chances again, and Works Progress Administration investments in construction of new government buildings, schools, roads, and other infrastructure created another boom that lasted from 1936 until the eve of World War II.

By 1940, Boone featured an eclectic mix of commercial and residential properties downtown, with new subdivisions and a rapidly expanding college hemming in the town on all sides. As the effects of the Great Depression ebbed, Boone also saw a new economic opportunity on the horizon—mountain tourism.

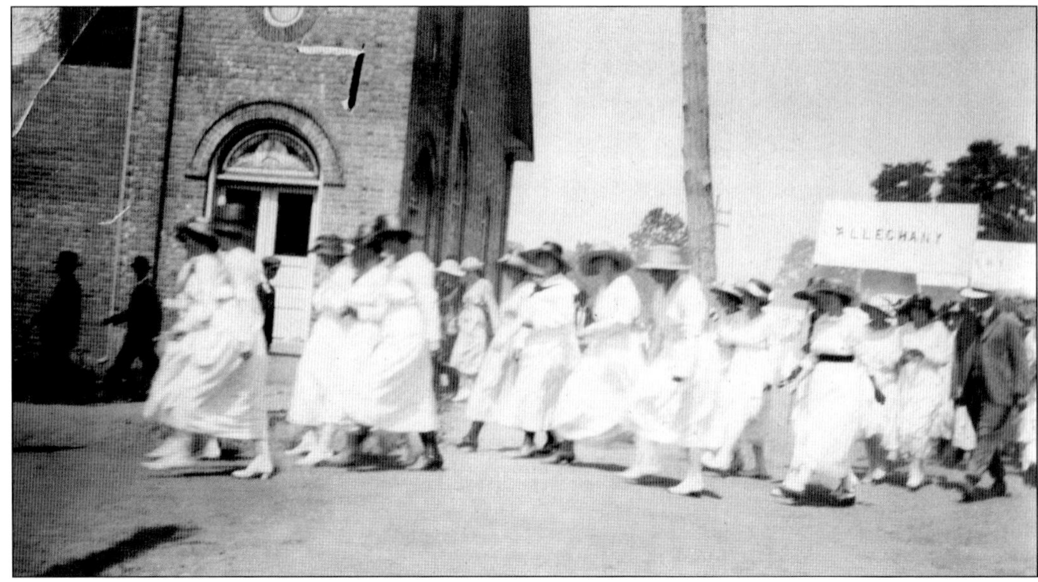

A large group of women dressed in white, likely advocating for passage of the Nineteenth Amendment, march past the Boone Baptist Church as part of Boone's July 4, 1919, festivities honoring veterans of the Civil War, the Spanish-American War, and World War I. Parade chair captain Edward Francis Lovill (1842–1925) supported women's suffrage despite holding less progressive views on racial equality. (H.L. and Gladys Coffey Collection.)

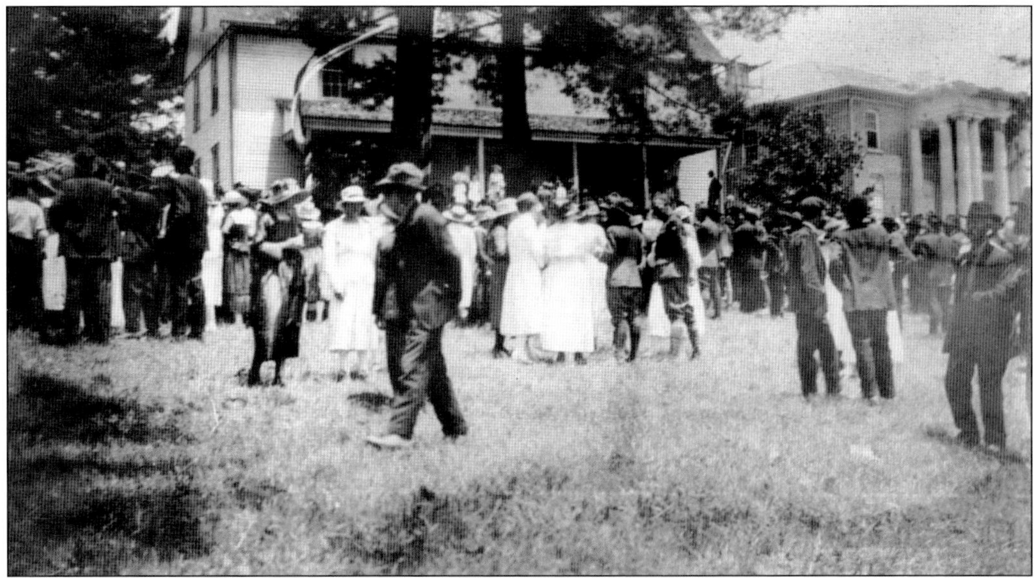

The July 4, 1919, parade progressed down King Street from the 1905 courthouse to the Appalachian Training School campus, where a large picnic lunch was served. This image shows parade participants gathered in front of the Watauga Academy building, with the first Science Hall (built in 1911) to the right. (H.L. and Gladys Coffey Collection.)

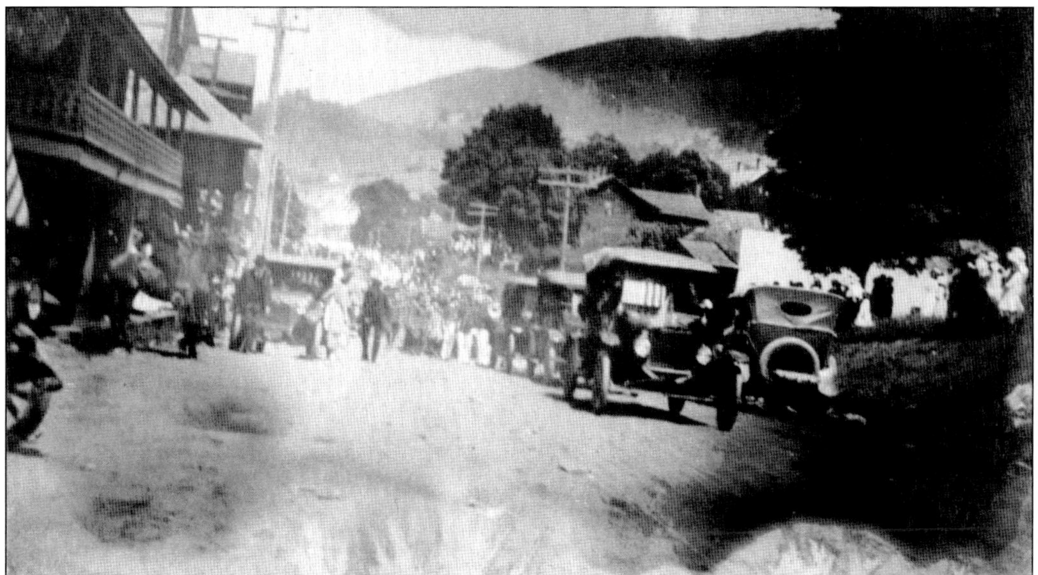

The July 4, 1919, parade moves east on King Street past the Critcher Hotel and the Old Brick Row at left. In the distance at right, between the first two telephone poles, is the J.D. "Crack" Councill House, with Dr. J. Walter Jones's office and drugstore behind the cars and onlookers at right. (H.L. and Gladys Coffey Collection.)

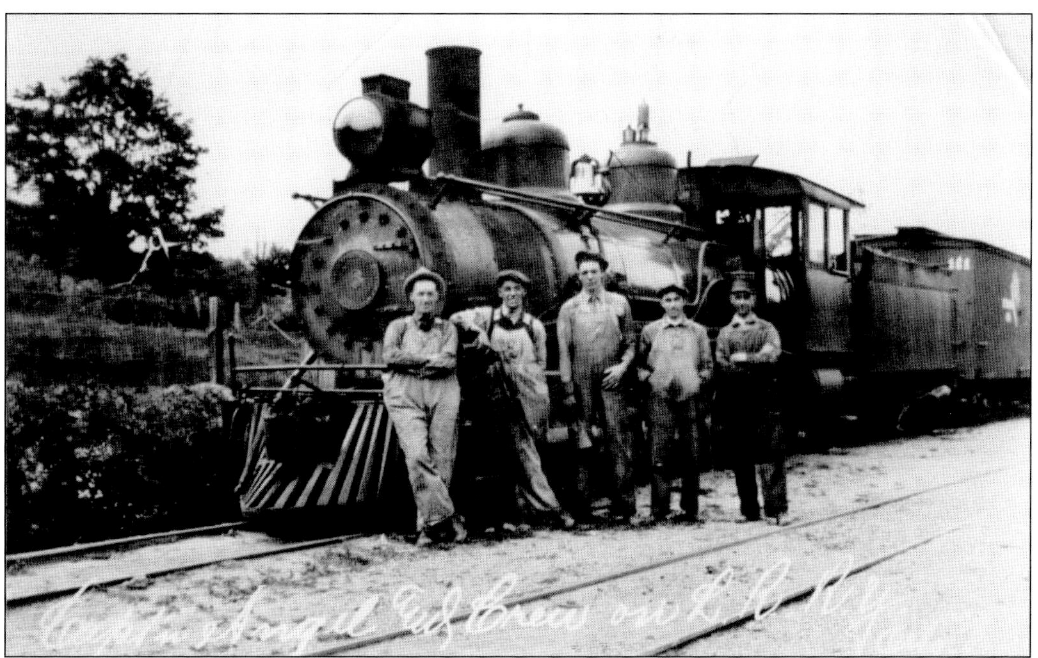

An extension of the Linville River Railway from Shulls Mill to Boone was completed in December 1918, transforming Boone's economy and architecture nearly overnight. Pictured in this October 1923 image of engine No. 6 at Boone are, from left to right, C.B. Angel, conductor; Paul Fletcher, brakeman; Ted Blalock, brakeman; Brownie Allison, engineer; and Mox Daniels. (Palmer Blair Collection.)

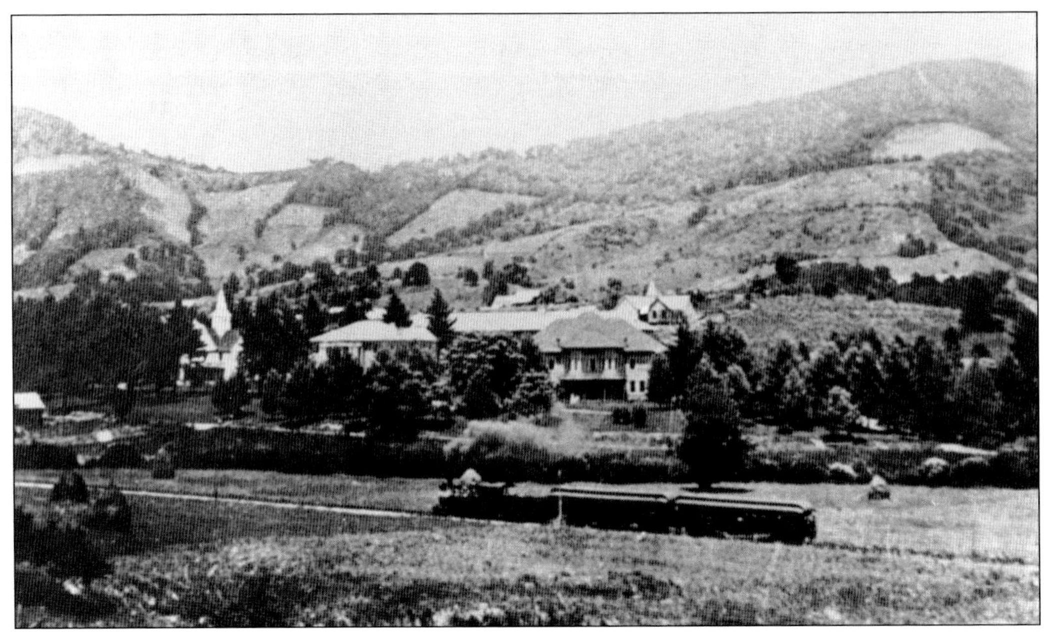

The Linville River Railway provided passenger and freight service to Boone, making high-quality brick, steel, and finished lumber readily accessible during the Watch Boone Grow campaign of the early 1920s. In this image, a passenger excursion train rumbles past the campus of Appalachian Training School on its way toward the Boone depot. (George Flowers Collection.)

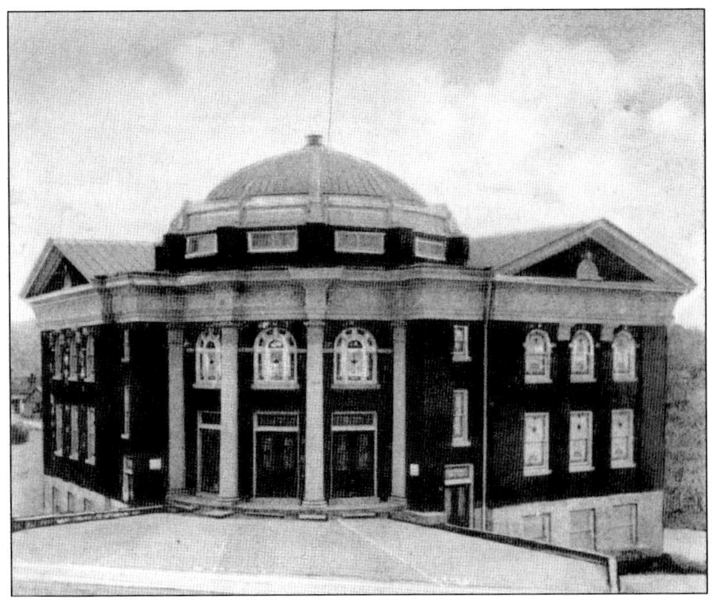

Wiley Gordon Hartzog (1885–1976) was the final contractor on the architecturally stunning, rotunda-form third Boone Methodist Church on King Street, replete with clerestory windows, dentiled entablature, and Corinthian columns. The church opened for services on July 29, 1923. This crop from a 1920s postcard shows the third church shortly after construction was completed. (Bobby Brendell Postcard Collection.)

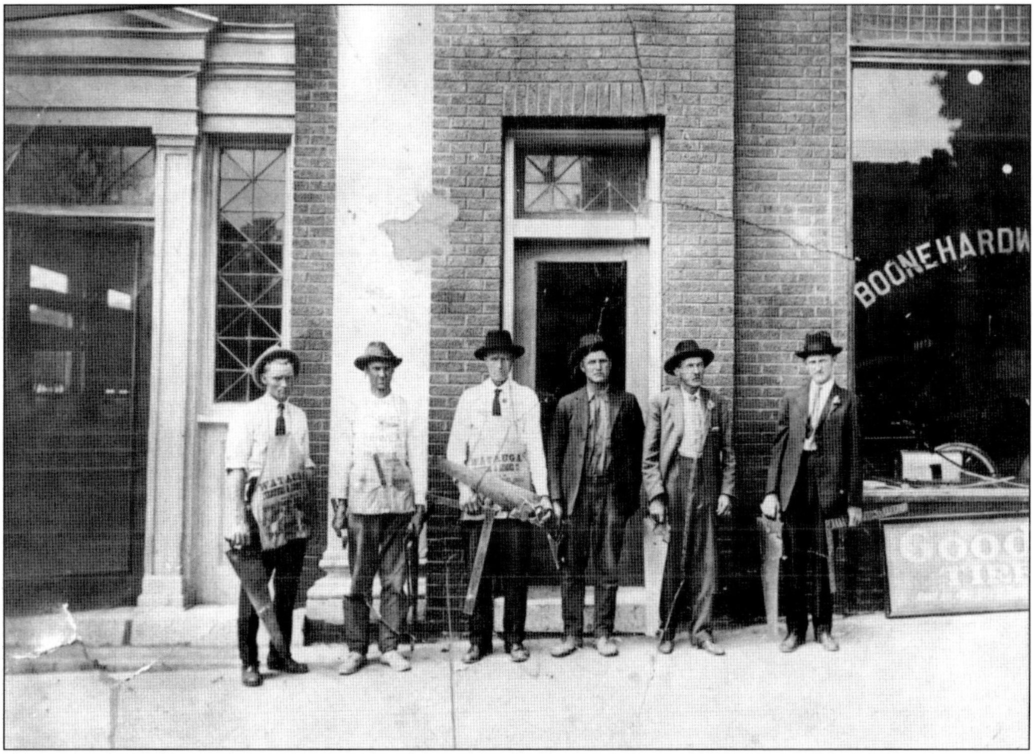

Carpenters on the Watauga County Bank, which was completed in 1923 from a design by Clarence B. Kearfott (1884–1977), take a break to pose in front of their handiwork. The workers are, from left to right, unidentified, Larkin Enzer Beach, Will Hodges, Frank Cullers, unidentified, and Pink Hodges. Will Hodges and McGhee Brothers were the primary contractors on the project. (Whitaker Family Collection.)

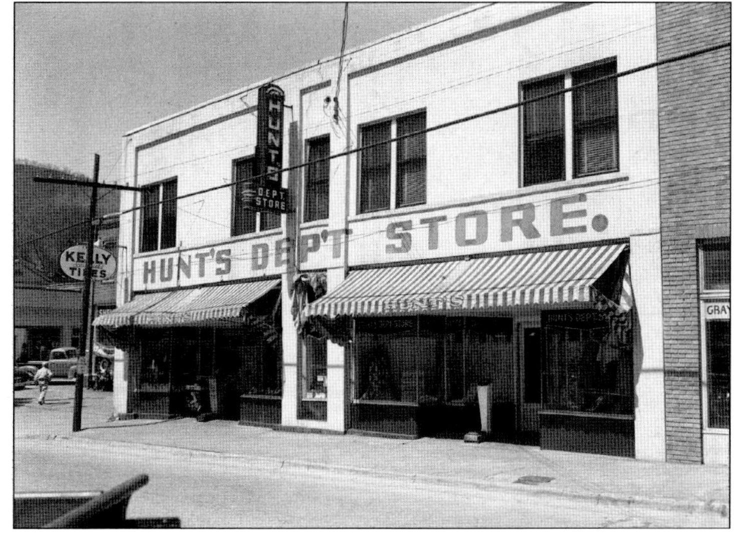

The J. Walter Jones block, completed in 1922 by Triplett and Poe of Lenoir, originally housed a bank, telephone exchange, lumber merchant, and dentist before it had a string of department stores as tenants. Hunt's Department Store, shown here in 1952, occupied the block from 1943 to 1987. The building has been the home of the Mast General Store since 1987. (Palmer Blair Collection.)

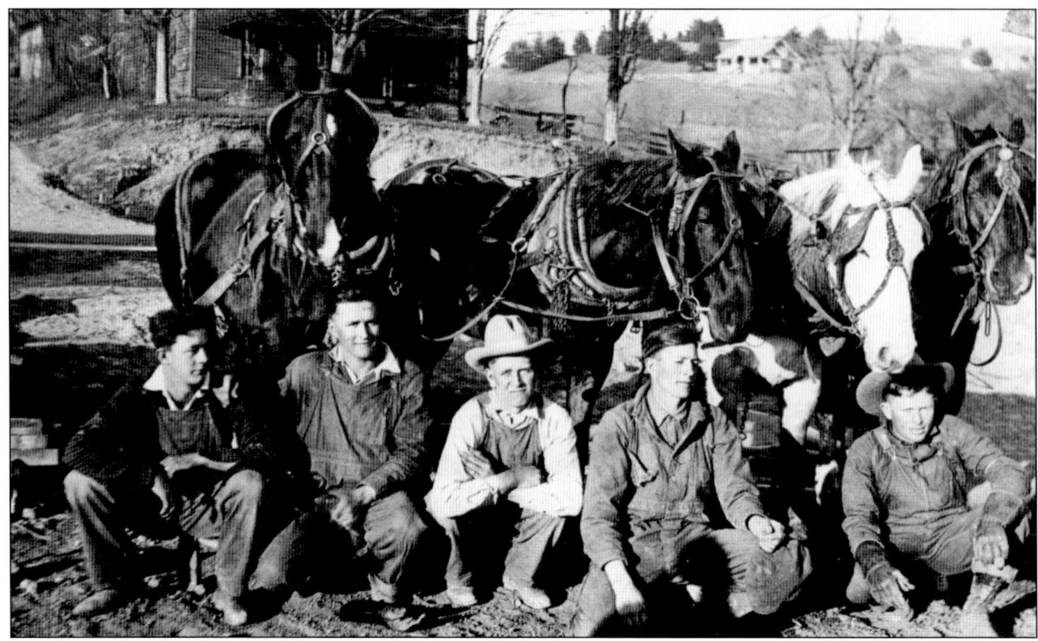

In this c. 1925 image, Willard Watson, Clyde Triplett, Ernest Hicks, Jess Laws, and Rob Boone pose with their horses in front of the J.D. "Crack" Councill House (the current site of the downtown Boone post office). The men may have been working on the Frank A. Linney Block at the time. The newly completed house at 224 Grand Boulevard is visible at upper right. (Historic Boone Collection.)

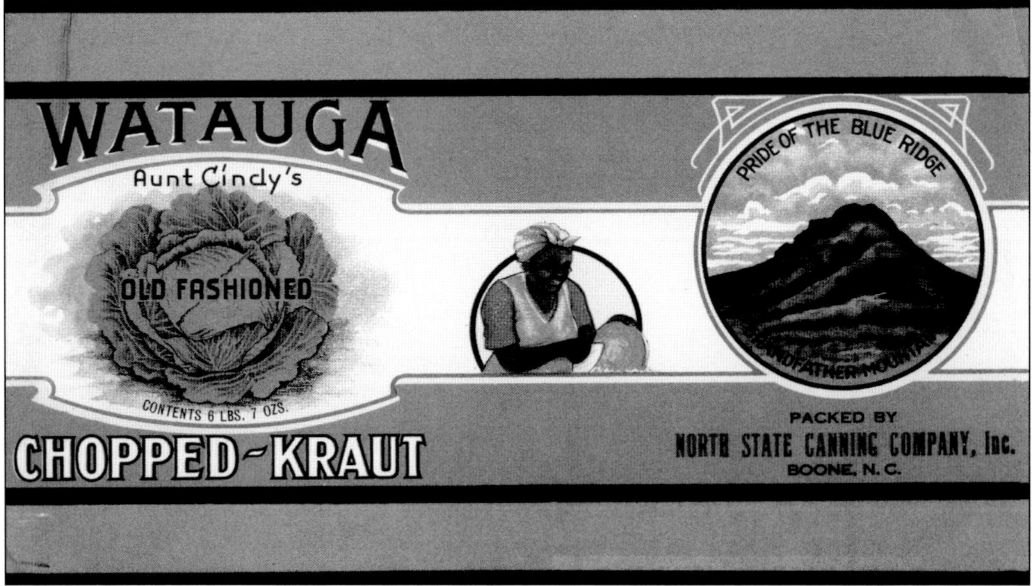

H. Neal Blair opened a canning operation at the west end of King Street in 1923, then leased it to the North State Canning Company, run by Dr. H.B. Perry and W.F. Miller, in 1926. It remained active into the 1980s. North State traditionally dumped runoff directly into Boone Creek, creating a foul odor that prompted locals to nickname the stream Kraut Creek. (Eric Plaag Collection.)

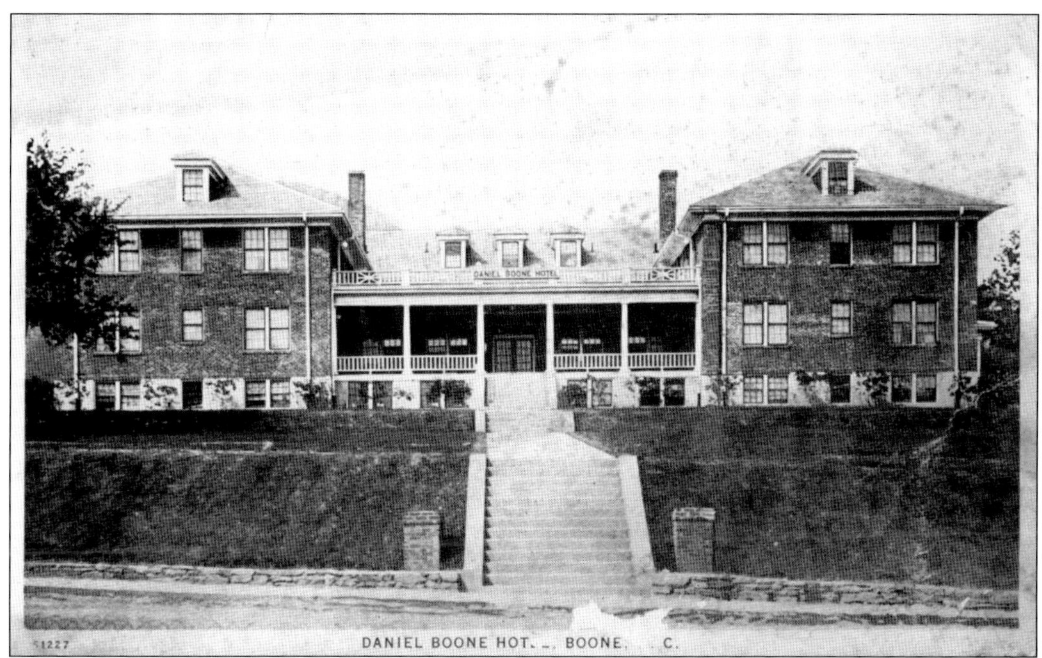

Completed in May 1925 on the site of the Jordan Councill Jr. home, the Daniel Boone Hotel, shown on this 1920s postcard, gave downtown Boone luxury accommodations befitting a county seat with a brisk commercial economy and a growing college. Sunday brunch was a major local draw for decades, and the large dining room hosted countless community events. (Historic Boone Collection.)

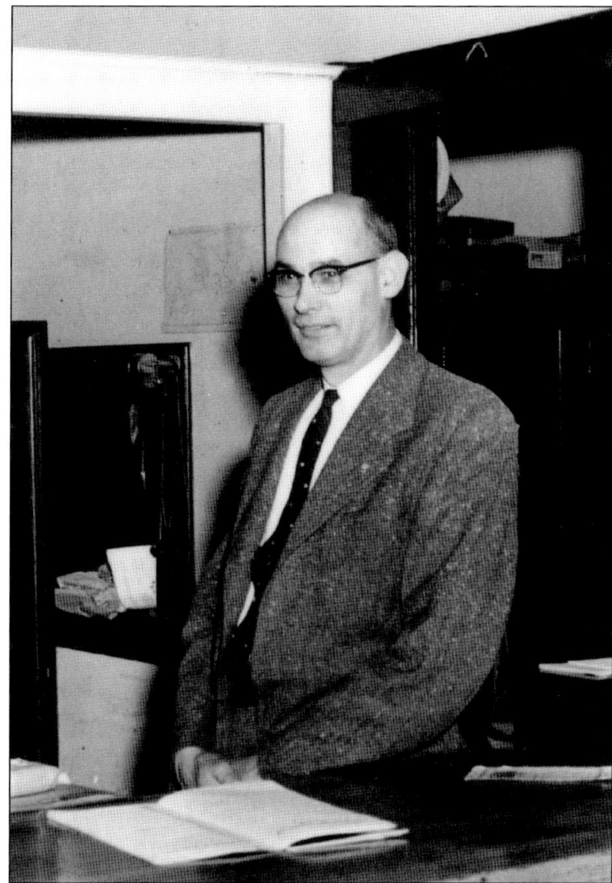

Clarence Alton Price (1904–1982) moved to Boone from High Point and took over as the assistant manager of the Daniel Boone Hotel in November 1939. He was promoted to manager a month later. Price and his wife, Louvenia "Billie" Etheridge Price (1908–2000), operated the hotel for the next 37 years. (Historic Boone Collection.)

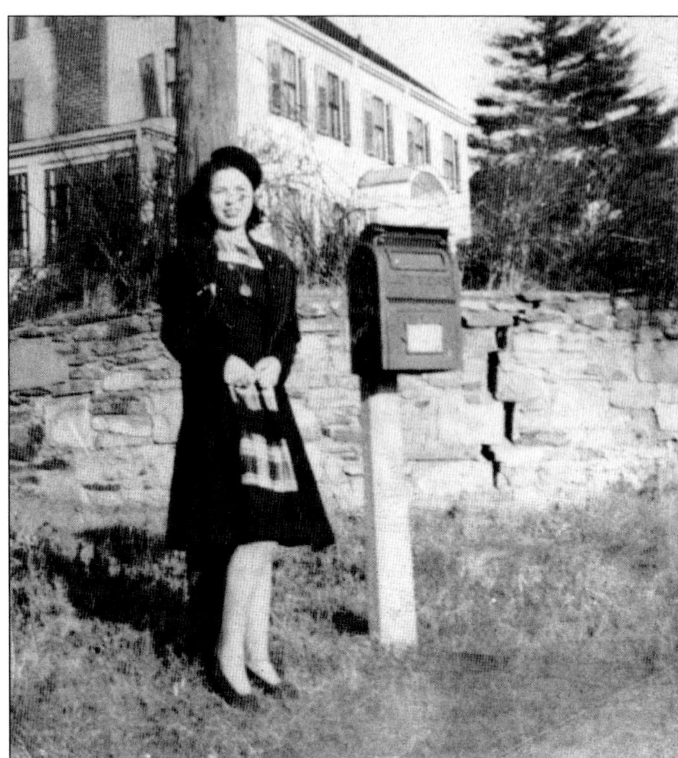

Jessie Timmons (later Norris) was born in Hickory but raised in Boone. Beginning in 1939, Timmons worked as the first switchboard operator for Boone Telephone Company in a building constructed for that purpose on Grand Boulevard. She is shown standing at the corner of Grand Boulevard and Queen Street in front of the Matheson House next to a postal box. (Jessie Norris Collection.)

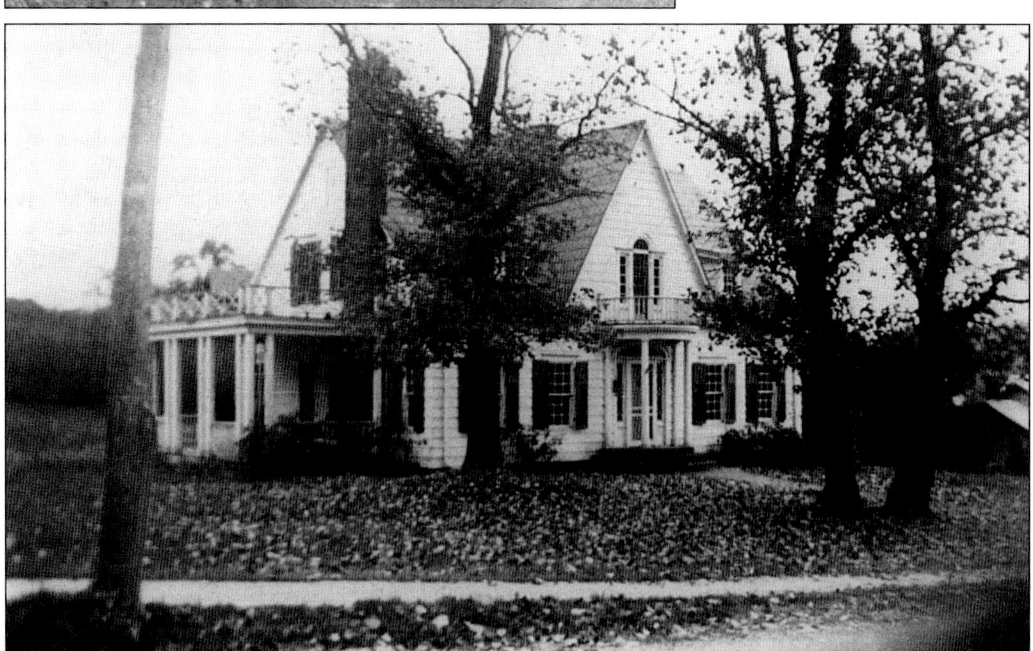

Built on North Water Street in 1926, the Oscar and Suma Hardin House was an outstanding example of Colonial Revival architecture that was unusually high style for Boone's domestic architecture. Blowing Rock mayor Robert Bogle "Bobby" Hardin (1910–1977) spent his late teenage years in this house until the untimely deaths of his parents in 1927 (Oscar) and 1931 (Suma). (Jones House Collection.)

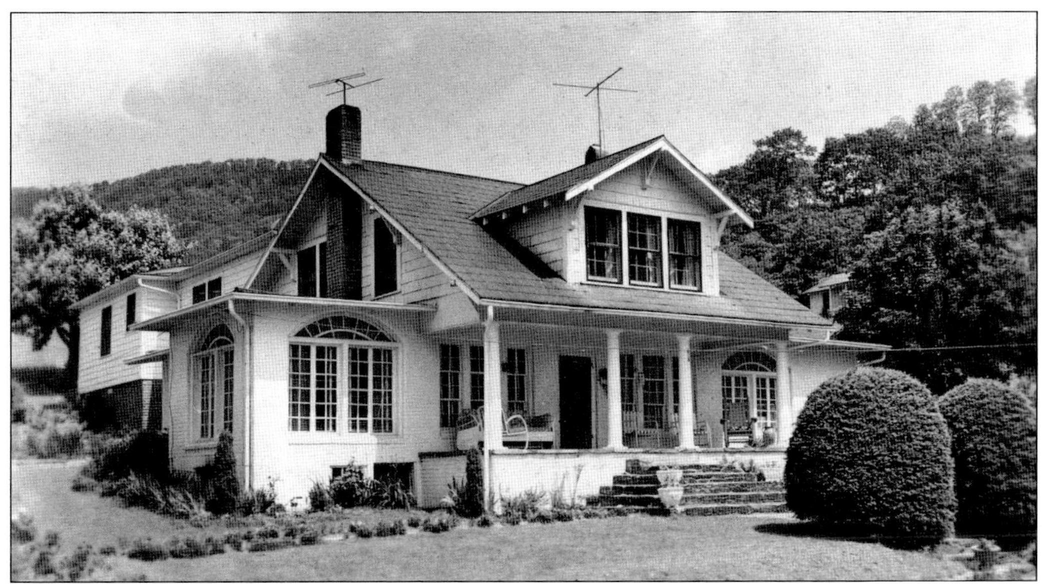

Aside from the Hotel Watauga, the Daniel Boone Hotel, and the Carolina Hotel in the Qualls Block, Boone offered few lodging accommodations in the early 20th century. By the mid-1930s, though, tourist homes like the Greene Inn and one owned by local banker and mayor Watt Harris Gragg (1887–1960) on Gragg Street offered weary mountain travelers bed-and-breakfast-style options as automobile tourism gained popularity. (Historic Boone Collection.)

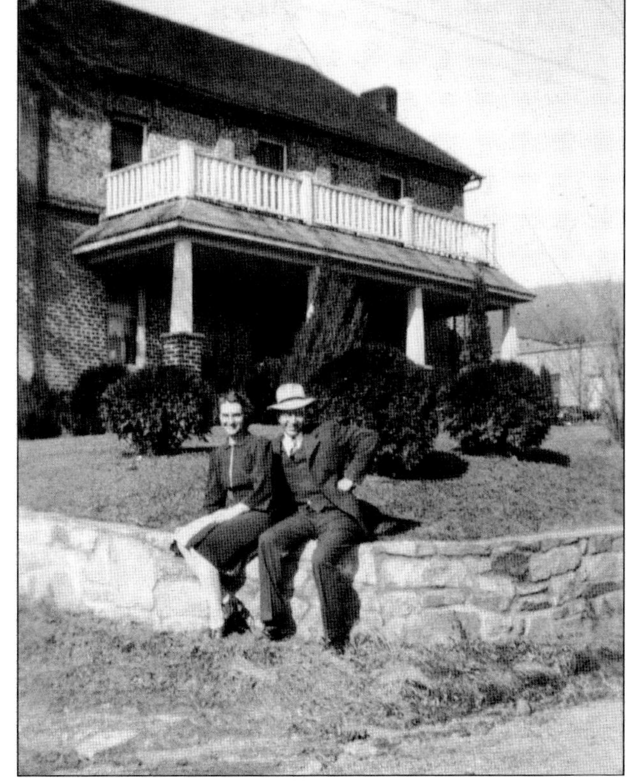

Built in 1889, Boone's fourth Watauga County Jail was on Burrell Street, with the jailer's family quarters at the front of the house and jail cells in the back. The county sold the jail in 1926 after a new one was built behind the courthouse. Louise Wyke Russell (left) purchased the building in 1937 for use as a residence. The building now houses Proper Southern Dining. (David Wyke Collection.)

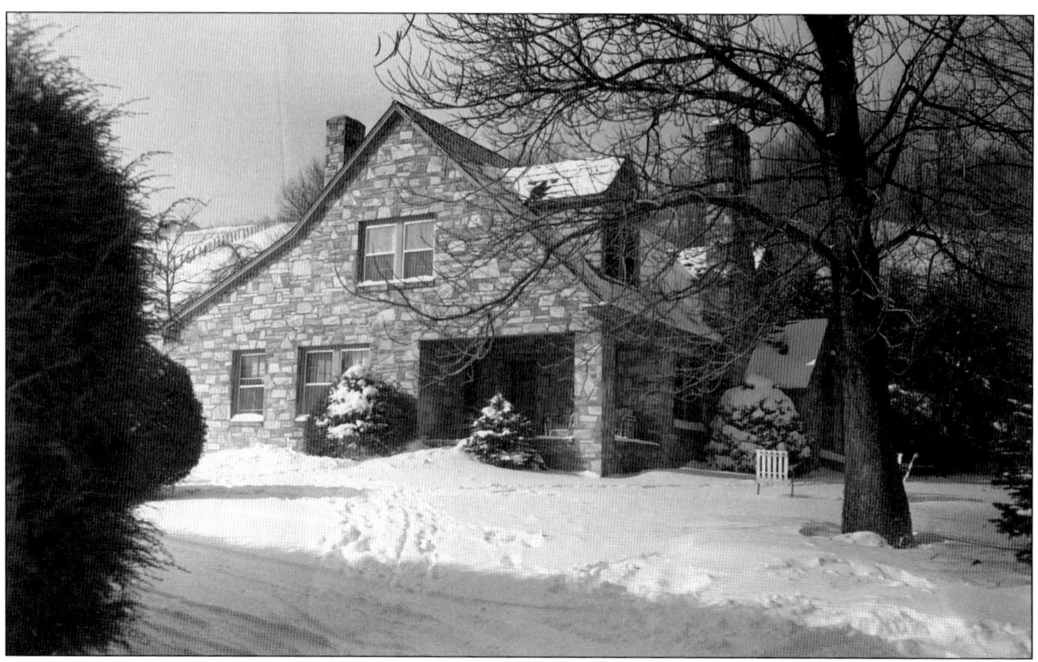

John L. Hickerson (1889–1938), a Black stonemason who built many Boone homes, likely built this house for Robert Luther Clay (1889–1945) in 1933. Clay sold the house to Robert C. Rivers Jr., publisher of the *Watauga Democrat*, in 1945, and it remained the Rivers family home until 1998, when Rachel Rivers-Coffey (1943–1999) and Paul Armfield Coffey (1934–2007) donated it to the Town of Boone. (Palmer Blair Collection.)

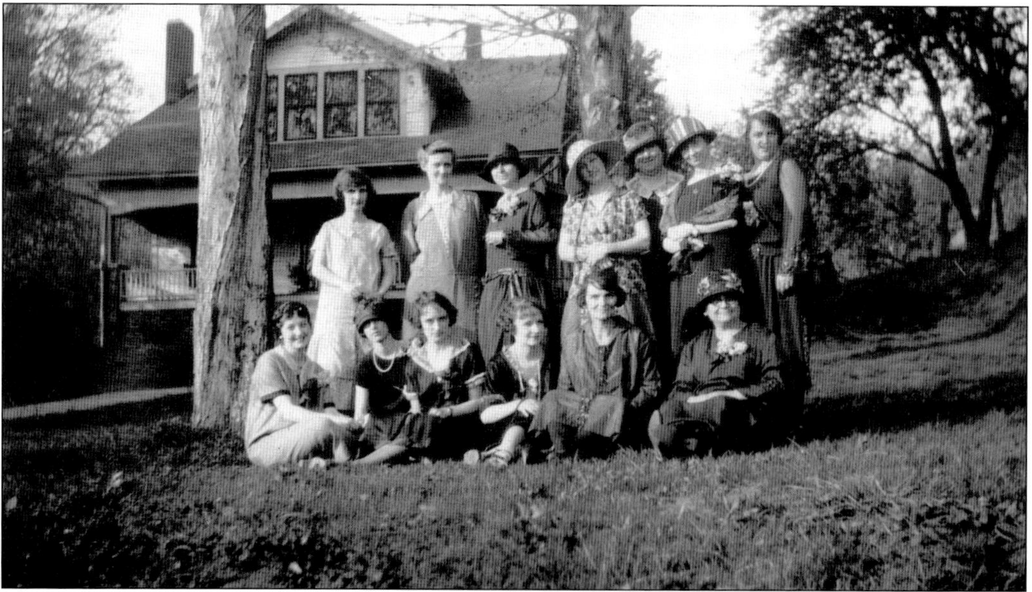

Members of the Friday Afternoon Club, a women's social club founded in 1918, gather on the lawn of MaeBelle South's home on North Water Street in the 1920s. From left to right are (seated) Grace Councill, Mrs. Dean Bingham, Mrs. David Green, Mrs. Cleve Johnson, Bessie Casey, and Mau Greene; (standing) Mrs. Mark Woosley, Tula Rankin, Mrs. Will Winkler, Mrs. Sproles, Hessie Linney, Annie Stansberry, and Jennie Critcher. (Historic Boone Collection.)

Paul Weston (1899–1962) was a Boston native who found modest success as a touring organist and pianist in the 1920s and 1930s before opening a photography studio in Boone in 1937. Thereafter, he alternated between photography and a revived musical career under the pseudonym Paul Weber and His Dancing Fingers. He is shown performing on Atlanta radio station WSB around 1937. (Paul and Ruby Weston Collection.)

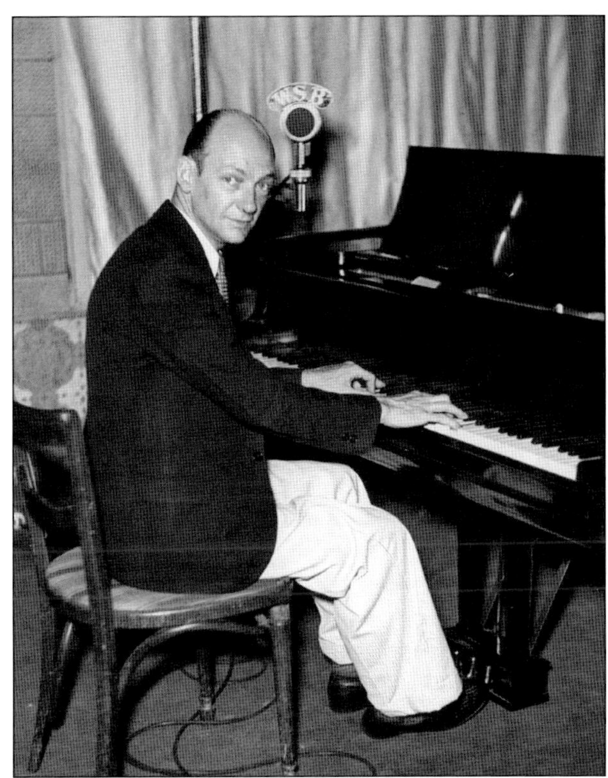

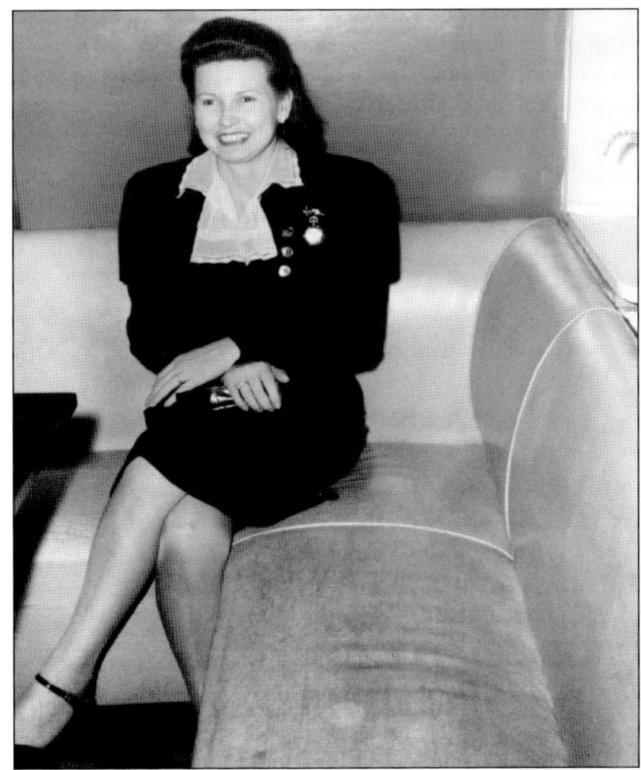

It is not clear how Ruby Cox (1913–2000) met Paul Weston, but they got married in January 1934 in Tennessee before settling in Ruby's home community of Todd. Ruby was a key partner in Paul's photography business and continued to operate the studio long after his death. She is shown here around 1940 in a Detroit club, probably accompanying Paul during one of his touring gigs. (Paul and Ruby Weston Collection.)

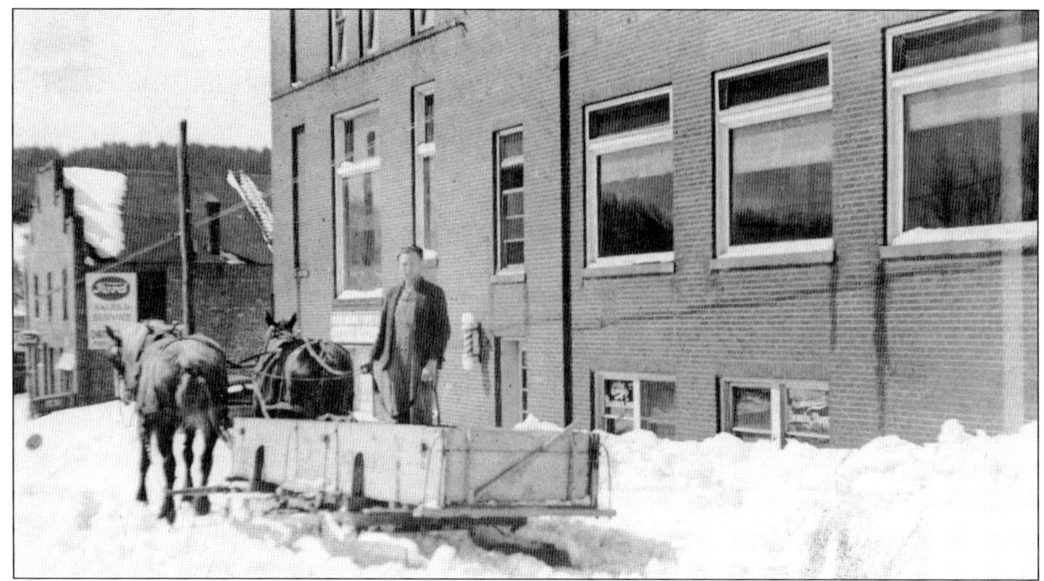

Heavy snowstorms have long been common in Boone, often disrupting travel for days. In this 1930s photograph, an intrepid soul guides his horse-drawn sled down South Depot Street past the Watauga County Bank and toward the Watauga Motor Company Building, which housed a Ford dealership and city hall beginning in 1932. (Historic Boone Collection.)

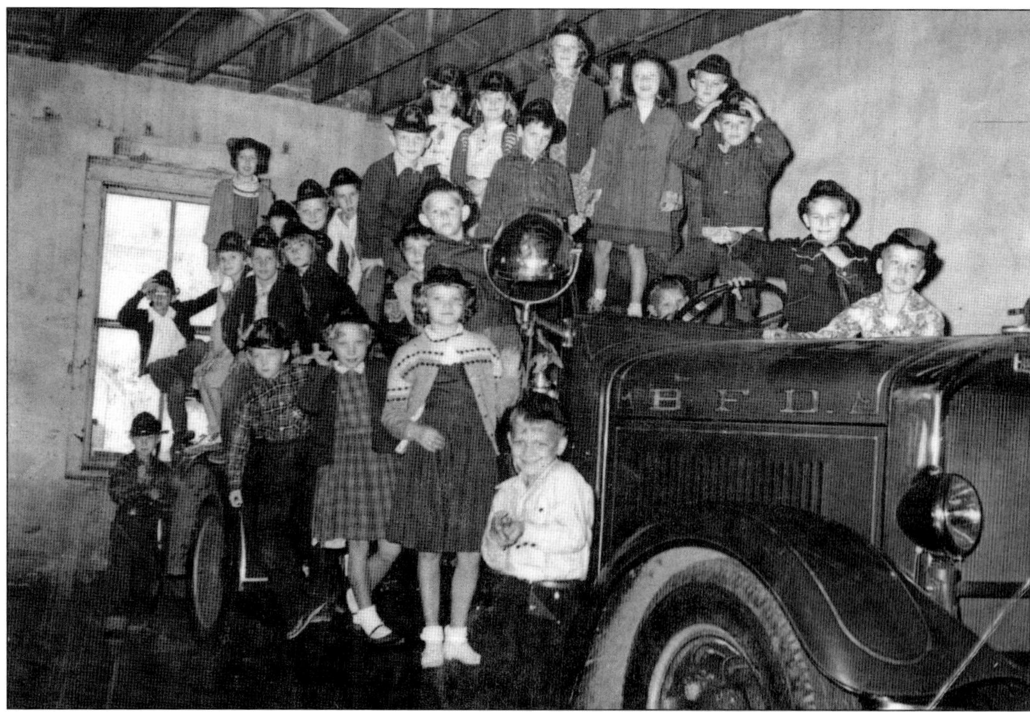

Boone Auto Sales, the last auto dealership to occupy the first floor of the Watauga Motor Company Building, moved to the Sebastian Building in 1936, allowing the Town of Boone to begin storing its firefighting equipment at city hall. In this photograph likely taken in the 1940s, schoolchildren pose atop one of the Boone Fire Department trucks. (Historic Boone Collection.)

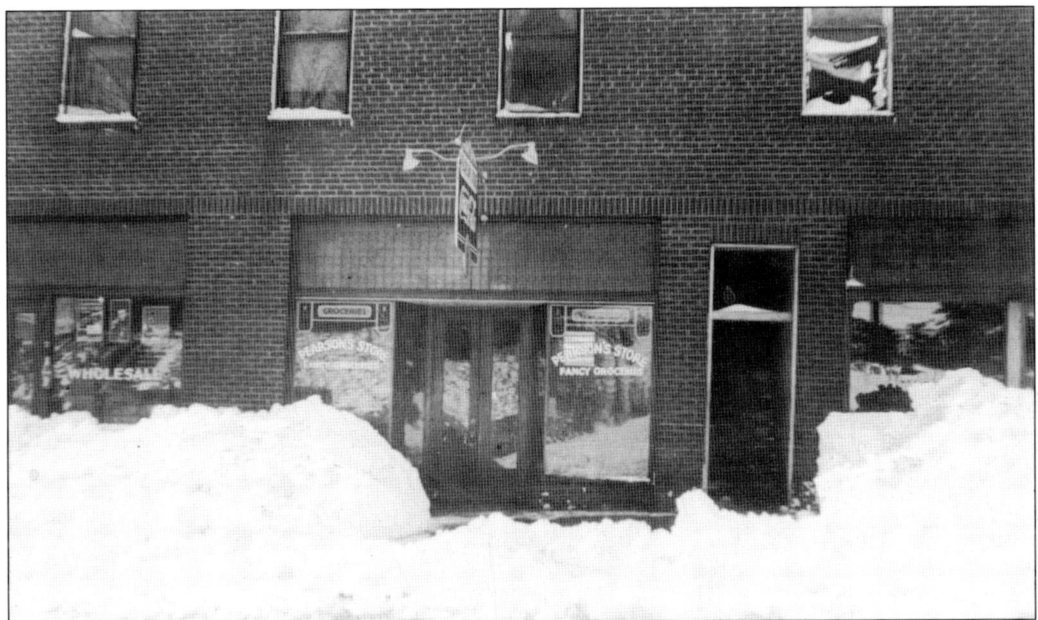

Pearson's Store, a grocery business that also provided some seed and feed options, occupied the second bay from the west of the Frank A. Linney Block, built by W.B. "Will" Hodges in 1924 on the former site of the Blair Hotel as part of the Watch Boone Grow campaign. Pearson's remained the principal tenant of this storefront from 1934 to 1941. (Historic Boone Collection.)

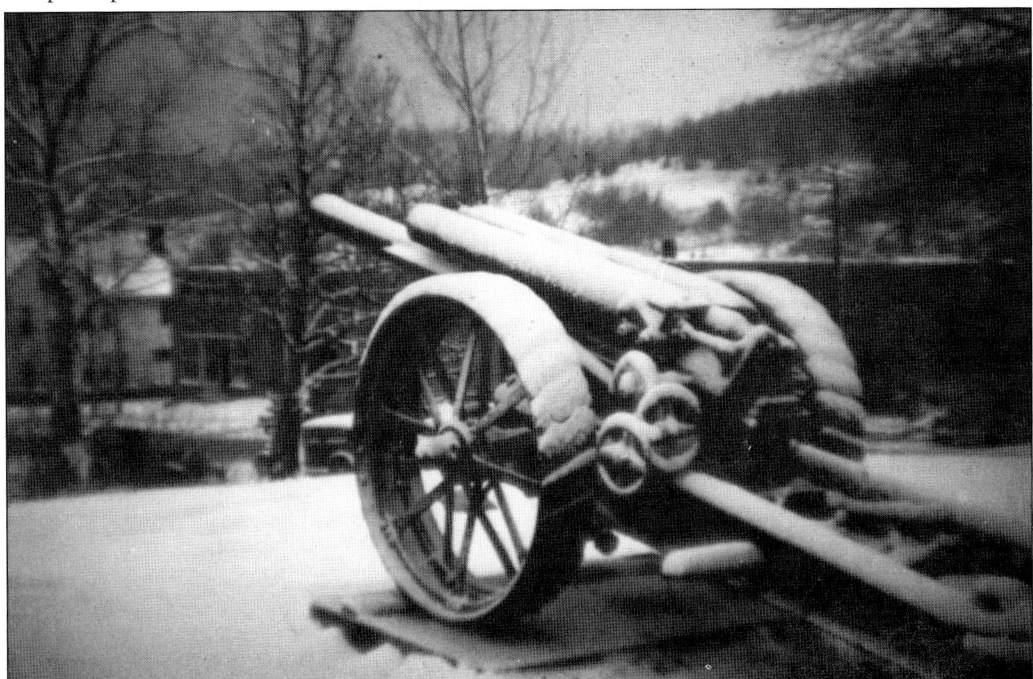

This World War I–era cannon was one of two that sat for many years on the lawn of the 1905 courthouse. Both cannons were scrapped in October 1942 to support US forces in World War II. At left, flanking Burrell Street, are the Rivers Old Home Place and the Sebastian Building, which was completed in 1931. (Rosalea Dorsey Collection.)

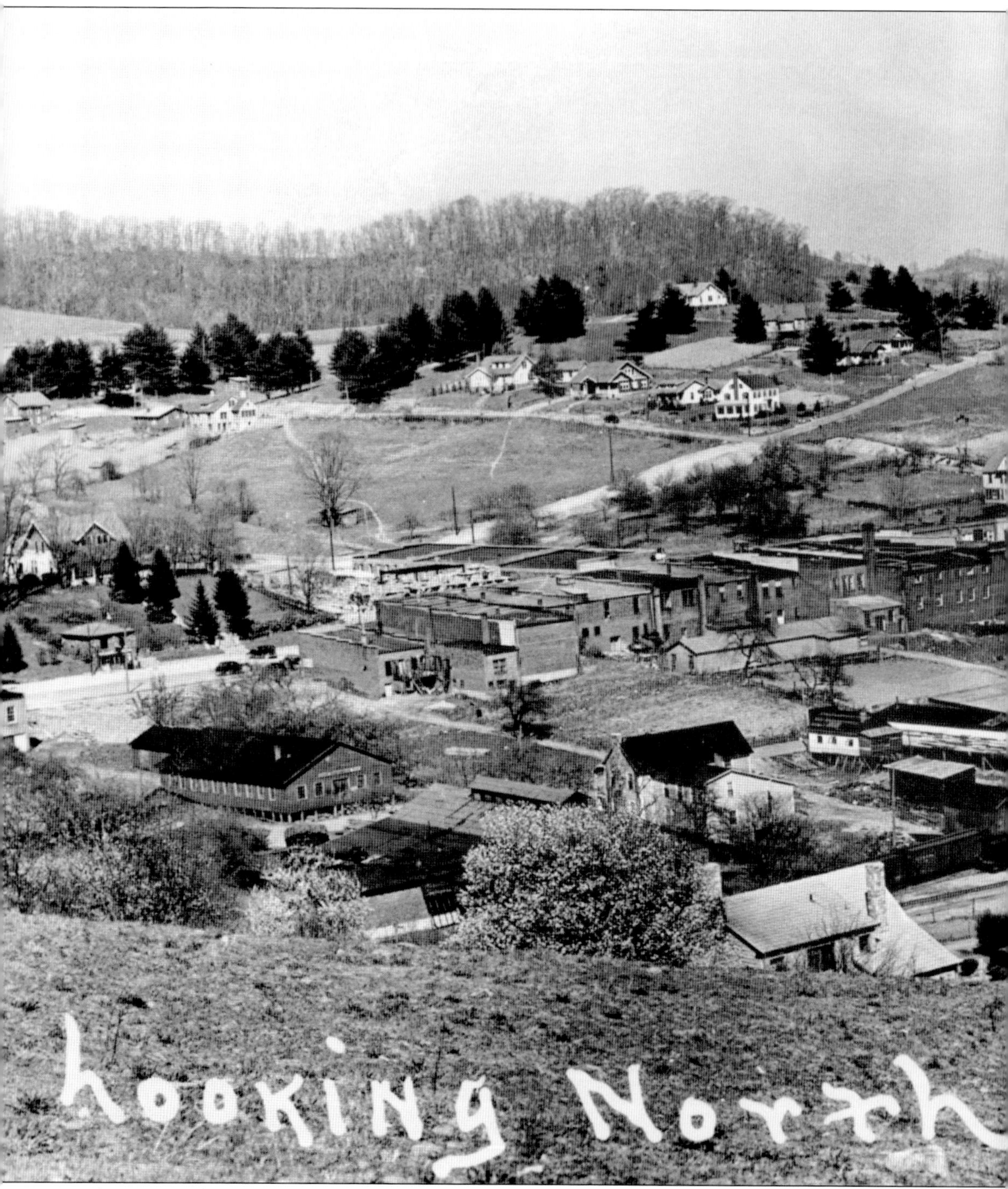

This view of downtown Boone in April 1939 was taken from a similar southwest vantage point as the c. 1885 Ramsour image on the bottom of page 10. Notable landmarks include the R.L. Clay House just below the hill at lower center left; the W.L. Bryan House, which had been moved from King Street to Howard Street in 1938; the Linney Law Office and Frank A. Linney House at extreme center left; city hall at dead center; the Jones House and Daniel Boone Hotel at

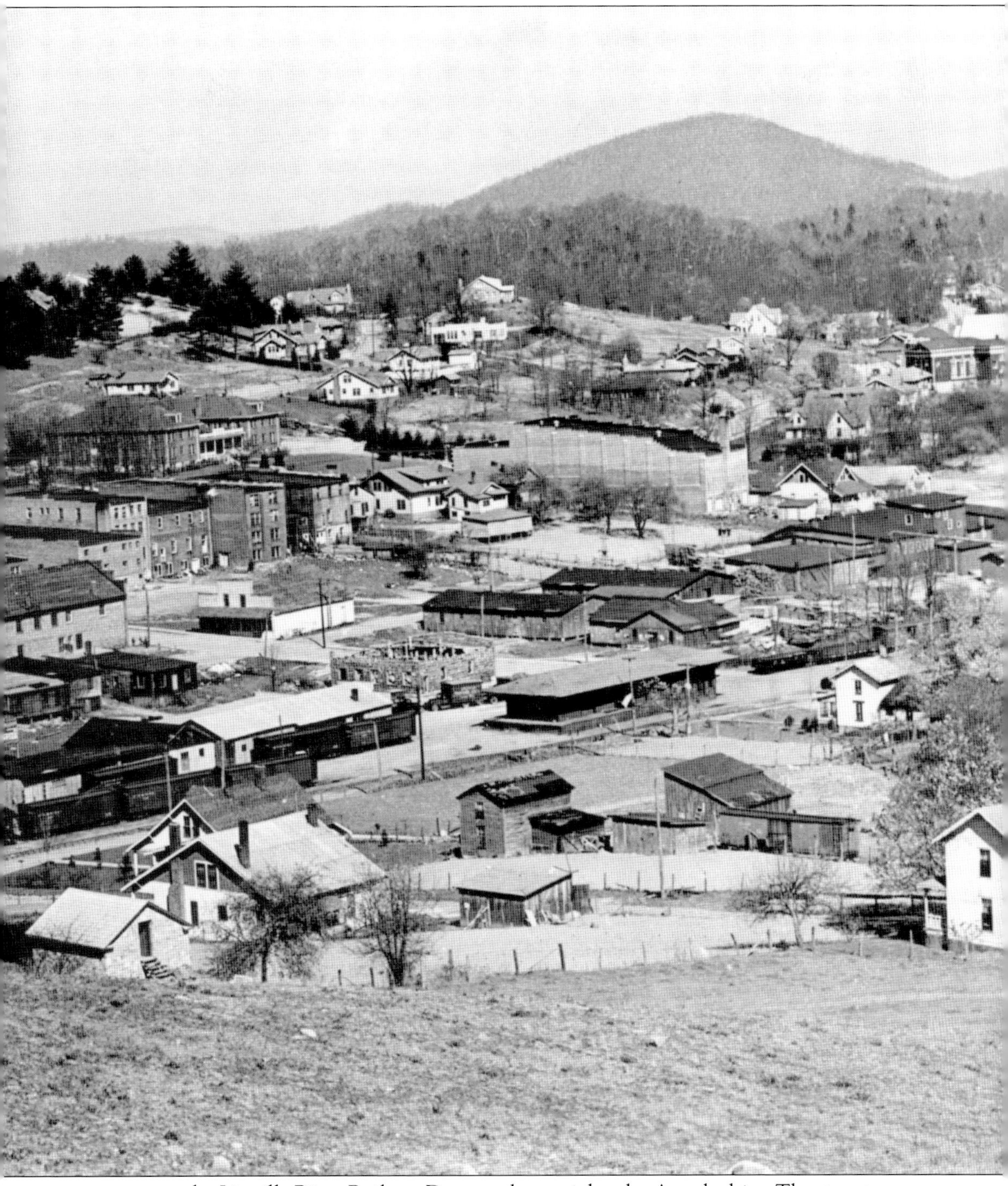

upper center; the Linville River Railway Depot at lower right; the Appalachian Theatre at upper right; and the E.S. Coffey House and Boone Methodist Church at extreme upper right. Grand Boulevard and Orchard Street homes (the Daniel Boone Park subdivision) occupy the hilltops in the distance. (Jones House Collection, Cy Crumley Scrapbook.)

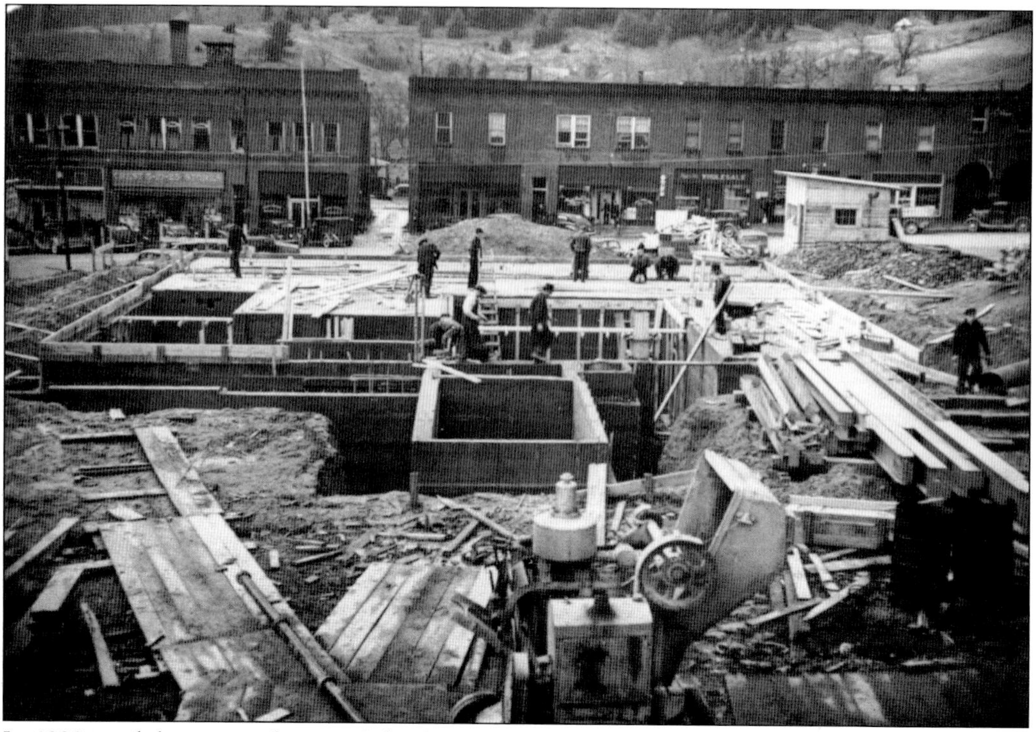

In 1938, work began on the new federal post office in downtown Boone. Funded by the Works Progress Administration, the Colonial Revival building featured native stonework by noteworthy Black stonemasons Earl and Clarence Lyons and carpentry by Willard Watson. Visible across the street are, from left to right, the Farmer's Hardware Block, Ice House Alley, Frank A. Linney Block, and Pastime Theatre. (Historic Boone Collection.)

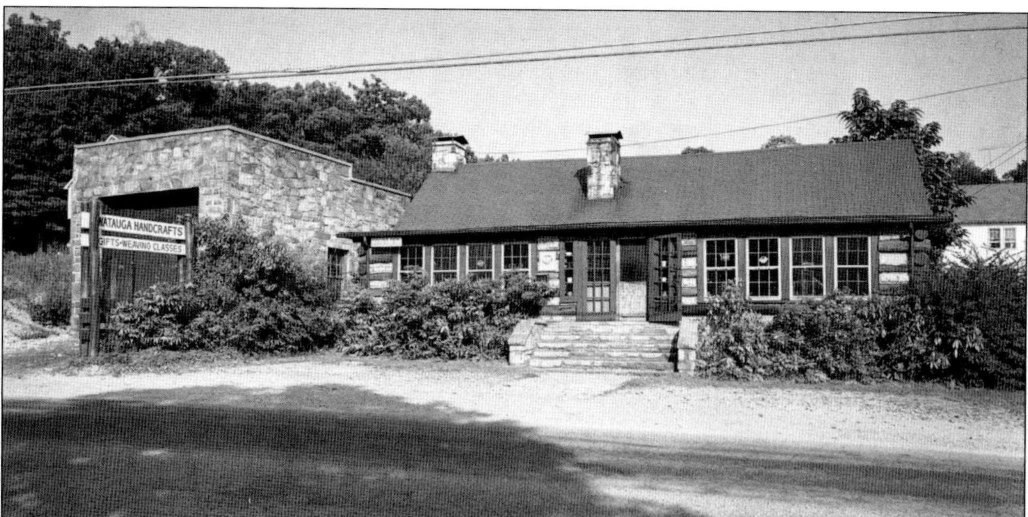

The Watauga Handicrafts Building, pictured in September 1955 on Hardin Street at the east end of town, was another Works Progress Administration–funded project completed in 1938 with stonework by brothers Earl and Clarence Lyons. The building was designed to provide training and income opportunities for locals interested in learning about and preserving local craft traditions. (Palmer Blair Collection.)

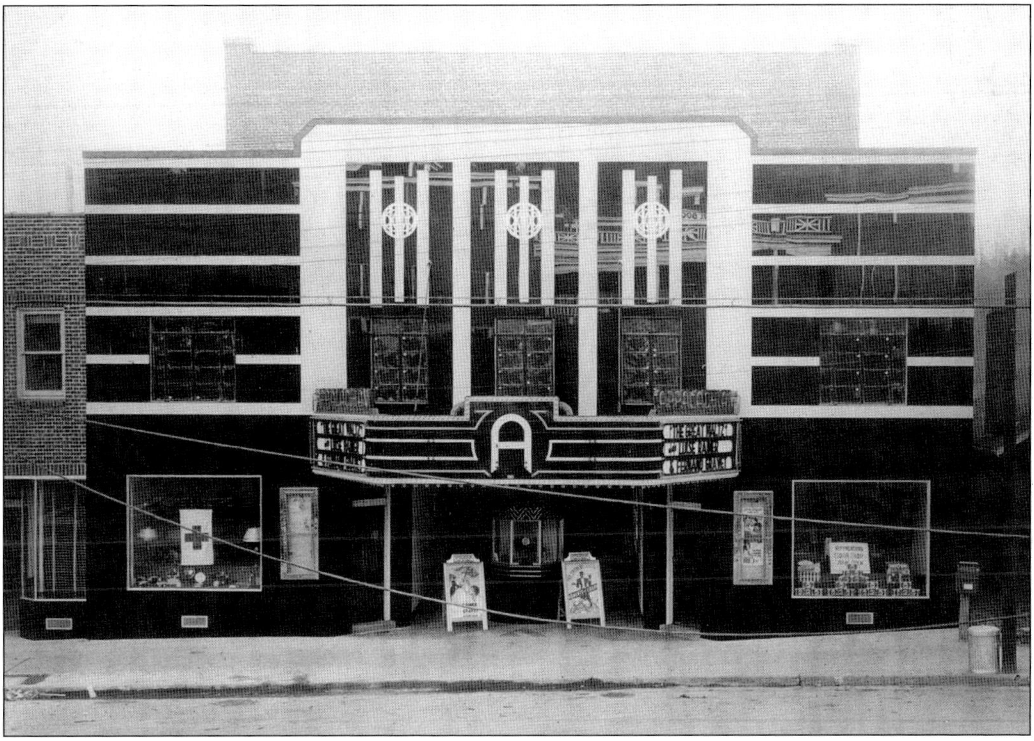

The Appalachian Theatre was another 1938 project, although it was funded by William Ralph Winkler (1900–1997) and Arthur Edward Hamby (1889–1945). Designed by Clarence Pickens Coffey (1906–1978) of Lenoir, the building featured Watauga County's first Art Deco design. Coffey, who had apprenticed with Frank Lloyd Wright, later designed the second Cove Creek High School and the 1968 Watauga County Courthouse. (Appalachian Theatre of the High Country Collection.)

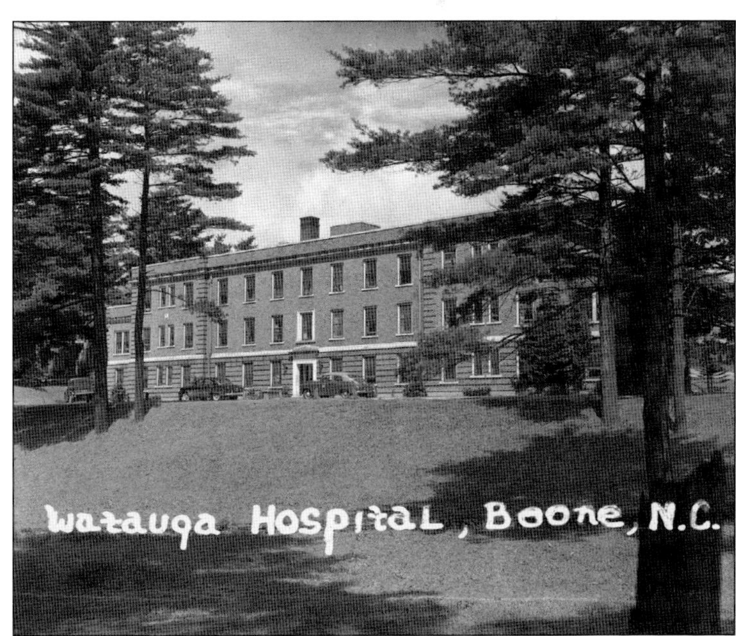

The Duke Foundation and Appalachian State Teachers College provided most of the funding for a new Watauga Hospital, which was built by contractor B.G. Teams (1902–1968) and based on a design by Robert Ferguson Coffey (1899–1935). The building was mostly constructed by 1933 but did not officially open until 1938, when it replaced the county's first modern hospital, which was located in the Dr. R.K. Bingham home on Hardin Street. (Palmer Blair Collection.)

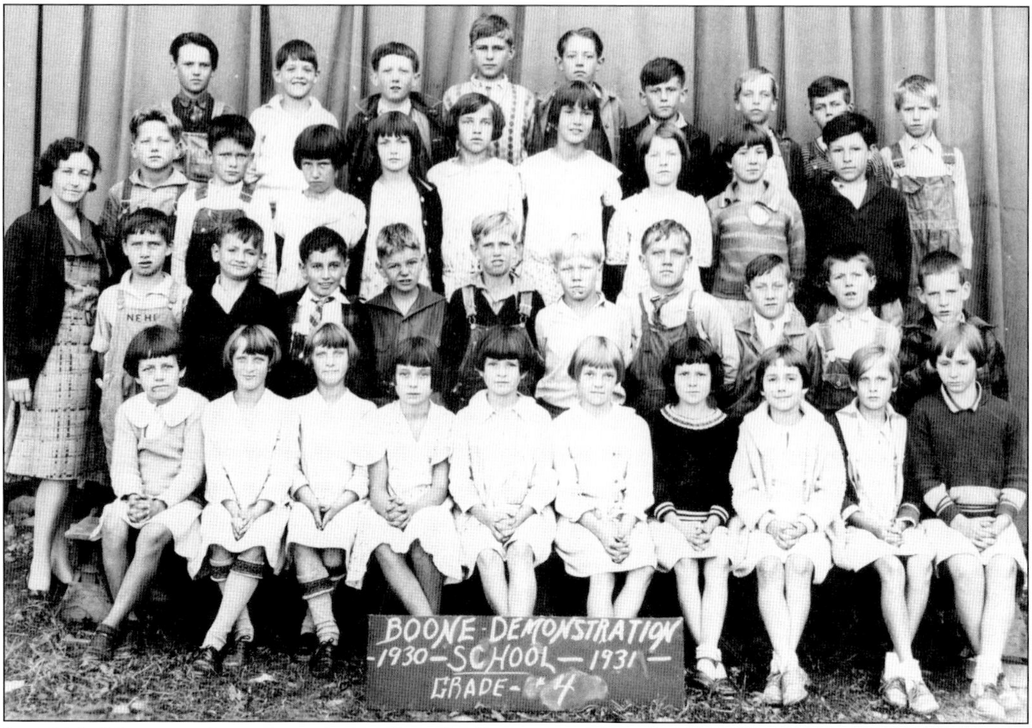

In 1925, Watauga County and the Appalachian State Teachers College created a cooperative program that led to the construction of the Boone Demonstration School, which allowed Appalachian students and teachers to educate local children. This image shows the fourth-grade class of 1930–1931 posing with their teacher. (George Flowers Collection.)

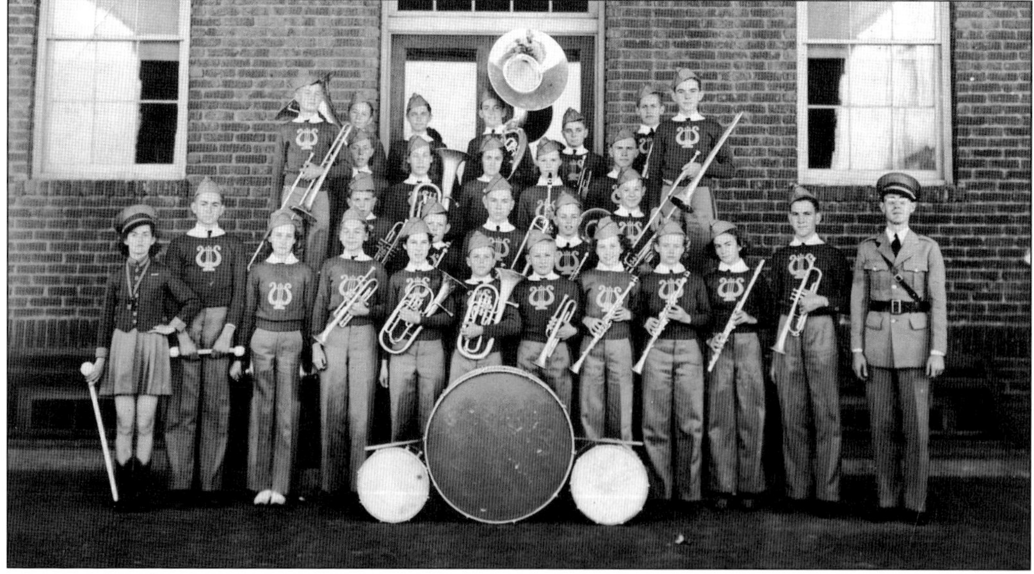

In 1938, local contractor Poly Carp Wyke (1884–1977) built a new, native stone Boone High School building on the ASTC campus as another demonstration school. Members of the Boone High School band pose with their director, Gordon Nash (1913–1985), for this real-photo postcard in 1939. A young Palmer Blair is second from left in the first row. (Historic Boone Collection.)

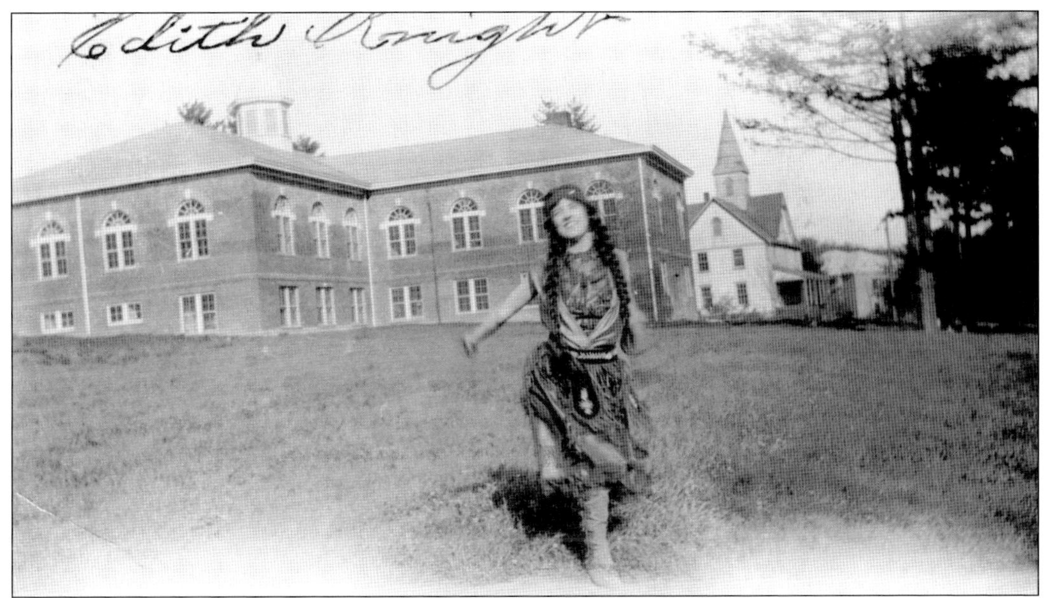

A young woman, possibly Edith Knight, clad in Native American clothing and long braids gambols in the late 1920s on the hillside behind the Central Dining Hall, built in 1925 on the Appalachian State Teachers College campus. The Watauga Academy building, with its distinctive cupola, is visible in the distance. (Historic Boone Collection.)

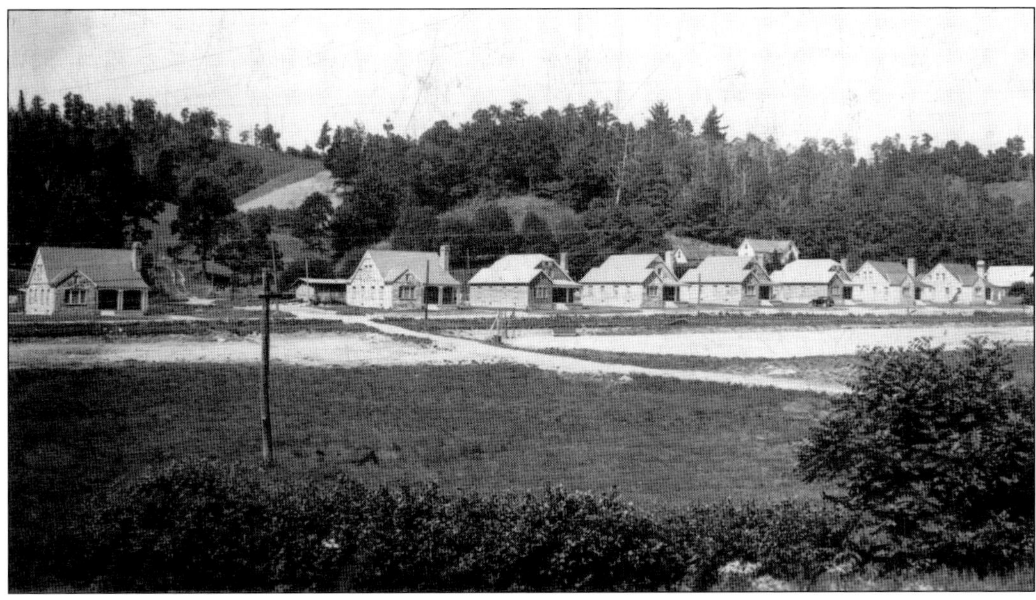

Shown here in the 1940s, the faculty houses along Faculty Street were constructed using funds from the Works Progress Administration. Contractor Poly C. Wyke completed the first six native stone and brick houses in 1938, with another ten finished by 1940. Appalachian State Teachers College auctioned off or demolished all 16 homes in the early 1990s. (Historic Boone Collection.)

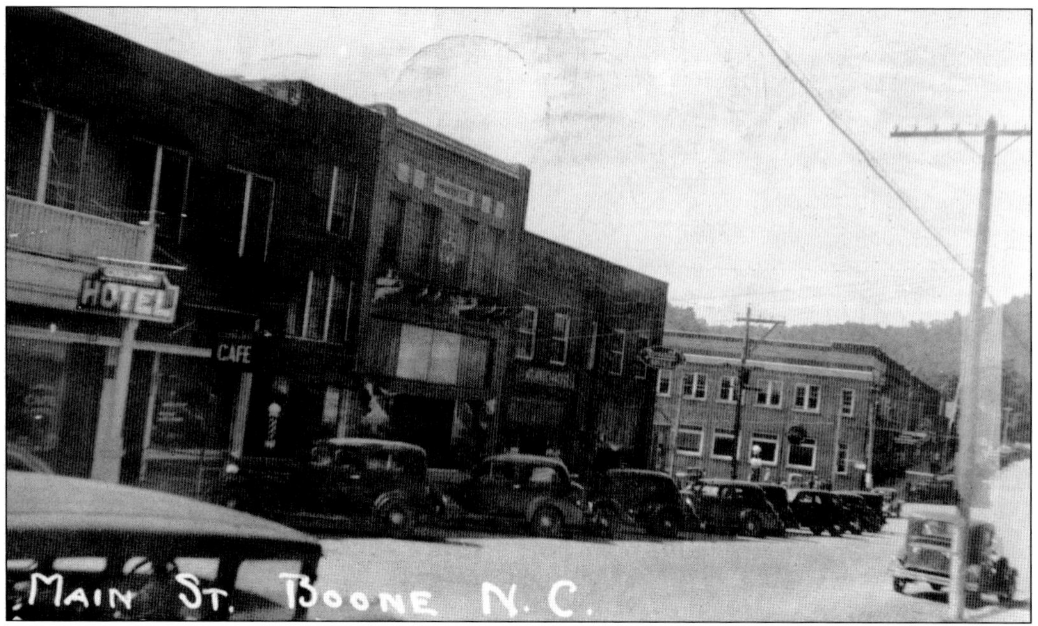

This c. 1936 real-photo postcard shows a key portion of the King Street business district as modern buildings were replacing the last vestiges of old Boone. From left to right are the J.L. Qualls Block (1922), Perry and Winkler Building (1929), H.W. Horton Building (1929), Boone Drug Company Building (1921), setback Shell Service Station (1936), and Watauga County Bank (1923). (Bobby Brendell Postcard Collection.)

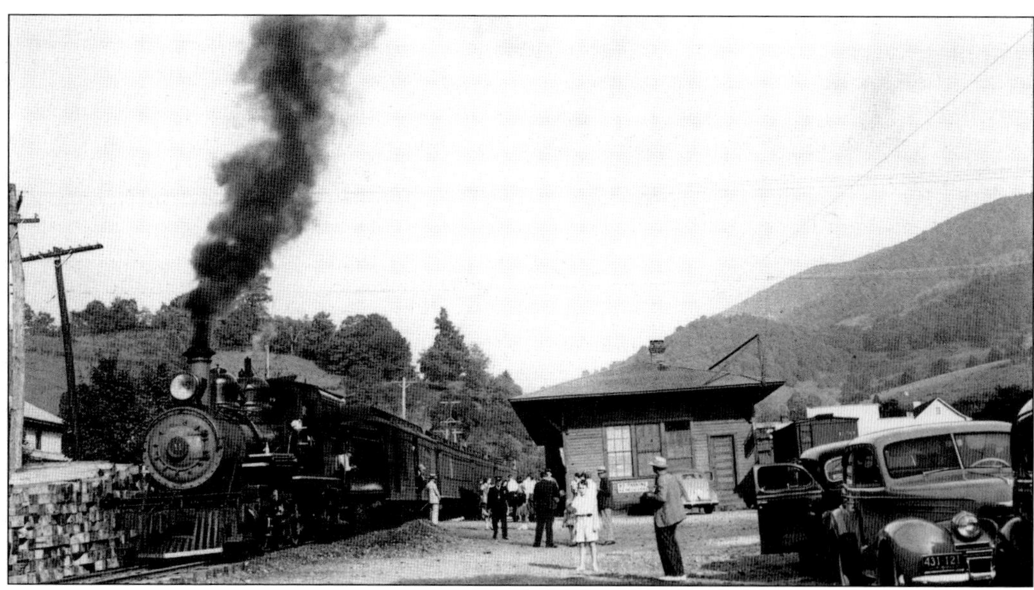

Tourists and locals board Engine No. 11 for one of its last advertised passenger excursions from Boone in this c. 1939 photograph. At lower right is the Linville River Railway (LRR) depot at Boone, which sat in the middle of present-day Rivers Street at Depot Street. The LRR cut passenger traffic to occasional excursions in the 1930s when the line shifted to bus and truck traffic as roads improved. (Jones House Collection.)

Three

Flood, War, and Rebirth 1940–1959

As Boone began to emerge from the effects of the Great Depression, it was slammed with two new setbacks. The first was the August 1940 flood that devastated much of Watauga County and forever ended train service to Boone. While roads had gradually improved during the late 1930s, allowing some heavy truck traffic to bring construction supplies up the mountain, the outbreak of World War II and the severe rationing that accompanied it meant that new construction—and many other forms of economic activity—dropped off during the war years.

Following the end of World War II, though, pent-up consumer demand, the availability of relatively cheap and reliable automobiles, and additional road improvements in the High Country meant a sudden spike in outsiders making their ways to Boone. Completion of new sections of the Blue Ridge Parkway in the area also encouraged tourists to stop in Boone. Recognizing the opportunity, town officials began looking for opportunities to draw tourists in. One such opportunity was a new outdoor drama, *Horn in the West*, which emerged from Watauga County's 1949 centennial celebration held primarily in Boone. Other nearby tourist sites, including the Daniel Boone Native Gardens and the Boone Golf Course, were created in the next decade, making Boone an ideal layover spot. Given the dearth of lodging opportunities in Boone after the war, this led to construction of new tourist courts, motels, restaurants, and other tourism-related infrastructure.

As a result of the postwar tourist boom, Boone again expanded its boundaries. To the south, along Blowing Rock Road, a new commercial corridor was forming, and several new industries looked to the corridor as a place to locate new factories and plants. To the east, along the highway to Wilkesboro, small bedroom communities like Perkinsville were gradually subsumed into Boone. Meanwhile, Appalachian State Teachers College continued to grow in both raw numbers and expansion of campus boundaries. In 1958, the town of Boone had nearly 50 percent more residents (3,600) than the 2,400 students at Appalachian. Over the next 10 years, however, Appalachian State's population would double, creating new pressures for Boone.

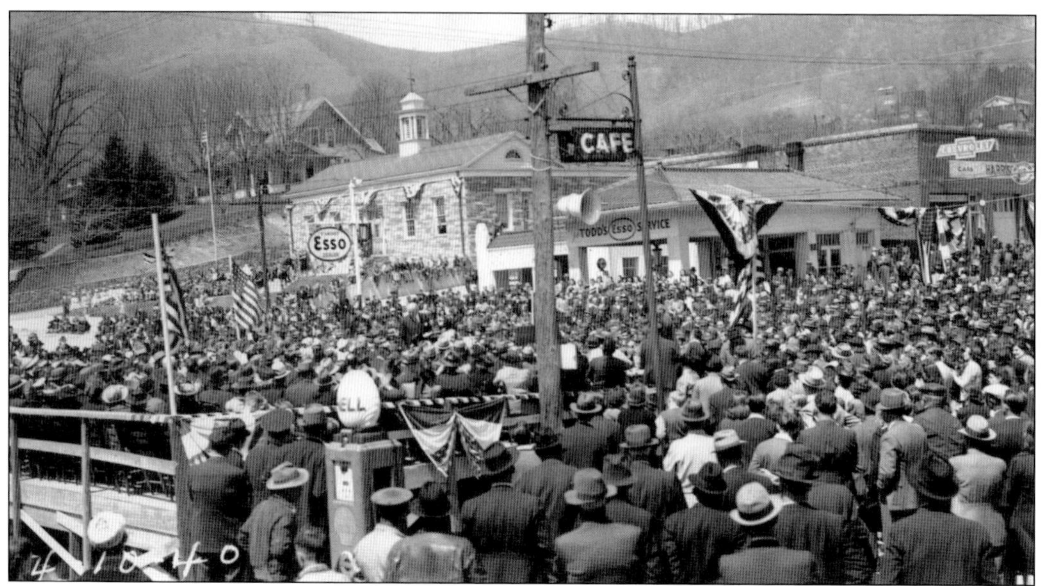

On April 10, 1940, townsfolk gathered at the intersection of Depot and King Streets for the official dedication of Boone's new federal post office. In the distance at upper left are the J.M. and Ida Moretz and Linney Houses. To the right of the post office are Todd's Esso Service and the Harrison Chevrolet building, on the site of the present town parking lot. (Jones House Collection.)

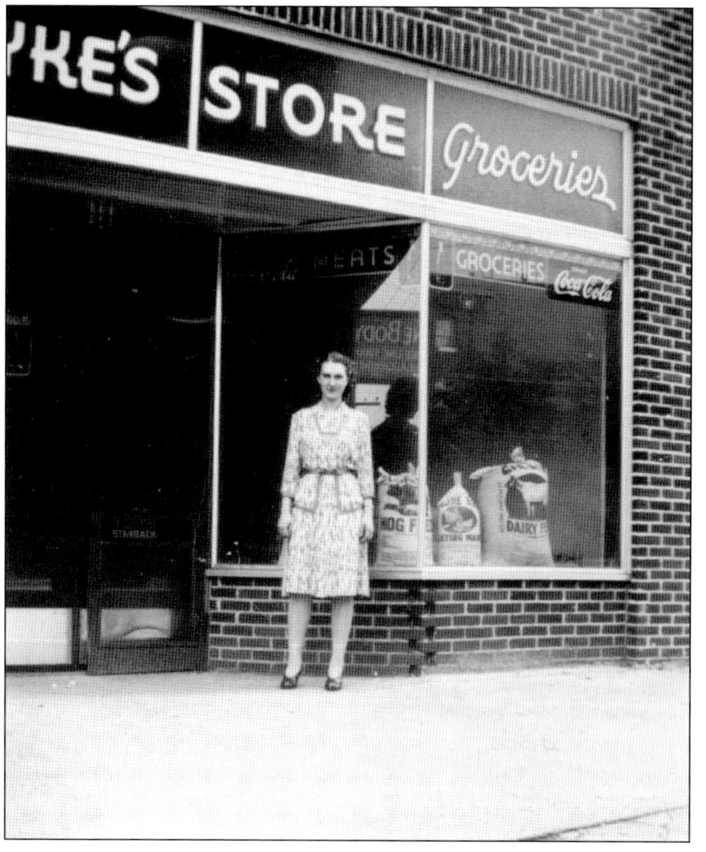

David Pinkney Wyke (1892–1948) opened Wyke's Store in July 1940, shortly after Joseph Edward Clay (1894–1986) constructed this small building opposite the 1905 courthouse. Wyke sold out to Clay's King Street Grocery, located one shop to the east, and briefly operated a feed store at the same location. Here, Louise Wyke Russell (1918–2010) stands in front of the store in the early 1940s. (David Wyke Collection.)

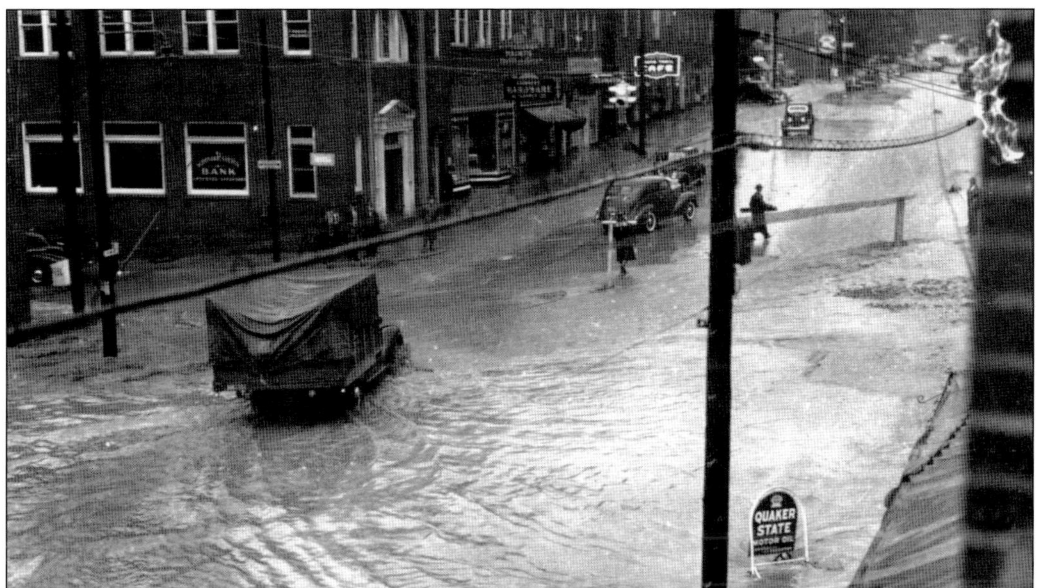

On August 13, 1940, up to 14 inches of rain from a stalled tropical system fell on Watauga County and Boone, triggering more than 2,000 landslides and inundating local communities. Shown here are floodwaters rushing down King Street as vehicles attempt to drive through the Depot Street intersection. Paul Weston captured this image from his studio in the Jones Building. (Paul and Ruby Weston Collection.)

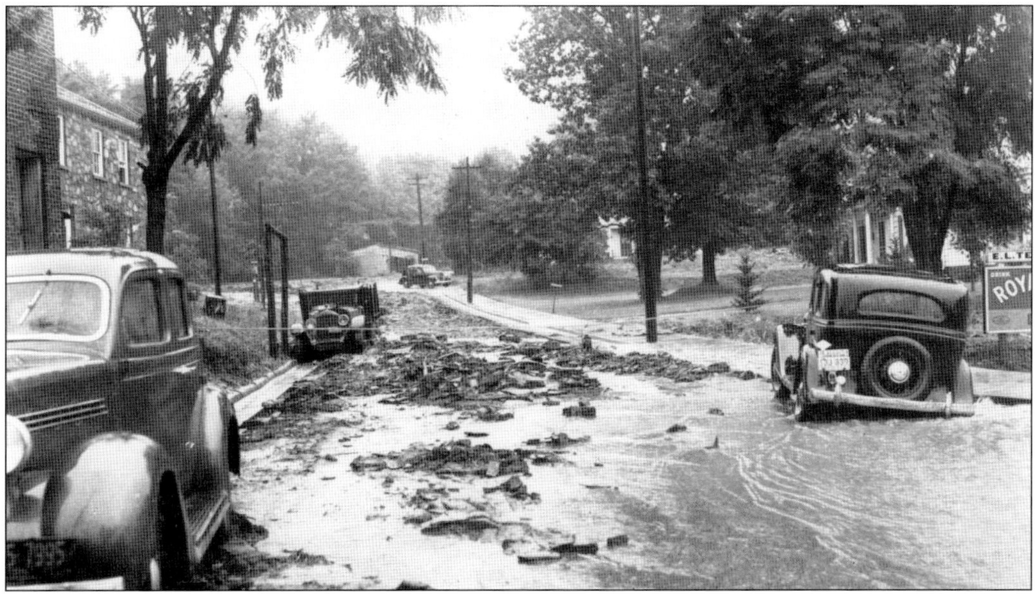

The damage from the August 1940 flood was so severe that Boone was cut off from the outside world for nearly two weeks. Paul Weston spent days walking through the county, documenting the damage, then walked his photographs to Wilkesboro to send them out over a wire service. This picture shows severe road damage to North Water Street, which took months to repair. (Paul and Ruby Weston Collection.)

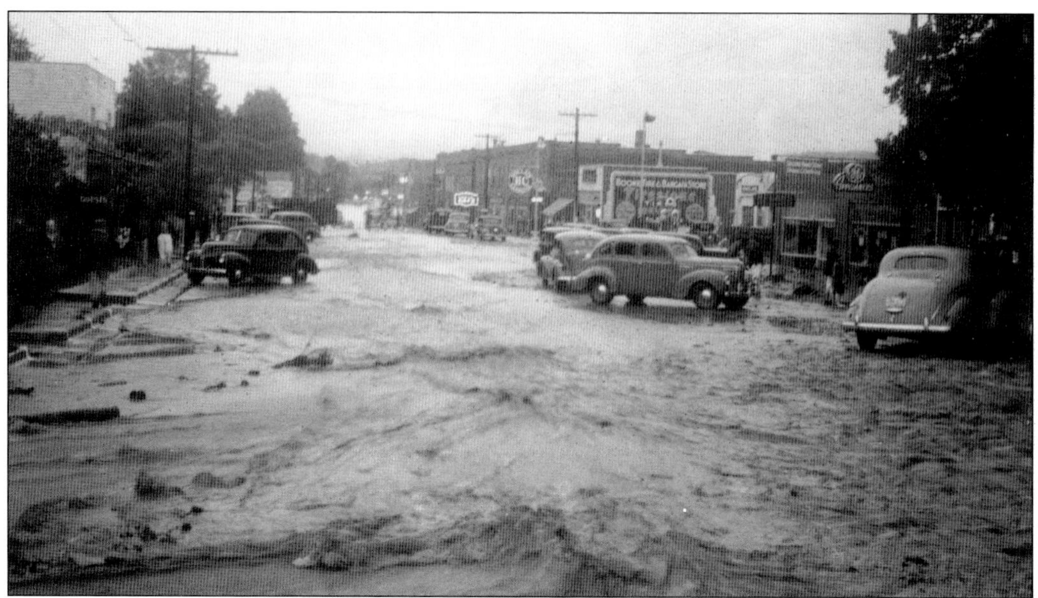

Floodwaters were so high on King Street, shown here looking east, that locals were able to catch trout that had washed downstream. The flooding also destroyed much of the Linville River Railway line, permanently ending train service to Boone. At left is the Jennie Coffey Store, with Hi-Land Cleaners and Watauga Hardware in the C.M. Critcher Building (1934) across the street. (David Wyke Collection.)

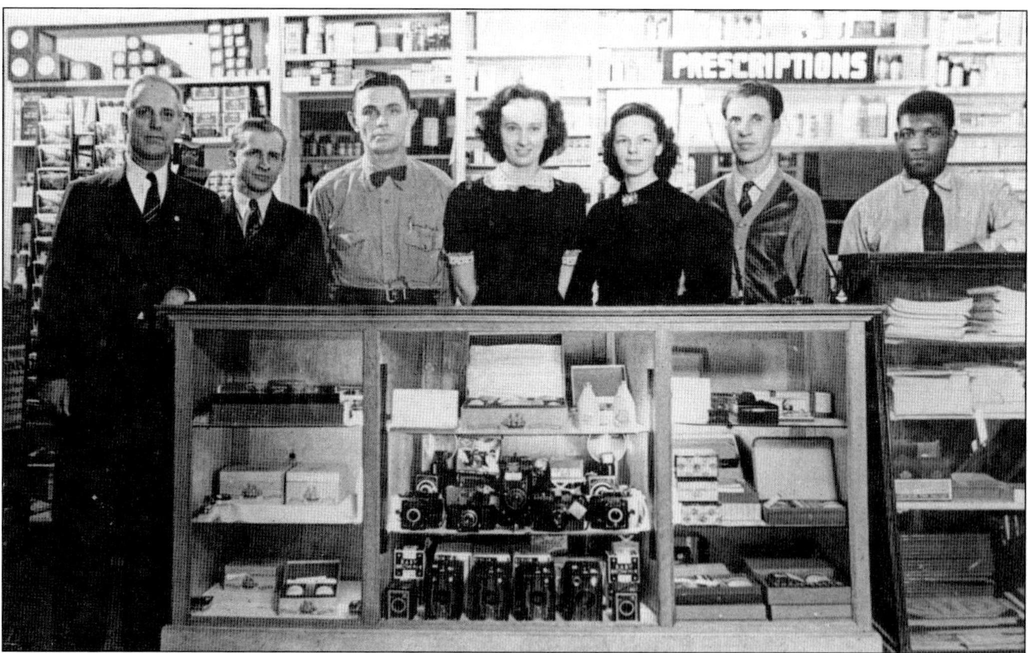

In the 1940s, many retail establishments in Boone employed Black workers, even as de facto and de jure racial segregation practices limited access to services for many Black residents of Boone. The staff of the Boone Drug Company is pictured here around 1940. From left to right are Dr. G.K. Moose, Dr. Wayne R. Richardson, Bob Agle, Eileen Jones, Delcie Moretz, Lige Bentley, and Haskell Flowers. (Historic Boone Collection.)

Rev. Ronda Horton (1895–1986) was born and raised in the Junaluska community. He boarded with the Mennonites at Elk Park for his early education, worked the coal mines of Virginia as a young man, then became a preacher in 1932, serving the Mennonite Brethren Churches in Vilas and Boone for decades. He also operated a small store on North Depot Street within Junaluska. (Historic Boone Collection.)

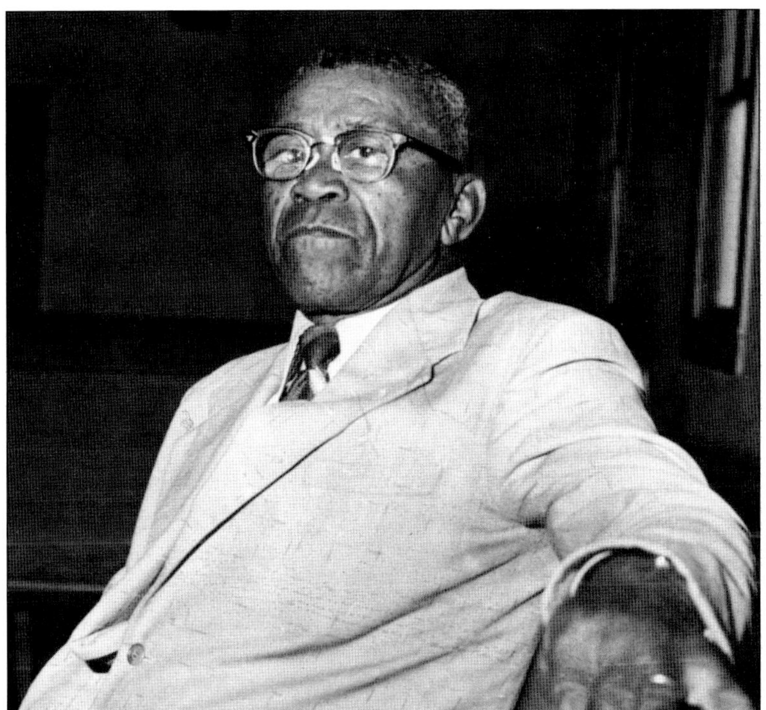

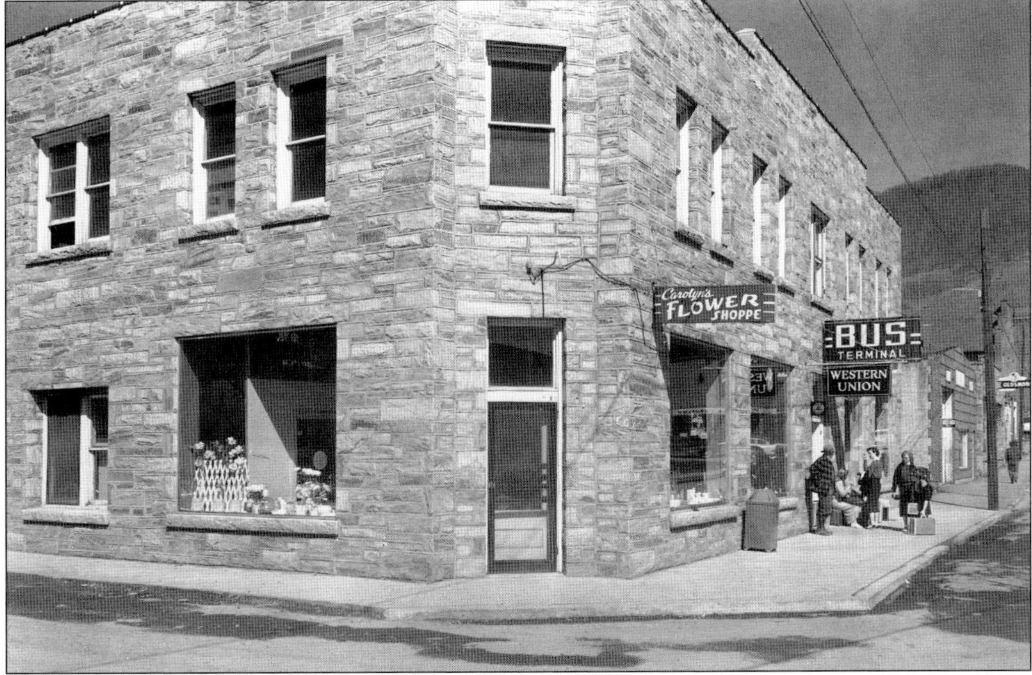

One Boone business that practiced segregation was the Terminal Roller Rink, which occupied the second floor of the Boone Bus Station, built in 1946 by W.G. Hartzog and shown here in 1955. Friday evenings were reserved for Black patrons. Both of Boone's movie theaters also either refused Black customers or corralled them into balcony seating, while many restaurants refused to seat Black people indoors. (Palmer Blair Collection.)

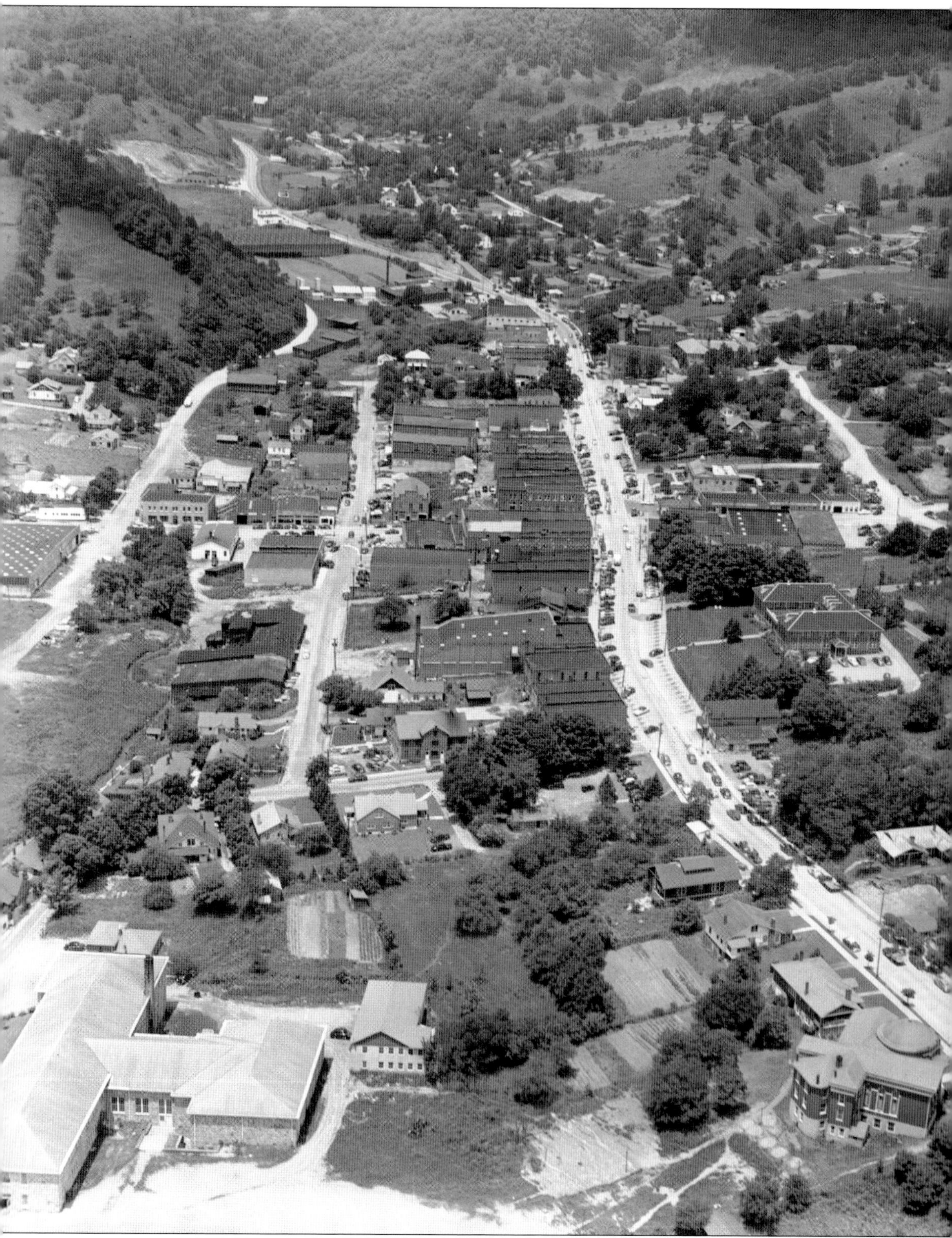

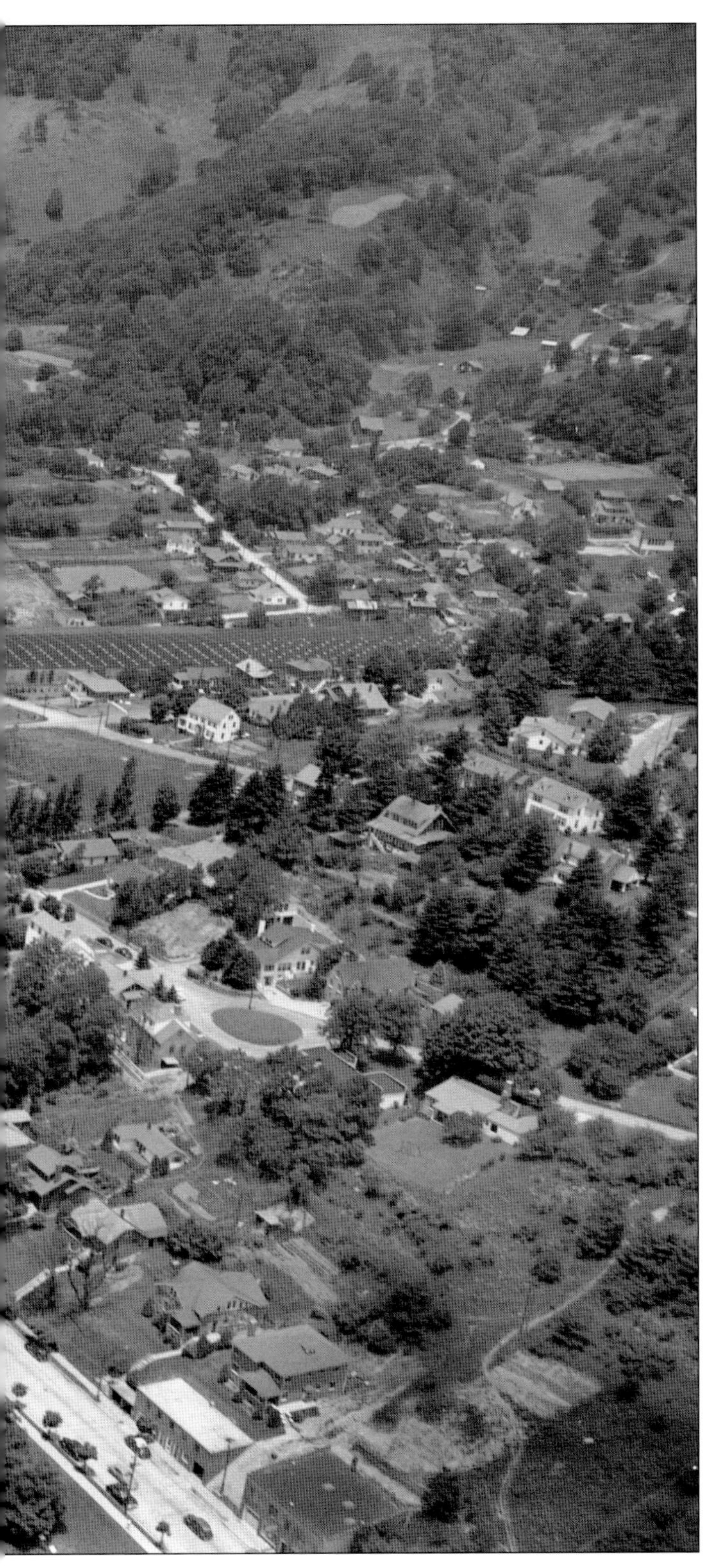

This June 1950 aerial view shows downtown Boone from the southeast and offers a different perspective on its development. Appalachian High School is at lower left, while the Daniel Boone Hotel is at center. King Street flows from upper left to lower right. Appalachian State faculty members originally built many of the homes at lower right on the north side of King Street, but in the 1950s, this area began to transition to a student housing cluster later known as Hippie Hill; many of the garage buildings along King Street expanded into apartment complexes. Note the three burley tobacco warehouses at center right, far center left, and upper left. Much of the Junaluska community, including the Mennonite Brethren Church, is visible at upper right just beyond the first tobacco warehouse. (Palmer Blair Collection.)

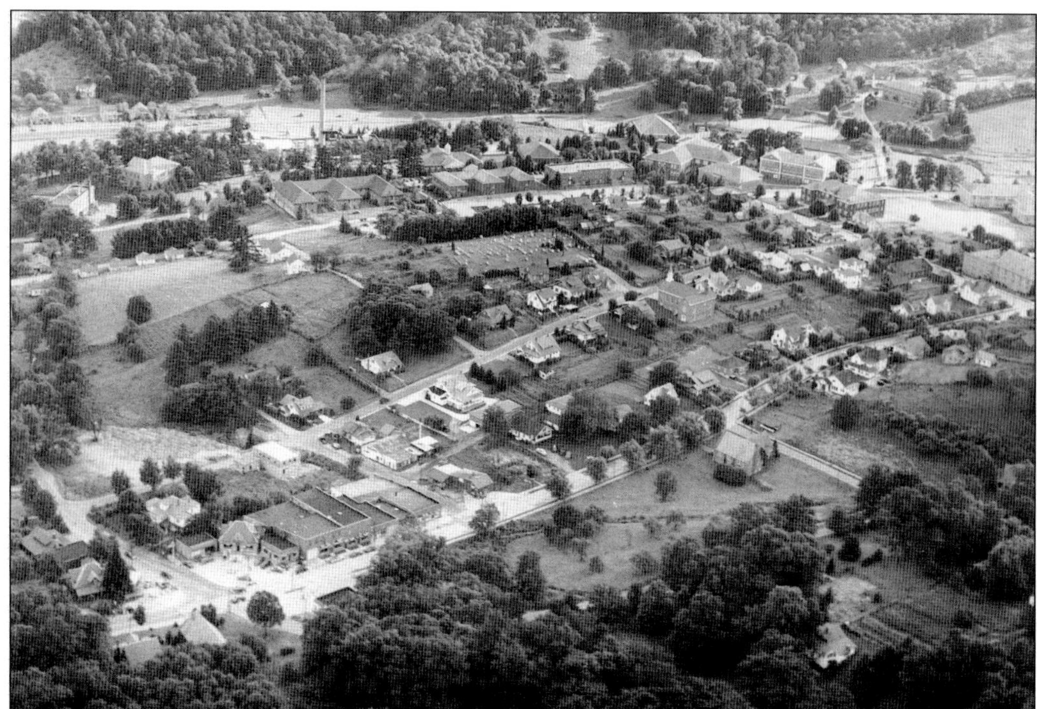

This June 1950 aerial view taken from the northeast shows the intersection of East King Street and Hardin Street—known as Greasy Corners—at lower left. Boone Cemetery, which was divided along racial lines between a well-maintained section for white people to the west and the overgrown Black section to the east—is at upper center, with the Appalachian State Teachers College campus just beyond the cemetery. (Palmer Blair Collection.)

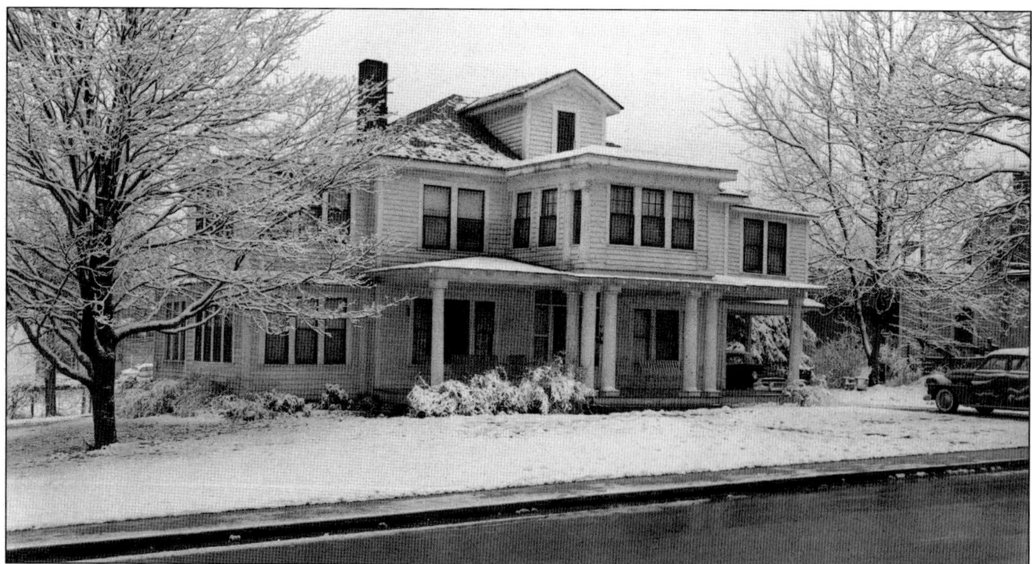

Pictured around 1950 after a light snowfall is the former Watauga Hospital, which had reverted to use as a residence by this point. Dr. Robert Knox Bingham (1877–1949) substantially enlarged his private home in 1922 to create Watauga County's first modern hospital facility, which remained in use until about 1936. (Palmer Blair Collection.)

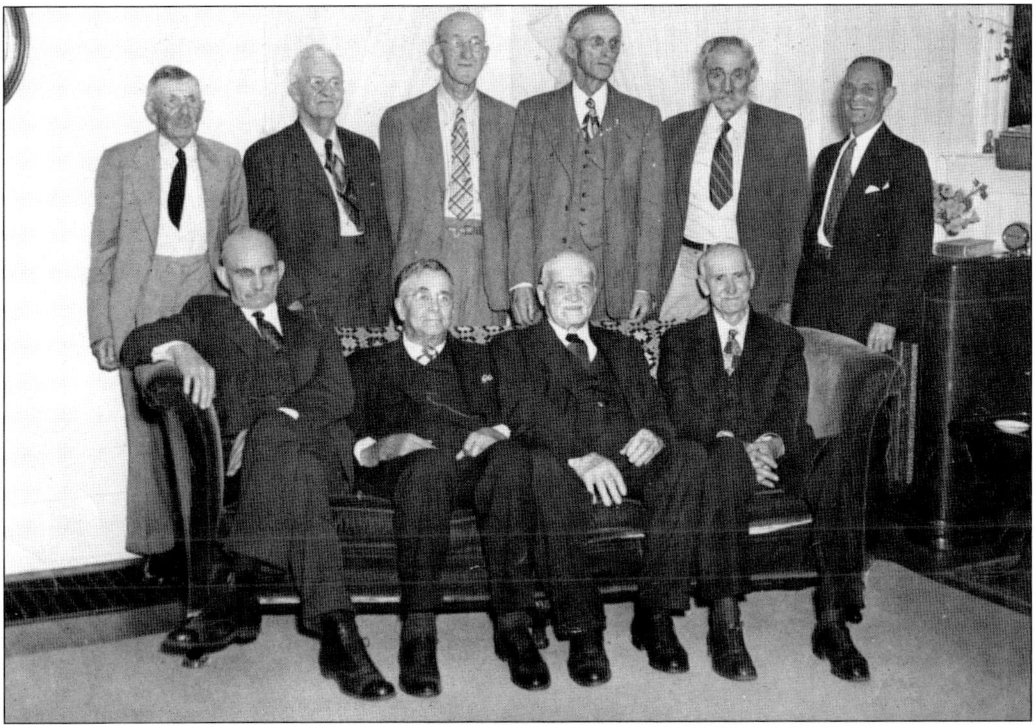

This 1949 dinner at the Linney House in many ways signaled the passing of the torch from Boone's old guard of leading men to a younger generation. From left to right are (seated) Dr. B.B. Dougherty, John W. Hodges, J.M. Moretz, and G.G. Wilcox; (standing) Will Todd, A.W. Smith, H.W. Horton, Tipton Greene, Will Carter, and Ed Cullers. (Historic Boone Collection.)

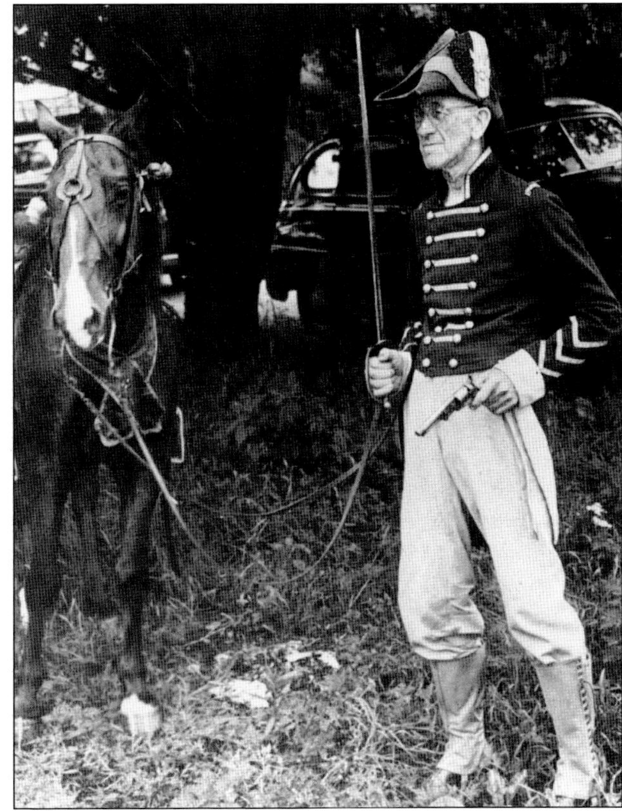

Henry Walter Horton (1873–1968), wearing his ancestor's military uniform, poses with his horse, which he rode for the length of the 1949 Watauga Centennial Parade on King Street. Horton, a prominent businessman, built the high-style H.W. Horton Building on the Old Brick Row site in 1929, only to lose it to foreclosure after the Wall Street crash. (Constance Stallings Collection.)

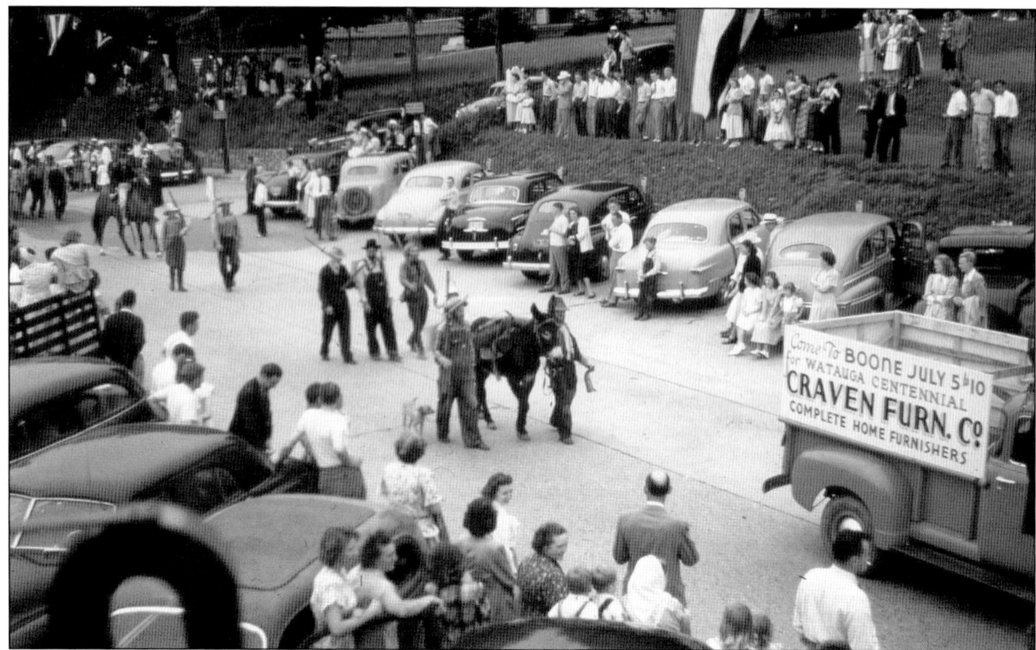

Dr. Edmond Theodore “E.T. “ Glenn (1907–1977) stood on the Appalachian Theatre marquee just outside his office window to take photographs of the 1949 Watauga Centennial Parade on King Street in July 1949. In this image, crowds line the street and terraces of the Daniel Boone Hotel as the procession moves through town. H.W. Horton is on horseback at upper left. (E.T. Glenn Collection.)

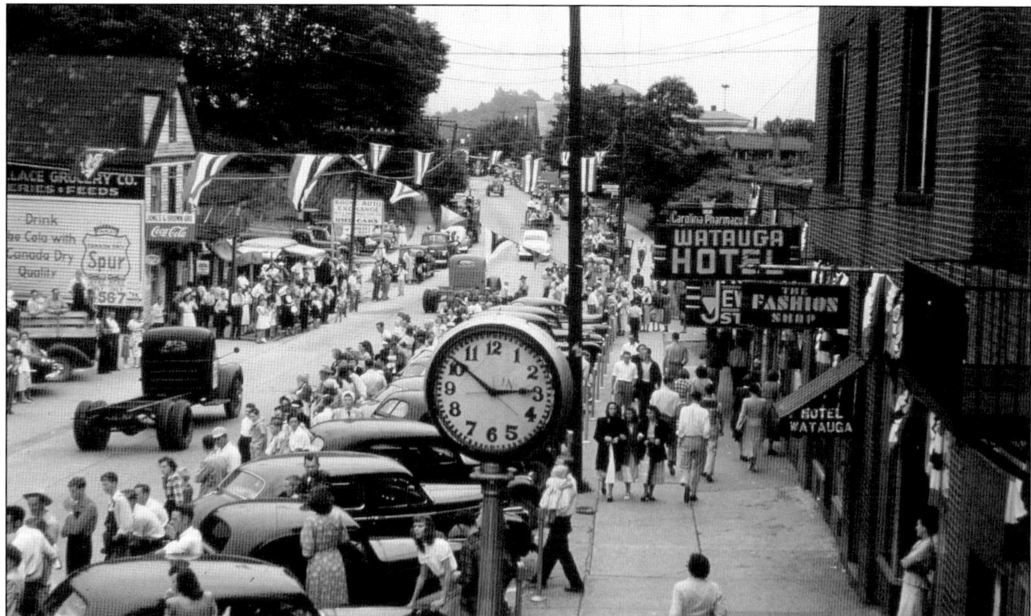

Dr. E.T. Glenn’s photograph from the marquee looking east on King Street shows the 1949 Watauga Centennial Parade procession passing the Stallings Jewelry clock just east of the theater. At left is the old Smithey’s Store, which was by then occupied by Jones and Brown Grocery. The dome of the Boone Methodist Church is in the distance. (E.T. Glenn Collection.)

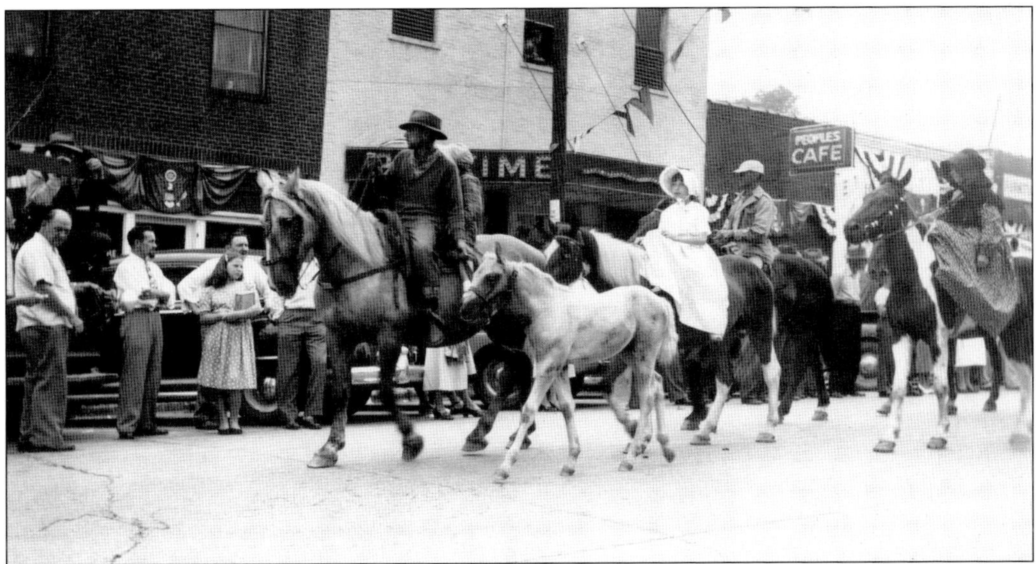

The Watauga Centennial Parade was accompanied by performances of a series of historical vignettes loosely organized under the name *Echoes of the Blue Ridge*. These were staged at the Appalachian State athletic stadium over five days. As a result, many parade participants dressed in their costumes, such as these folks passing the Pastime Theatre (1924) opposite the Linney House. (Paul and Ruby Weston Collection.)

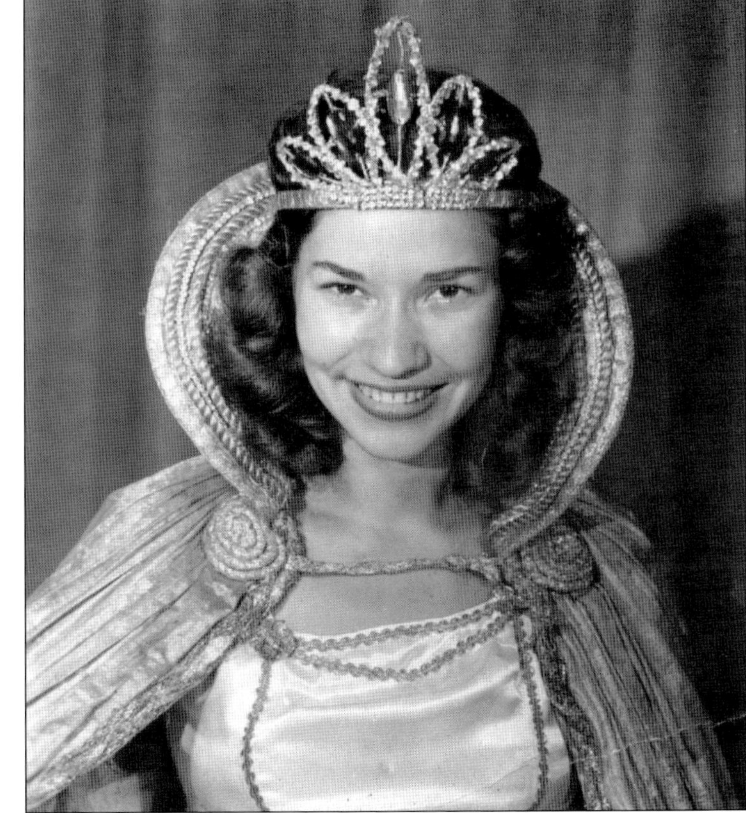

As part of the centennial celebration, Boone locals voted on a Centennial queen, selecting 23-year-old Mickey McGuire (later Hagaman), who handily beat her competitors. McGuire, an employee at Boone Drug Company, was described in the local press as "one of the town's most popular young ladies." (Von and Mickey Hagaman Collection.)

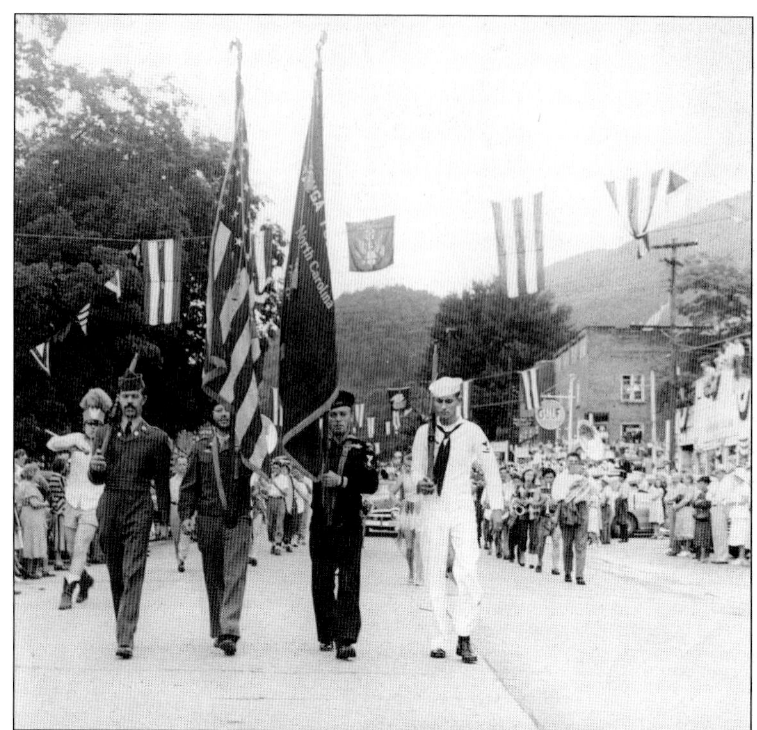

Looking west toward the intersection of Water and King Streets, the color guard leads the 1949 Watauga Centennial Parade. From left to right are an unidentified recruiter, John Thomas King II (1923–1995), Robert Von Hagaman (1925–2016), and Gene Lewis Reese (1927–2001). The E.L. Teague Gulf station and the 1875 courthouse are at right. (Von and Mickey Hagaman Collection.)

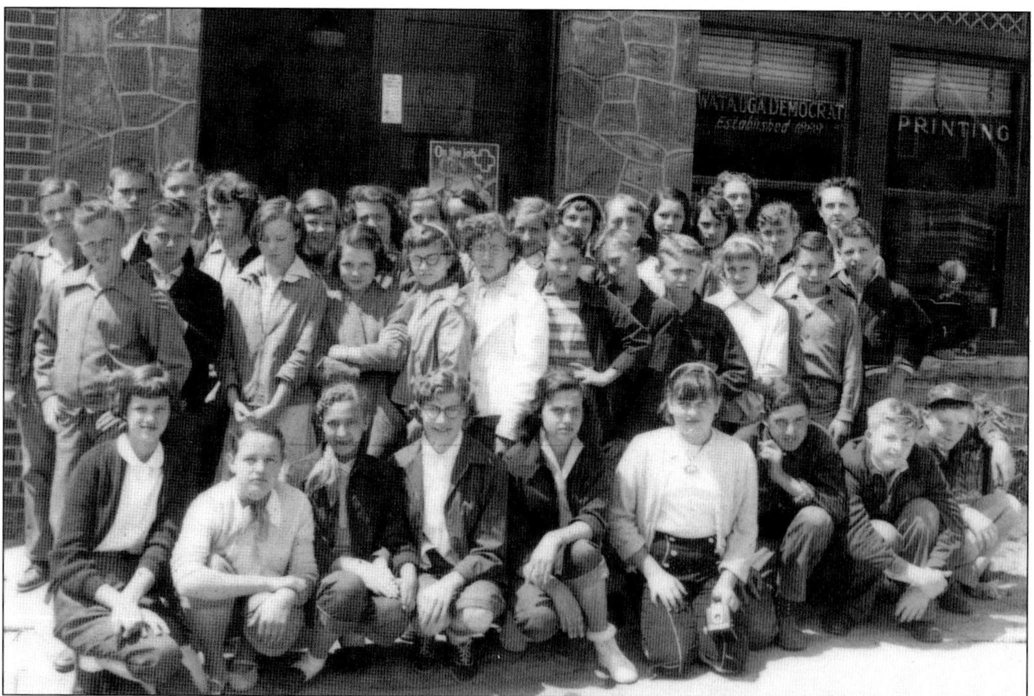

The Watauga centennial festivities and subsequent interest in boosting Boone tourism through historical pageantry also served as an incentive for area children to learn more about—and take pride in—their community. Shown here around 1950 are schoolchildren visiting the third *Watauga Democrat* building (1937) on King Street. (Historic Boone Collection.)

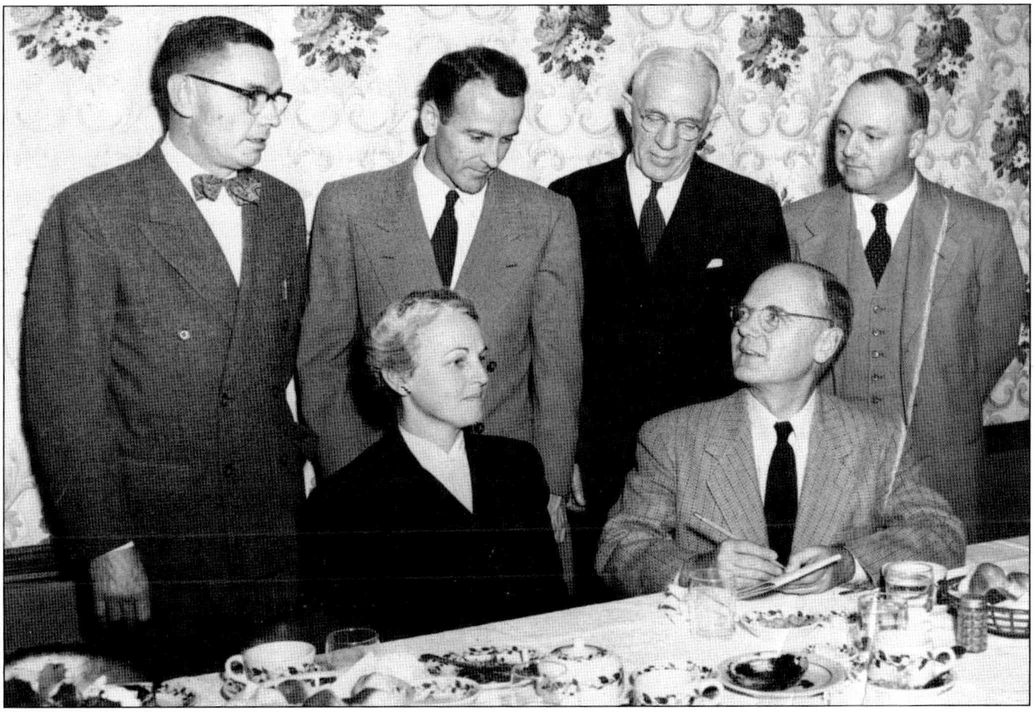

Following the success of the Watauga centennial pageantry, members of the Southern Appalachian Historical Association recruited playwright Kermit Hunter to write a new outdoor drama, *Horn in the West*. Pictured from left to right are (seated) Constance Shoun Stallings (1904–1982) and Samuel Sheldon; (standing) Robert Edward Agle (1911–1981), Hunter (1910–2001), Dr. Isaac Garfield Greer (1881–1967), and Dr. Daniel Jay Whitener (1898–1964). (Historic Boone Collection.)

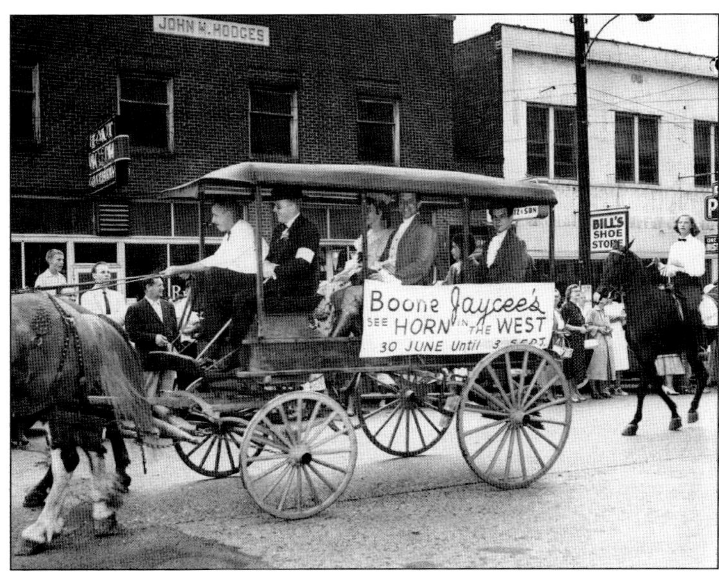

Kermit Hunter's *Horn in the West* debuted on June 27, 1952, at the Daniel Boone Amphitheatre, built on farmland donated by James Bennett Winkler (1896–1978). Winkler later donated land for the Daniel Boone Native Gardens and Daniel Boone Park. This undated image shows actors in a parade promoting the production as their wagon passes the Qualls Block and John W. Hodges Building. (Historic Boone Collection.)

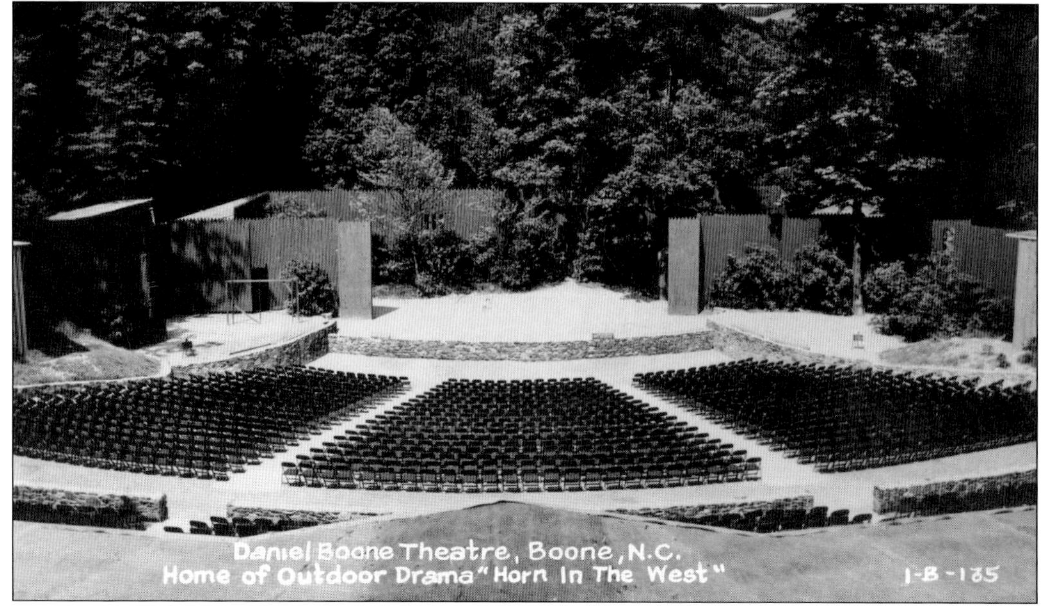

The Southern Appalachian Historical Association's production of *Horn in the West* and the nearby Hickory Ridge Living History Museum remain significant tourist draws during summers. The amphitheater has changed little since this real-photo postcard was produced in the early 1950s, although modern improvements and a partnership with the Town of Boone, which owns the land, have recently produced innovative ideas for programming beyond summer performances. (Bobby Brendell Postcard Collection.)

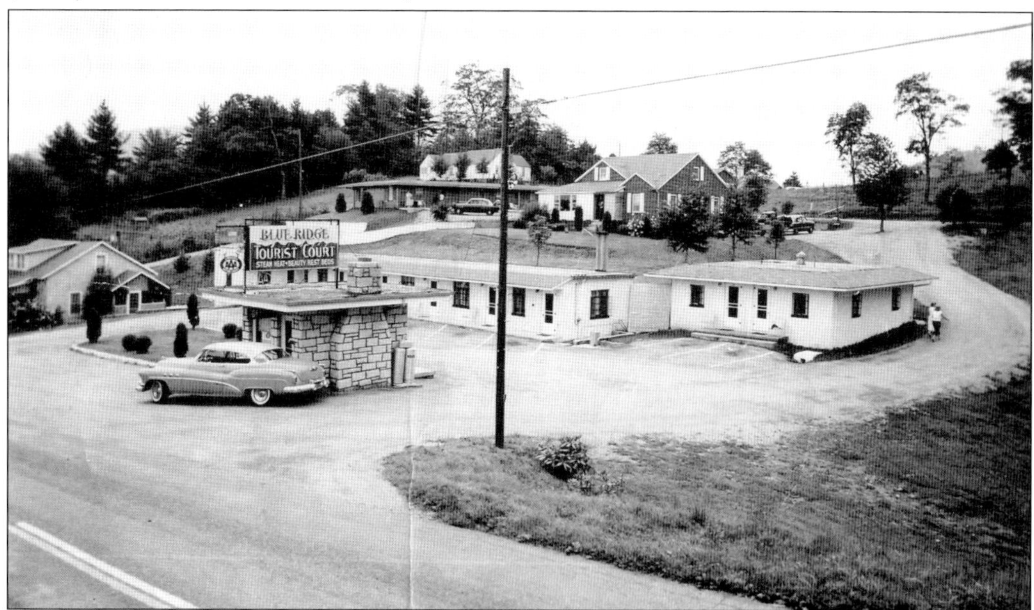

At the end of World War II, increased automobile tourism to the High Country, coupled with new tourist attractions like *Horn in the West* and the Blue Ridge Parkway, left Boone short on accommodations. In response, Estel G. Wagner (1920–2011) built the Blue Ridge Tourist Court in the Perkinsville area in 1950. Currently undergoing restoration, it is the only surviving Boone tourist court from the 1950s. (Estel G. Wagner Collection).

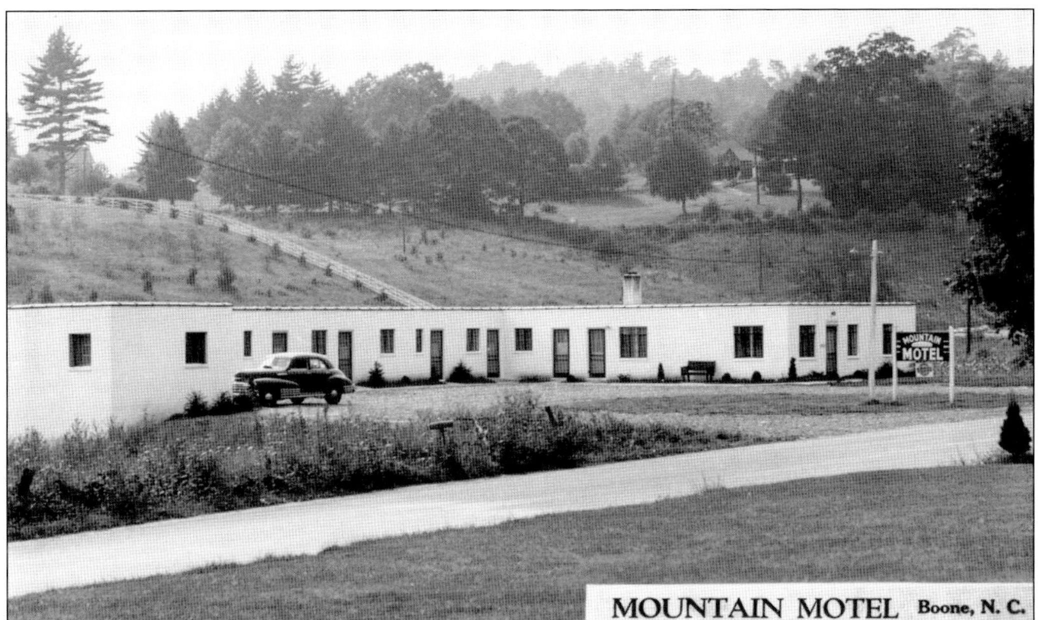

Another early roadside motel built in reaction to tourism demands was the Mountain Motel, completed by L.T. Tatum in 1948 on Blowing Rock Road on what is currently the site of a McDonald's. By 1960, Blowing Rock Road had nearly a dozen motels and tourist courts between King Street and Deerfield Road. (Bobby Brendell Postcard Collection.)

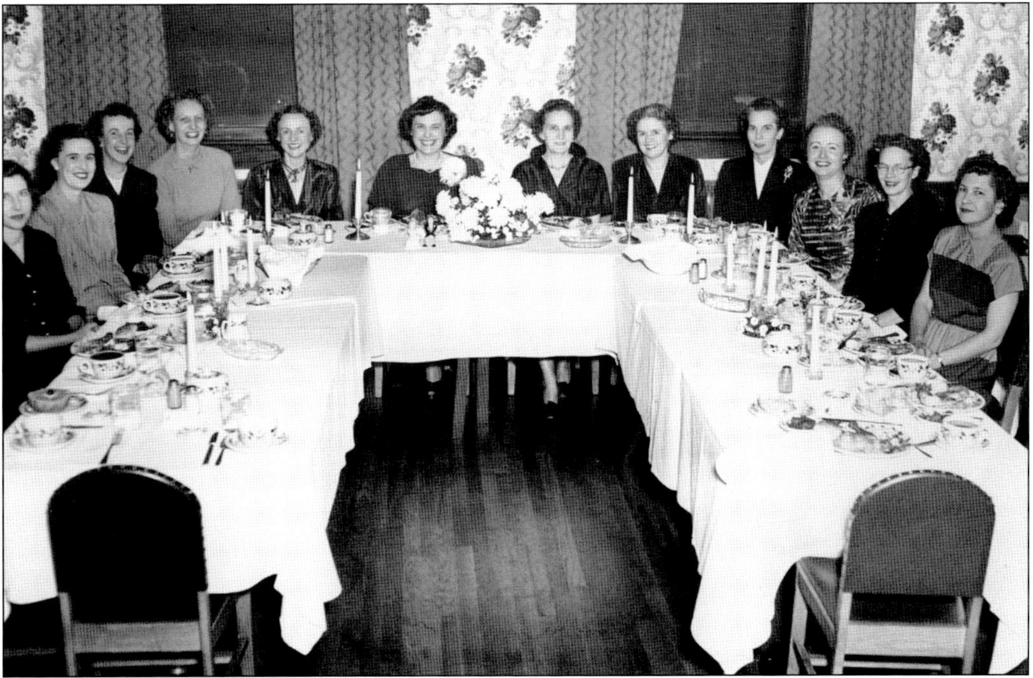

As Boone grappled with increased tourist traffic from *Horn in the West* and the completion of portions of the nearby Blue Ridge Parkway, the Junior Women's Club and other women's groups advocated for new roadside accommodations for tourists. This image shows a Boone businesswomen's luncheon at the Daniel Boone Hotel in the mid-1950s. (Historic Boone Collection.)

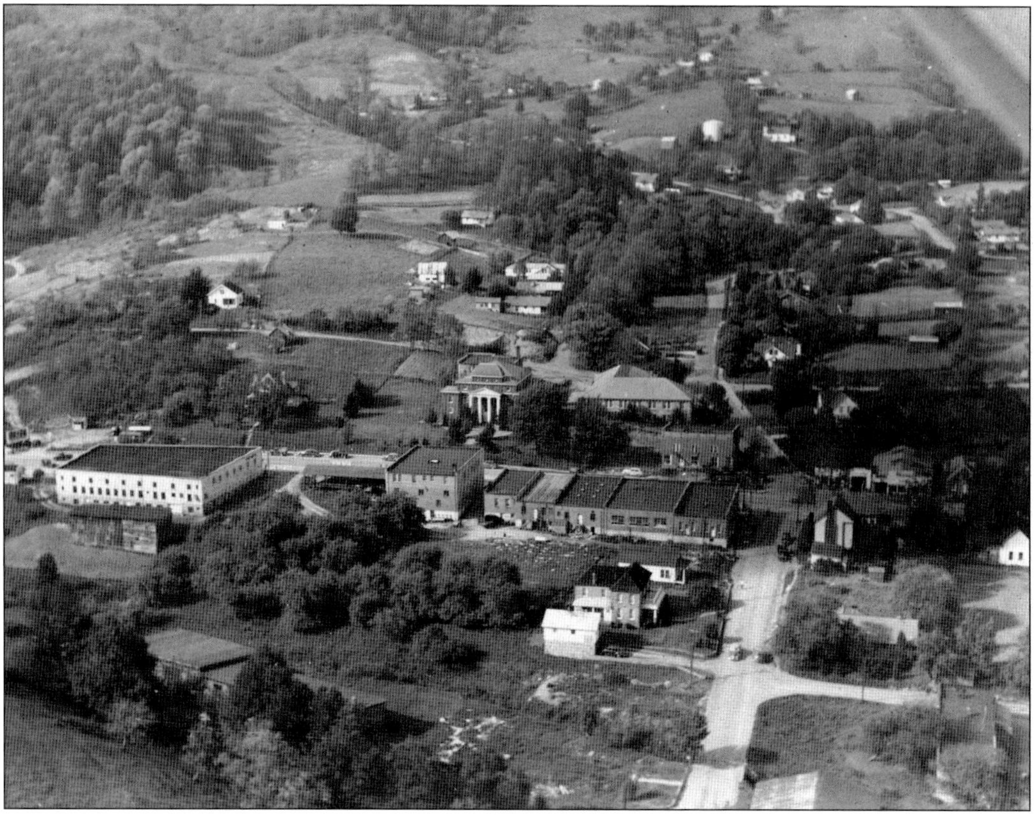

In this July 1948 image, Water Street is shown running south to north from the bottom. The 1940 Smithey's building is visible at left, while the 1938, WPA-funded courthouse annex building is between the 1905 courthouse and the 1875 courthouse. The long building in the left foreground, often misidentified as the "Tweetsie shed," was the Boone Furniture and Lumber Company warehouse (1929); the structure was demolished in 2018. (Crate Teague Collection.)

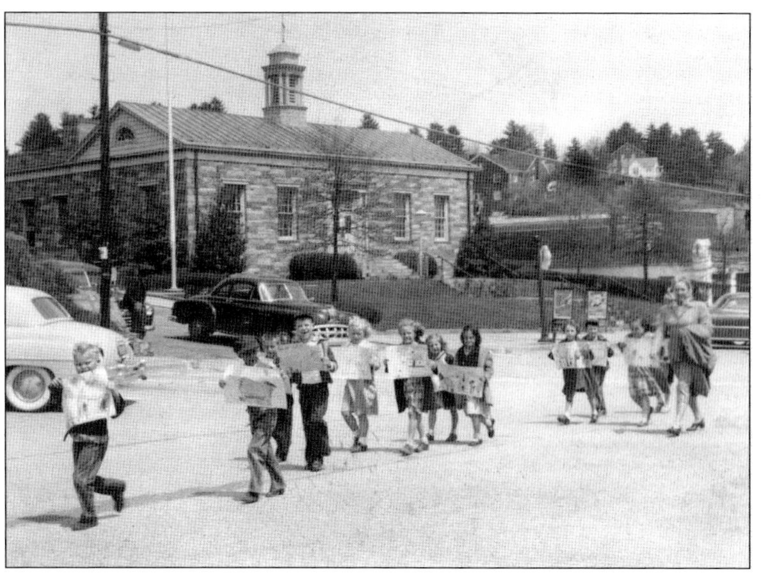

In preparation for the premiere of *Horn in the West* and thousands of expected tourists, Constance Stallings and Mayor Gordon Winkler (1903–1981) organized a "Clean Up, Paint Up, Fix Up" parade to be held on April 28, 1952. These young schoolchildren carry drawings as they parade past the Boone post office. (Constance Stallings Collection.)

Guitarist and songwriter Arthel Lane "Doc" Watson (1923–2012) was born in nearby Deep Gap. At a young age, he lost his sight. To earn extra money, he took to busking with his guitar on the streets of Boone while also working as a piano tuner. He is at right holding his Les Paul Goldtop guitar in this October 1954 photograph of the Charles Osborne Band. (Palmer Blair Collection.)

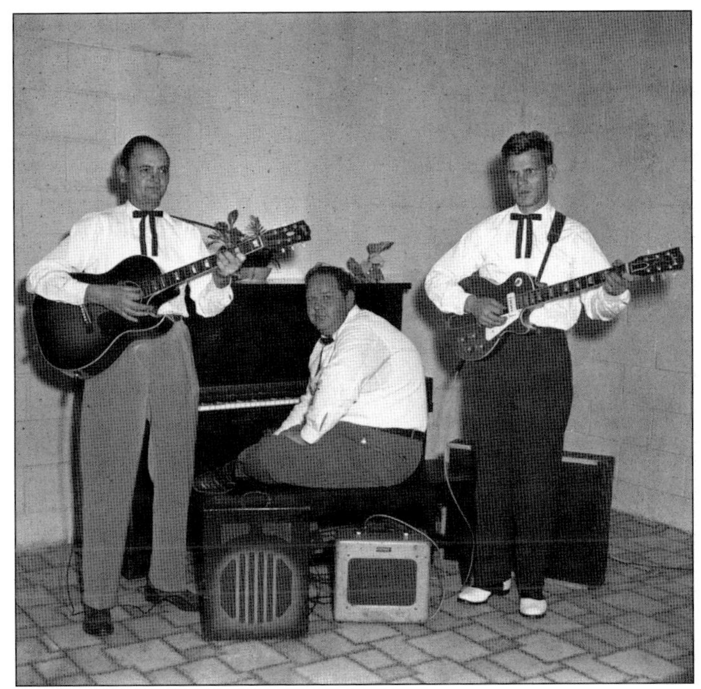

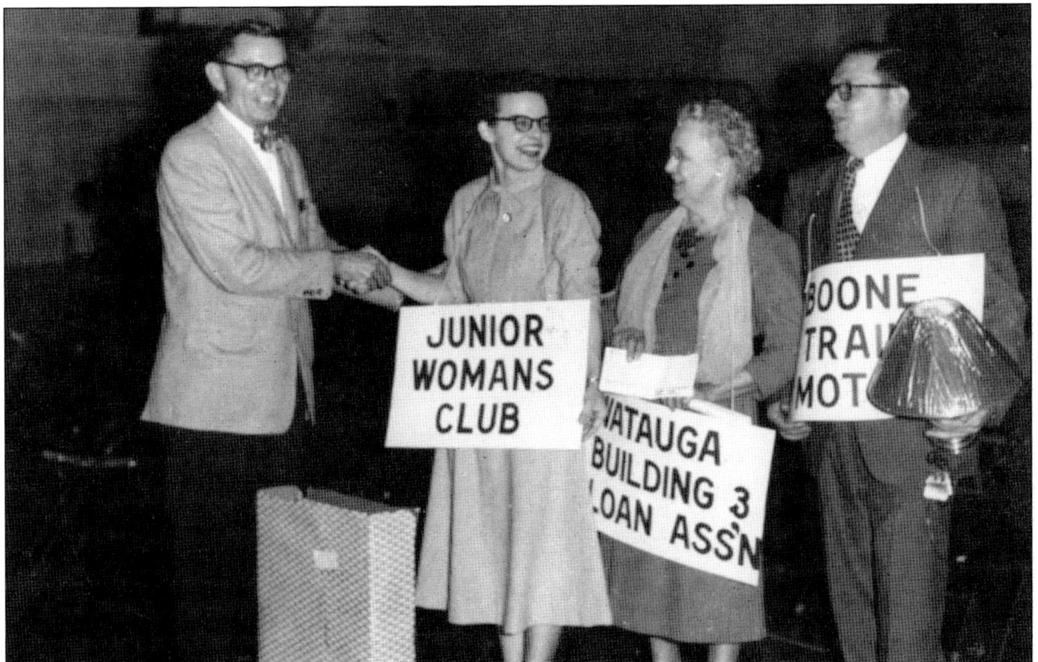

Contests were common in Boone during the 1950s, ranging from beauty pageants to talent shows to commercial giveaway stunts. In this November 1953 image documenting a spelling bee to benefit the Appalachian Band Parents Association, from left to right, Bob Agle congratulates Carrie Lee Farthing Dickerson (born 1926) as Pearl Mae Leonard Bingham (1886–1975) and Rev. George Shuford look on. (Historic Boone Collection.)

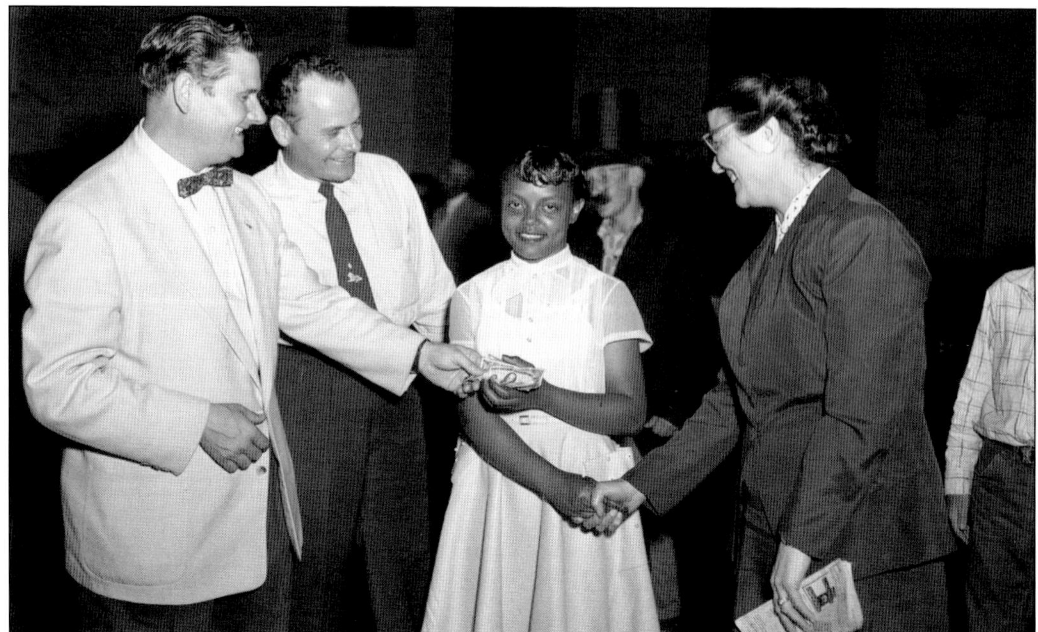

Another contest was the Arthur Smith Talent Hunt, a regional competition culminating in a Charlotte television appearance for the winner. In this May 1954 image, 12-year-old Sherry Grimes (later Horton; 1941–2010), of the Junaluska community, is accepting her prize from Arthur Smith as Sonny Smith and Grimes's vocal teacher, Maebelle Casey South (1897–1984), look on. Doc Watson finished second. (Palmer Blair Collection.)

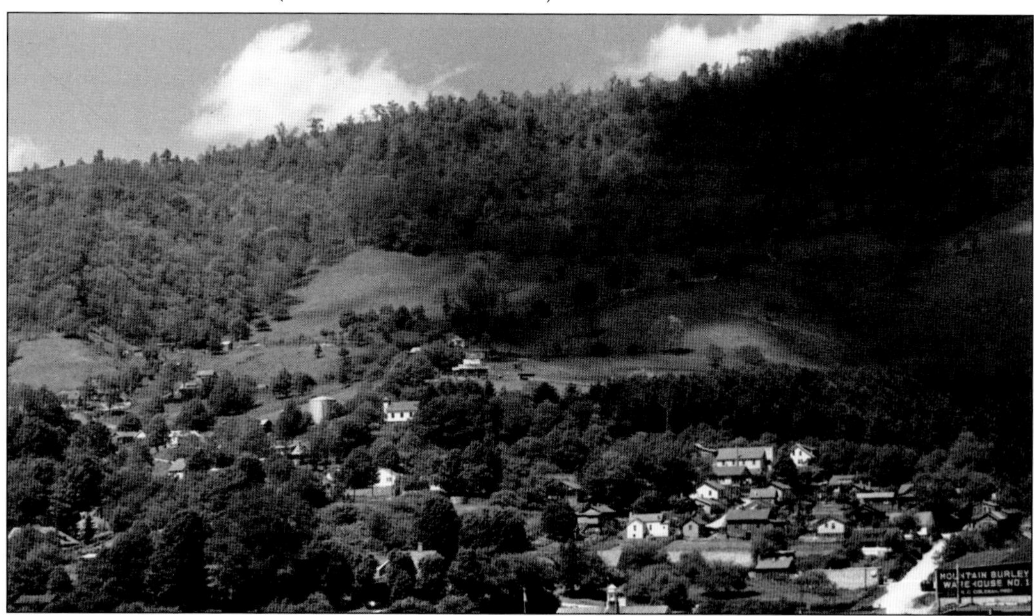

This 1954 image shows the Junaluska community spread out across the Rich Mountain hillside. At center left is the Boone Chapel, while the Chocolate Bar, a popular community hangout, is at lower right across the street from the Mountain Burley Warehouse. The Mennonite Brethren Church, with its front tower, is diagonally up the hill and to the left from the Chocolate Bar. (Palmer Blair Collection)

With no public kindergartens in the 1950s, locals relied on private settings for early childhood education. Louise DeLima ran a popular kindergarten sponsored by the Junior Women's Club in her home on Hardin Street during that time. David Richardson, son of Dr. Wayne Richardson and Melissa Richardson, is seated at left wearing a cowboy hat in this Palmer Blair photograph. (Richardsons of Boone Drug Collection.)

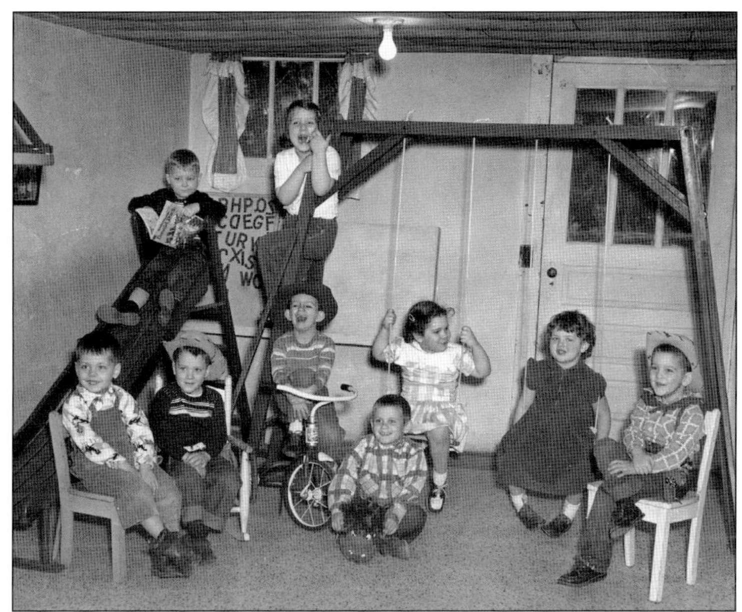

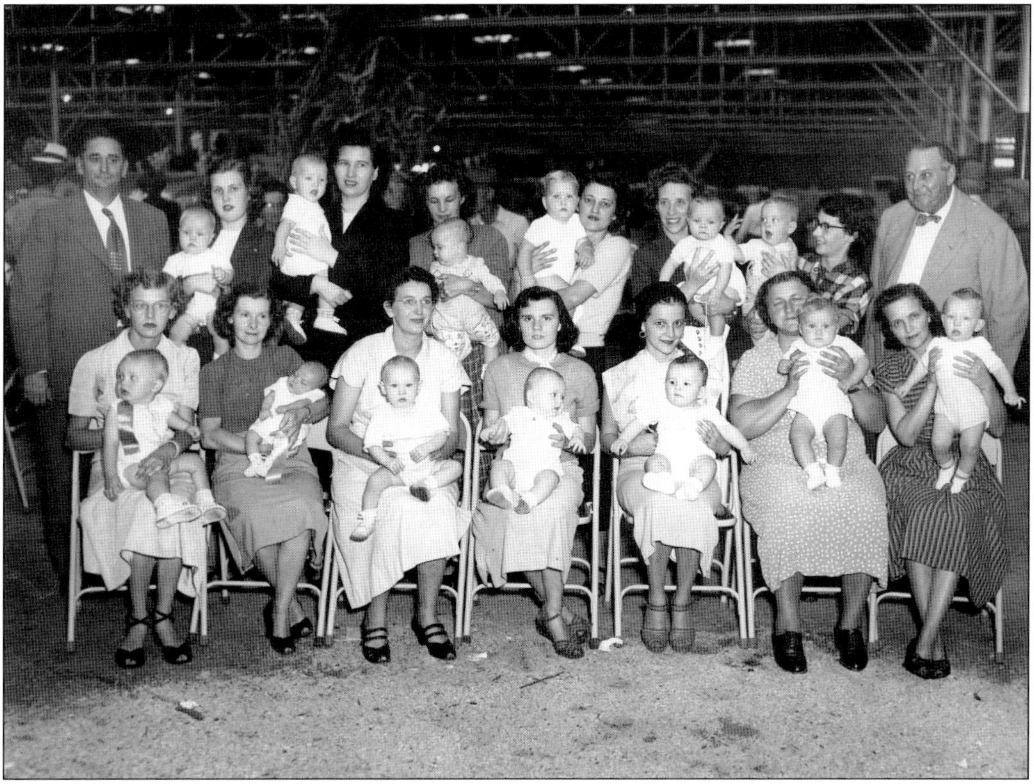

Baby contests were an enormously popular event with baby-boomer parents at the annual Blue Ridge Agricultural Fair. Shown in 1953 are the annual judges, Barnard Dougherty (1909–1965; left) and Watt H. Gragg (right), while mothers hold their babies. Melissa Crouse Richardson (1915–1994) is the third mother from the right in the back, holding her son David Wayne Richardson (born 1951). (Richardsons of Boone Drug Collection.)

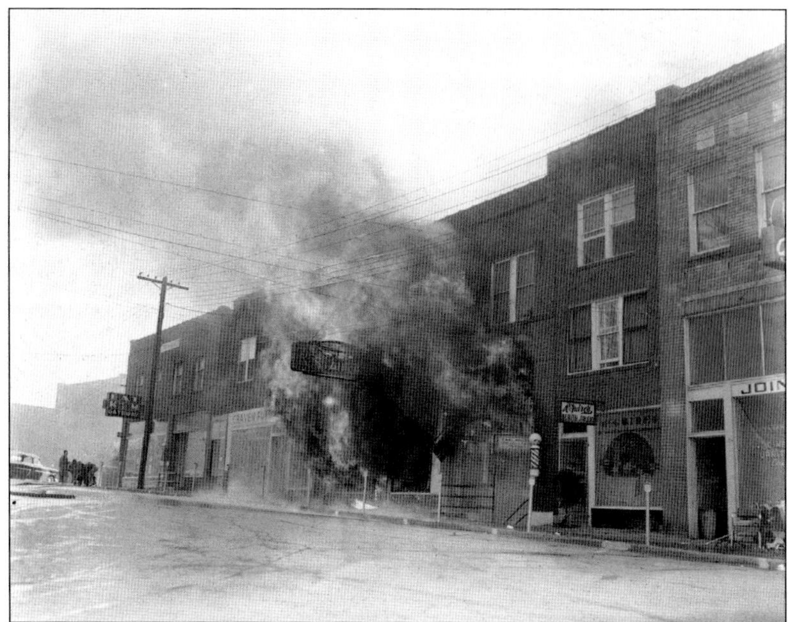

Fires remained a major source of anxiety in Boone throughout the middle of the 20th century. This Christmas Day 1952 fire in the Qualls Block not only destroyed six businesses in the building, it also cut electrical power for most of Boone's residents. The fire permanently ended the Carolina Hotel's operations in the building. (Palmer Blair Collection.)

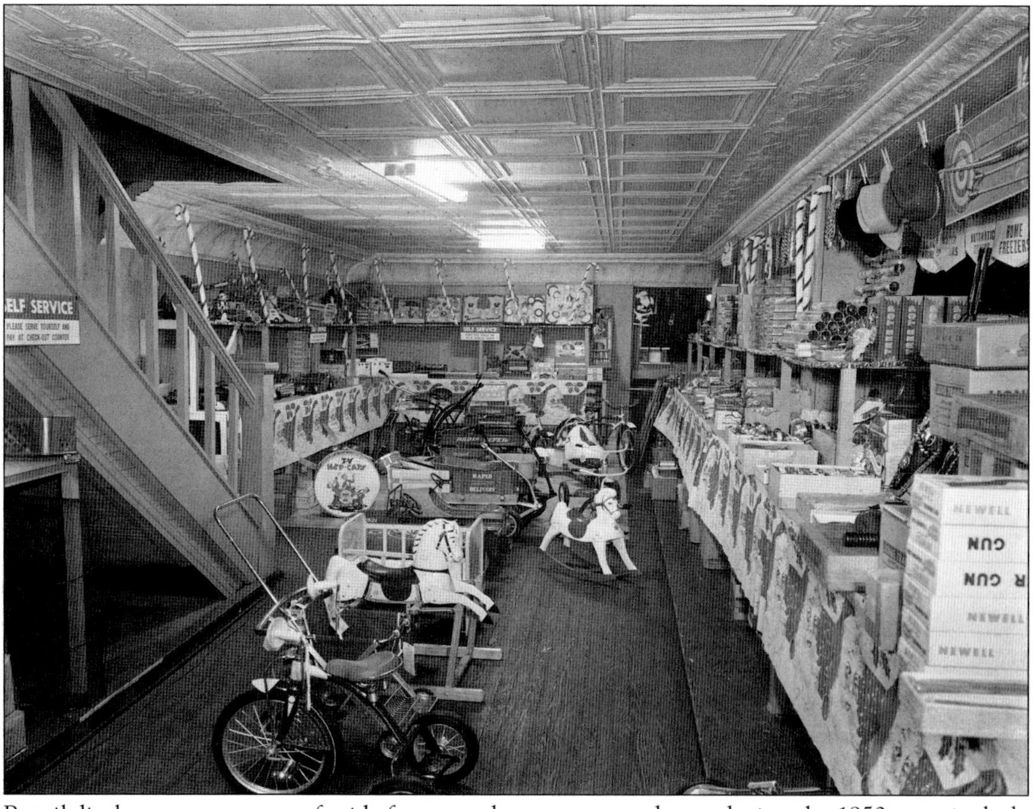

Retail displays were a source of pride for many downtown merchants during the 1950s, particularly as the busy Christmas season approached. This November 1954 publicity image for Farmer's Hardware shows the store's Christmas toy display in the basement level of the building, with signs urging customers to utilize "self service" for their shopping. (Palmer Blair Collection.)

Initially chartered in 1953, the Boone Golf Course finally started coming to fruition in late 1957 as Wade Edward Brown (1907–2009) took the reins as president of the operation. The course, designed by Ellis Maples and located between the Middle and South Forks of the New River, was expected to be a major tourism draw for Boone. It opened in July 1959. (Henry Dewolf Aerial Surveys of Watauga County Collection.)

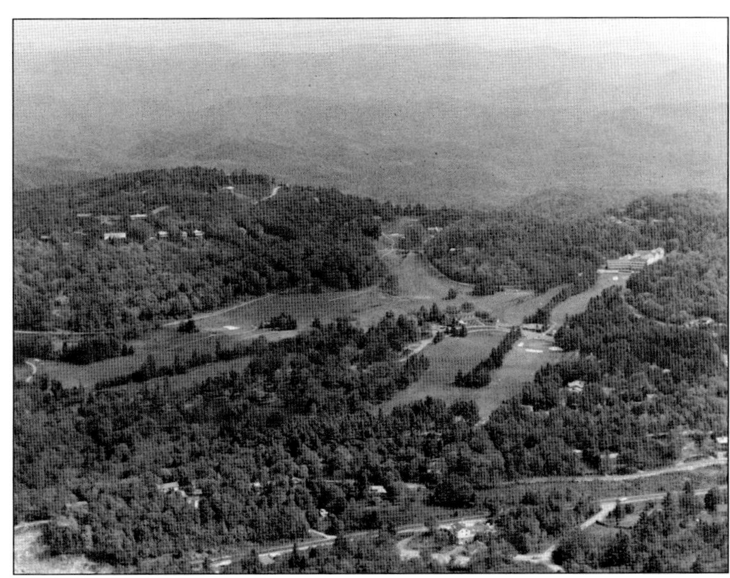

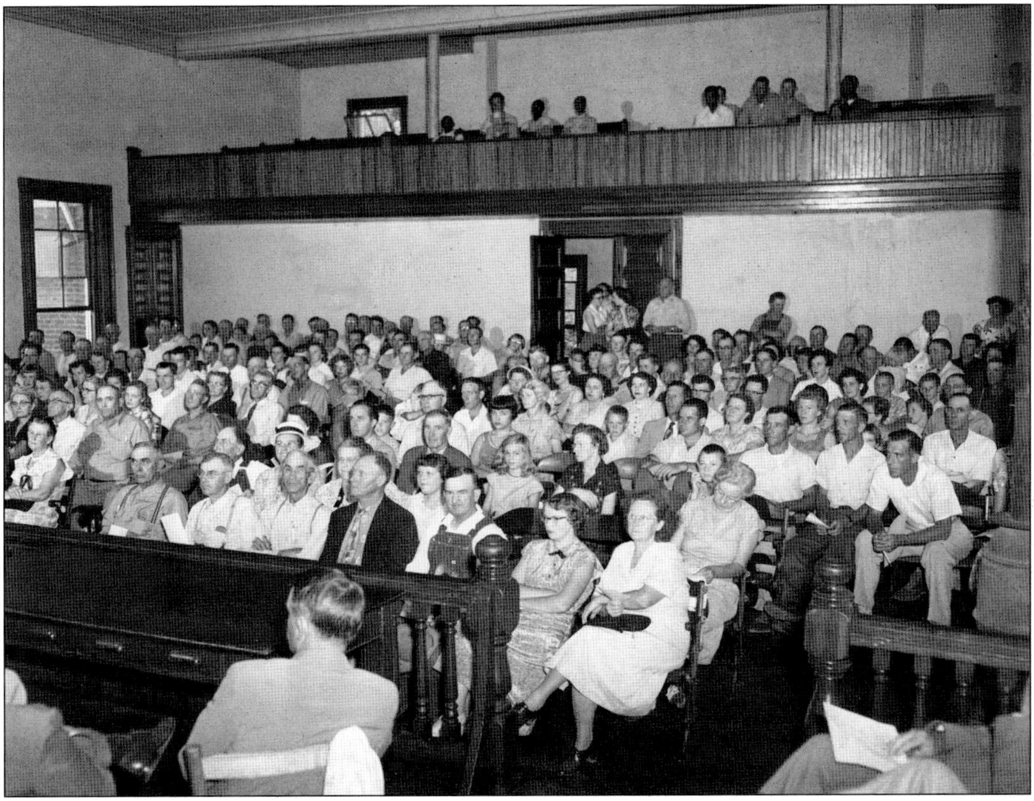

A large crowd listens to a speaker at a Farm Bureau meeting in August 1954 in the courtroom of the 1905 Watauga County Courthouse. Racial segregation, both de jure and de facto, remained the order of Boone into the 1960s, with Black farmers from Boone and Watauga County relegated to the courtroom's balcony seats. (Palmer Blair Collection.)

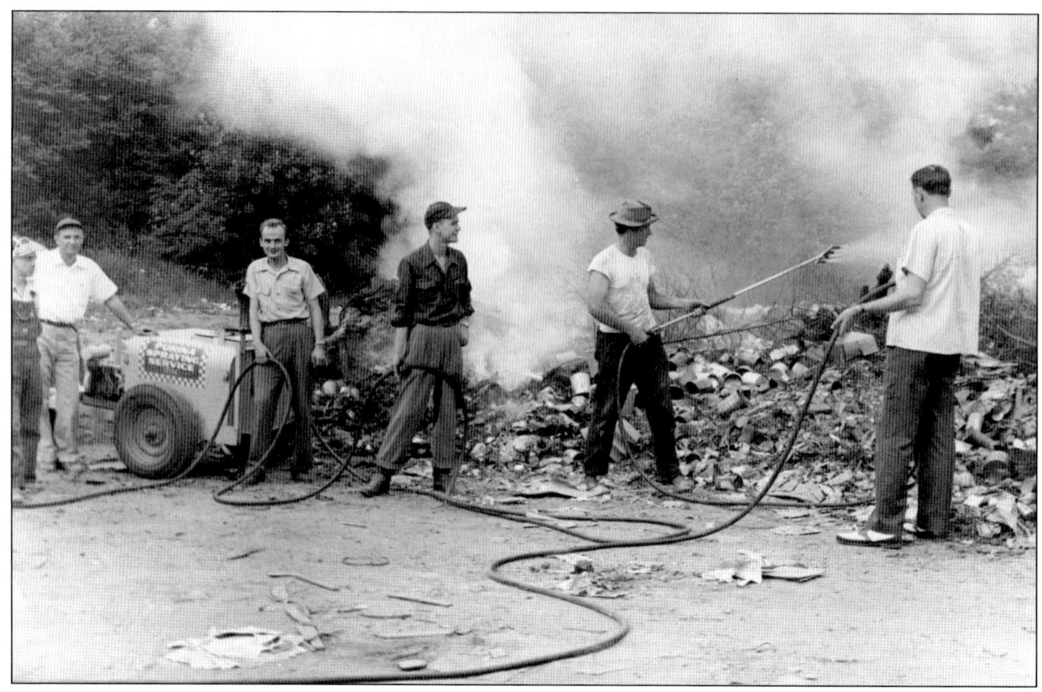

Wharf rats and inextinguishable fires were long considered major issues at the town dump. This 1948 image shows the Jaycees taking on a new pest at the dump, which was located at what is now the site of Appalachian State University's chancellor's residence. From left to right are Lawrence Wilson, Joe Michael, Cecil Farthing, R.D. Hodges, Perry Greene (spraying DDT to quell a fly infestation), and Fred M. Gragg. (Historic Boone Collection.)

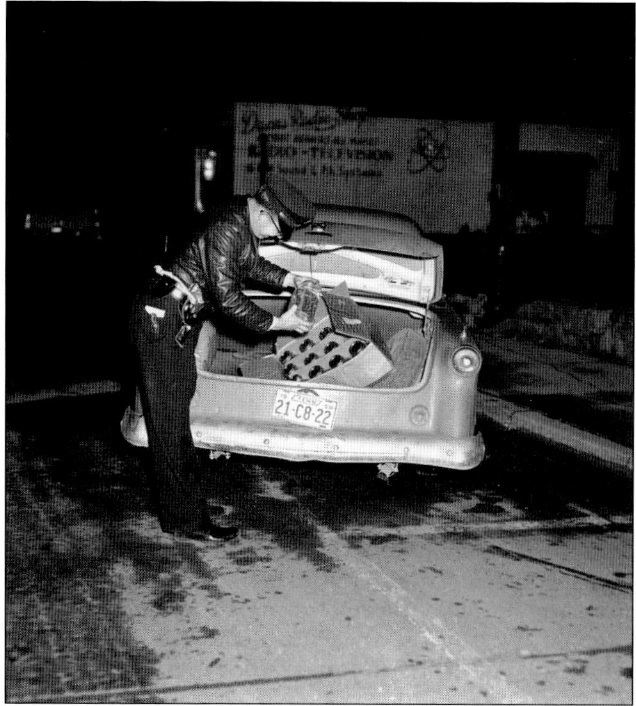

Boone had a long history of being a dry town, with activities ranging from the Ku Klux Klan aiding local authorities in the 1920s to stop the liquor trade to cabbies making booze runs to Calhoun Falls for locals as late as the 1980s. In this 1958 image, officer Max Adams Fox (1931–2013) makes a moonshine bust on a car occupied by three residents of Mountain City, Tennessee. (Palmer Blair Collection.)

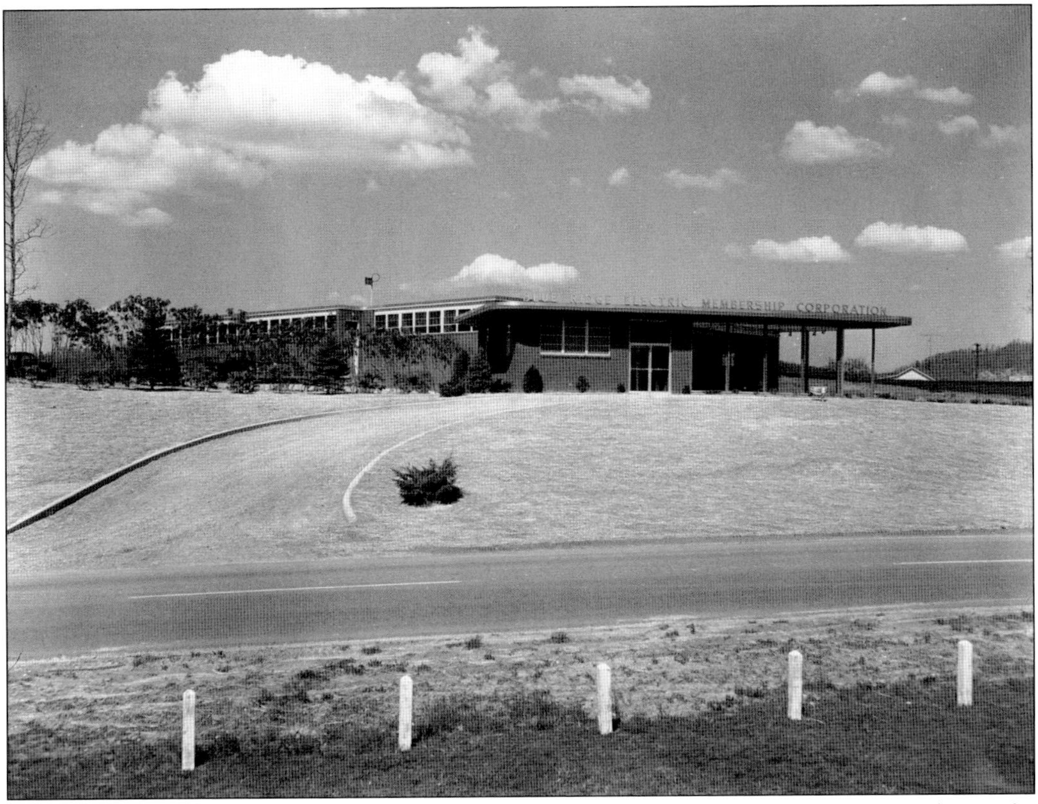

During the 1950s, many Boone businesses began looking beyond the downtown business district for more room or newer accommodations. One was the Blue Ridge Electric Membership Corporation, the local rural electric cooperative, which moved to this new building on Blowing Rock Road in May 1957. The site is currently home to Boone's state liquor store. (Palmer Blair Collection.)

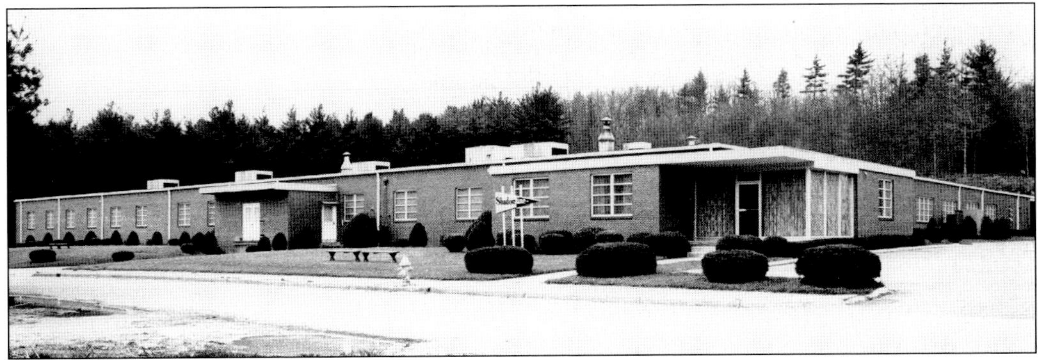

Local business interests also worked hard to draw new industries to Boone in the 1950s. One such enterprise was Shadowline Inc., a lingerie company that opened this plant just off Blowing Rock Road in July 1957, promising to employ more than 600 workers. Watauga Industries Inc., a local concern, served as the leaseholder and stock-issuer to get the plant started. (George Flowers Collection.)

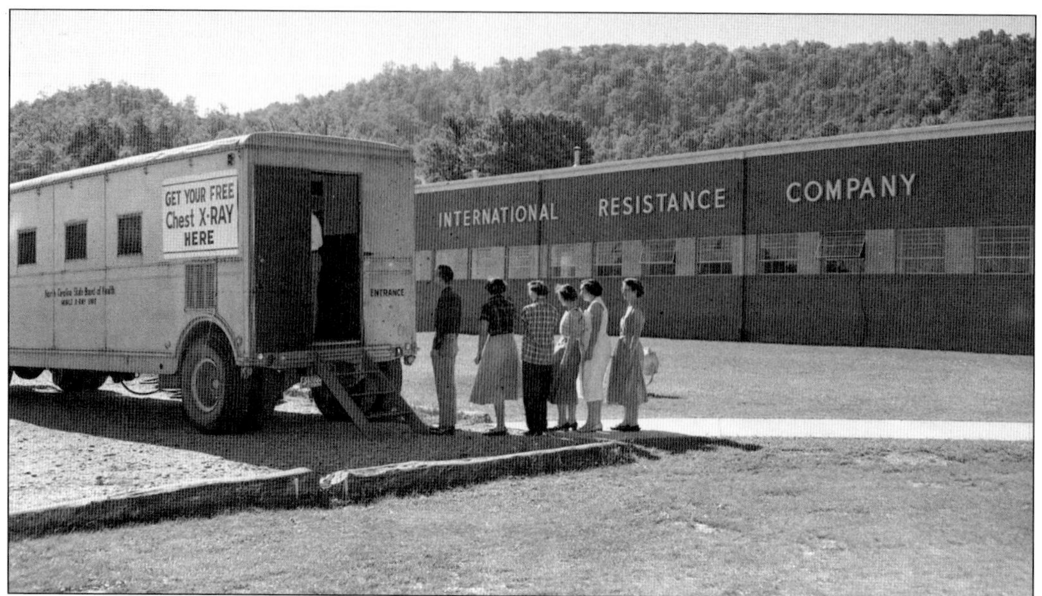

The International Resistance Company, manufacturer of electronic resistors, opened its plant in January 1954 on Greenway Road with promises to employ up to 450 people. This 1956 photograph shows employees at the plant lining up for a tuberculosis screening chest X-ray during a widely publicized public health campaign. (Palmer Blair Collection.)

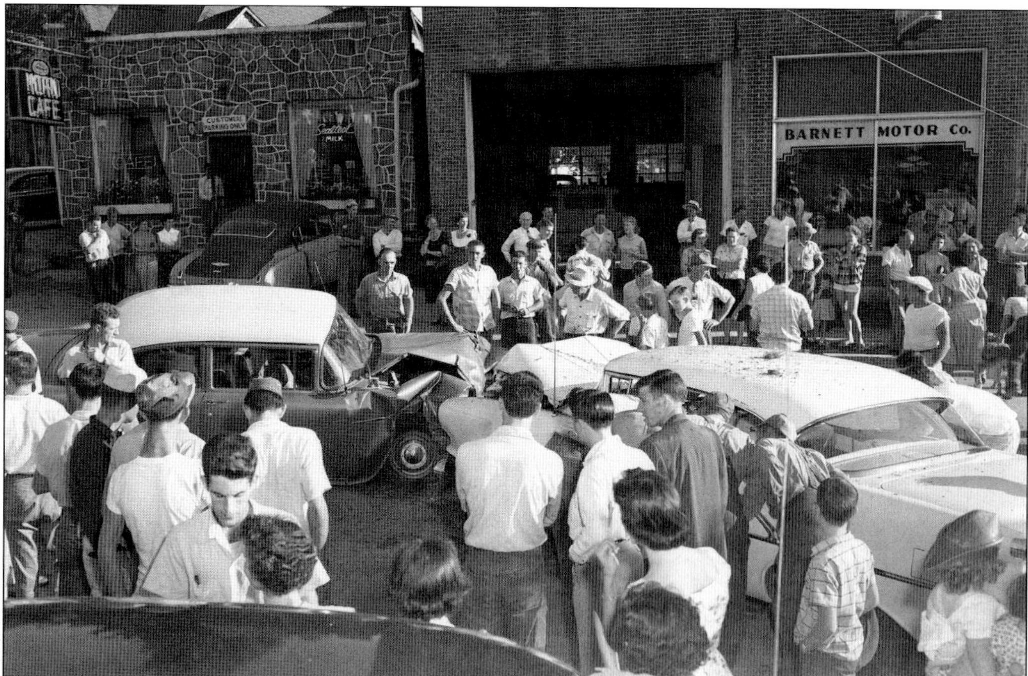

Car accidents were major news throughout the 1950s, with many of them ending tragically because of the lack of modern safety equipment. This September 1956 image shows the Emma Isaacs–E.J. Hardin wreck in front of the Horn Café and Barnett Motor Company at Greasy Corners. Isaacs was the owner of the Horn Café; her daughter Velma Isaacs Rhymer died from her injuries. (Palmer Blair Collection.)

Four

Workers of Boone 1950s

Much of what today's residents know about Boone, its architecture, and its people around the middle of the 20th century comes from the stunning images shot by Boone photographer Palmer Blair during the late 1940s and 1950s. In addition to his work as a studio photographer, Blair took countless stringer gigs for the local paper and promotional jobs for local businesses. The sheer volume of events, people, and places that Blair photographed between 1947 and 1957 is enough to leave one wondering if he ever ate or slept.

According to his widow, Sarah Lynn Spencer, Blair was often frustrated that the news cared little about regular folks and instead focused on wealthy men and the businesses they operated. To correct that deficit, Blair began a photograph series called Workers of Boone, in which he visited most of the businesses in Boone and outlying areas and photographed the people working there. All told, about 400 images Blair captured in 1952 as part of this project survive. They offer an intimate glimpse of the people he wanted to acknowledge and honor, as well as exceedingly rare views of the interiors of the places where they worked and, often, the interactions they had with others while working. As far as the author of this book knows, none of these images were published during Blair's tragically short career.

Blair's eye for detail and the character of his subjects reflects the compassion and grace with which he approached the workers of Boone and photography in general. Unlike the town itself at the time, Blair's work was not racially segregated—he sought out subjects of all backgrounds and occupations. This chapter includes 44 images from the series, all of which are found in the Digital Watauga Project's Palmer Blair Collection. The chapter also includes two special images—the first is one of Blair's self-portraits, while the other is a studio portrait of an individual who probably would have been otherwise overlooked and forgotten if not for Blair's keen eye. Everyone in town knew George Horton in the 1950s, yet his story is not the kind that usually makes it into history books.

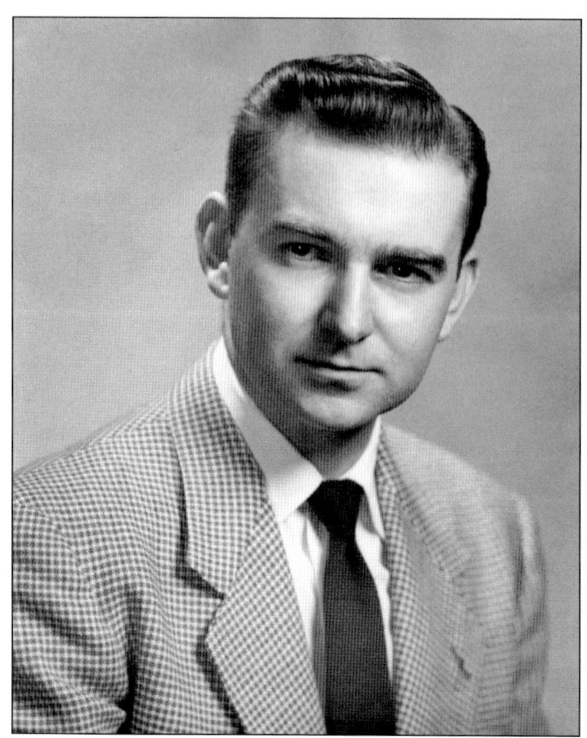

Palmer Sligh Blair (1922–1957) was a Boone native and a graduate of Appalachian State Teachers College. Together with his wife, Sarah Lynn Rives Blair (born 1927), he opened their first photography studio as Palmer's Photo Shop in 1947. Blair and his cousin Hudson C. Sisk were killed when the engine failed on the plane Sisk was piloting while the men were on a commissioned aerial photography excursion on March 21, 1957.

Velma Rose Combs Burnley (1921–2019), a native of Vilas, North Carolina, is shown working as a cashier at the Northwestern Bank in 1952. She later became the bank's first female vice president, president of the chamber of commerce, and Boone's first female mayor, serving from 1989 to 2005. She was a powerful force in Boone's economic development during the late 20th century.

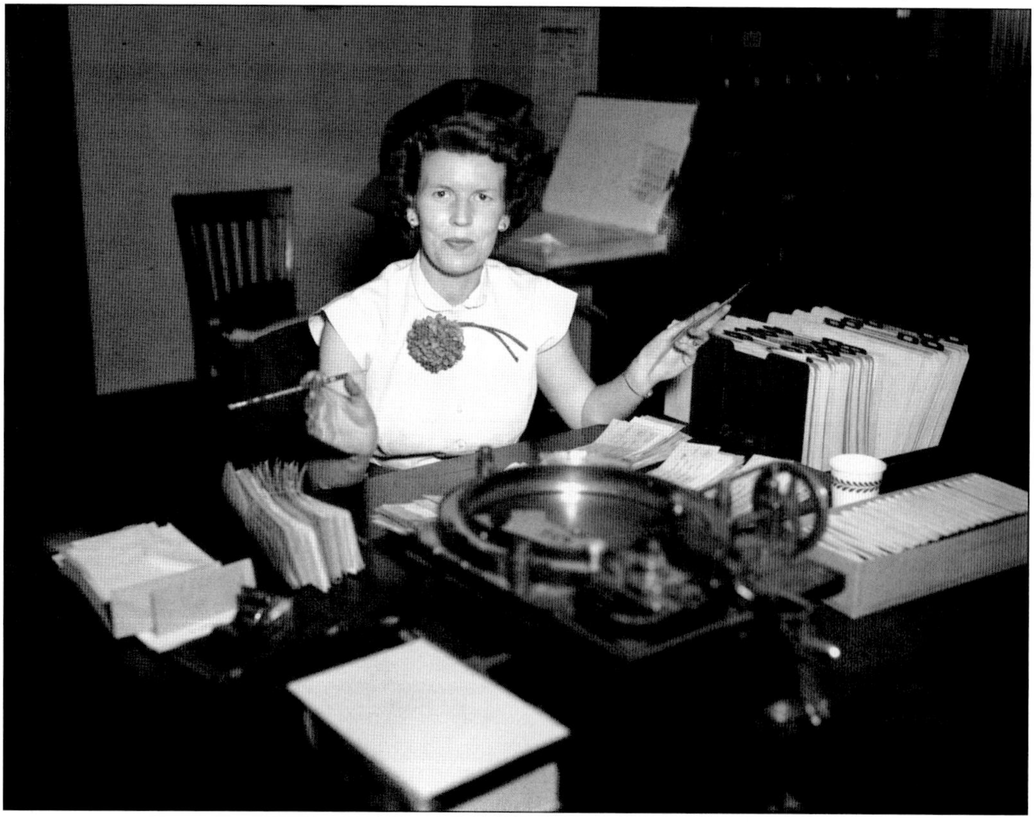

Alice Lenore Councill Robbins (1916–1977), a longtime ticket-seller at the Appalachian Theatre, glares at the camera in this 1952 image that shows a behind-the-scenes glimpse of her "office." Like many of the employees at the Appalachian, Robbins was inextricably connected to the theater in the public's memory as a result of her decades of service there.

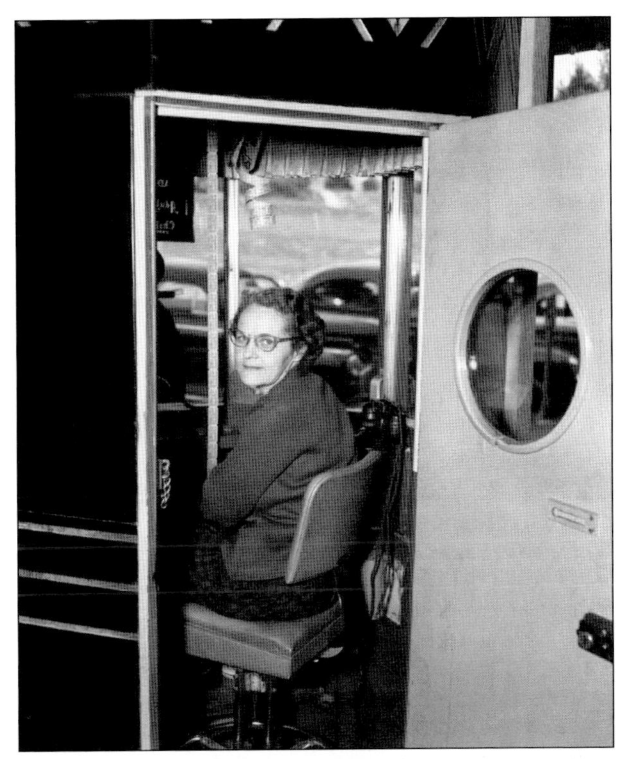

Bob Agle spent much of World War II working for a dairy company in Tennessee, but he returned to Boone in August 1945 to take a position as manager of the Appalachian Theatre, later rising to general manager of its parent Statesville Theater Corporation. He is pictured in his tiny office on the mezzanine of the Appalachian Theatre in April 1952.

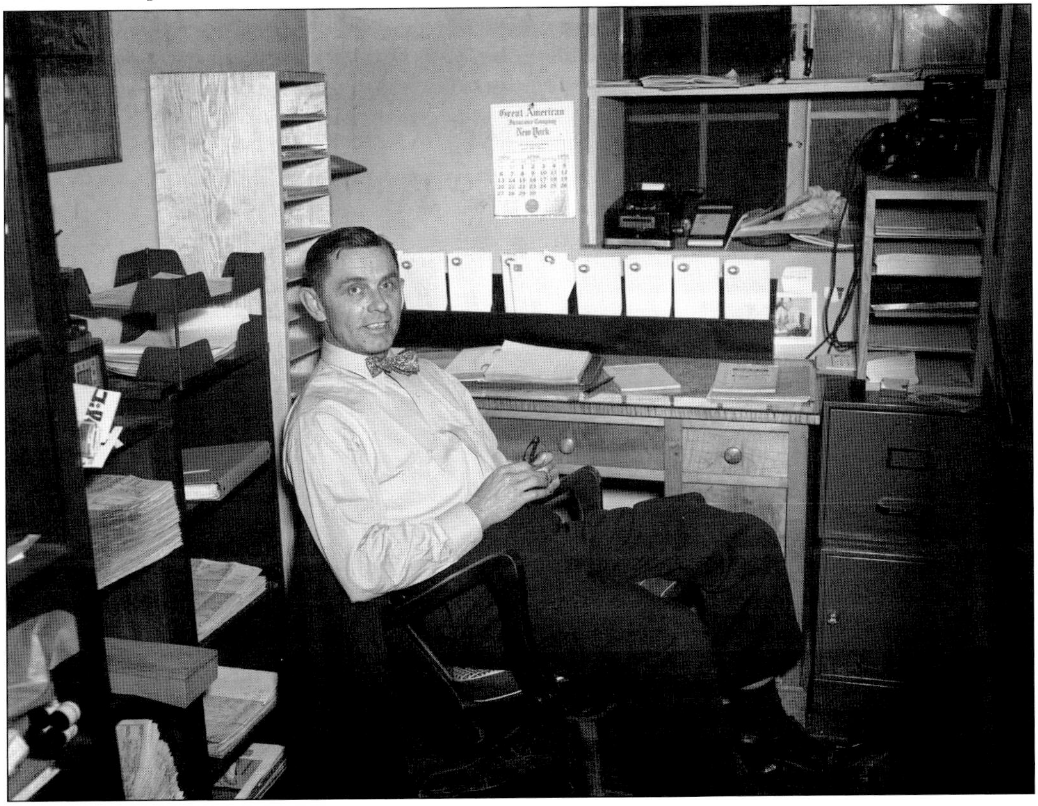

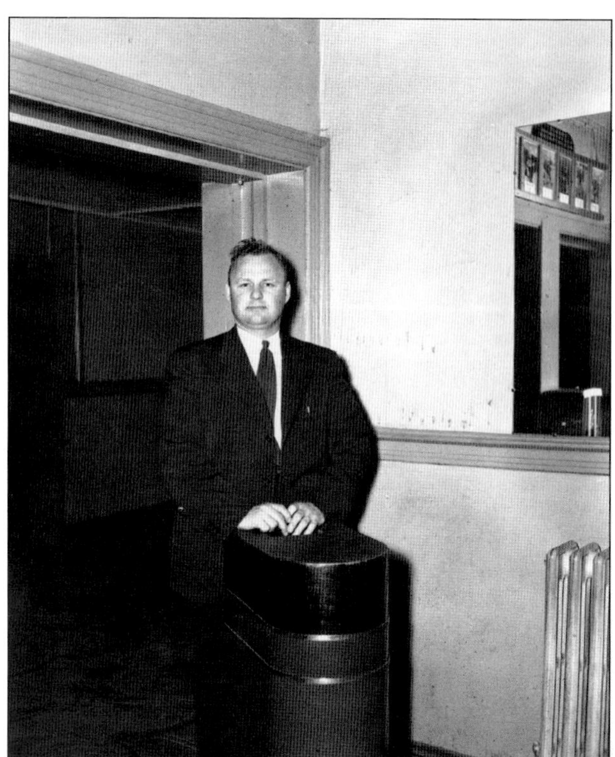

Following Bob Agle's 1948 promotion to district manager, Jay William Beach (1922–2002) took over as manager of the Appalachian Theatre. He quickly earned a reputation as the best babysitter in town, given that many parents would drop their children off at the theater on Saturdays, effectively leaving them in Beach's care while the parents completed their shopping. Beach is shown at the theater's ticket stand.

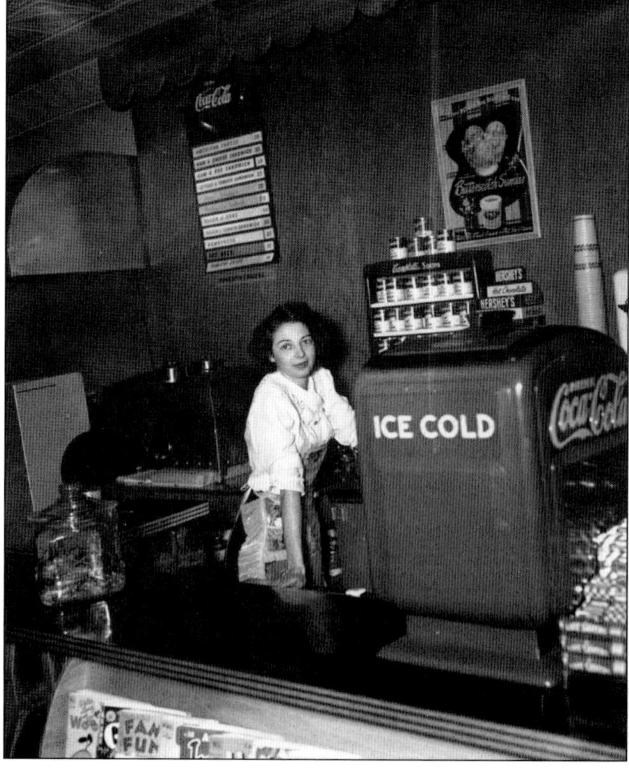

Nellie Mae "Nell" Matheson Redmond (1928–2018) is behind the counter of the Appalachian Soda Shop, which she ran with her husband, Thomas Broadus Redmond (1908–1995), from 1950 to 1991. They acquired the business in the Appalachian Theatre building shortly after the devastating 1950 fire that nearly destroyed the theater. The shop was famous for its tasty cheeseburgers.

George William Horton (1920–1973) was a notorious but beloved character on Boone's streets during the 1950s, when Palmer Blair set up this studio portrait. A hard worker who took odd jobs throughout town for decades, Horton was renowned for his kindness but also struggled with poverty, alcoholism, legal challenges, and homelessness. He died during a blizzard in December 1973.

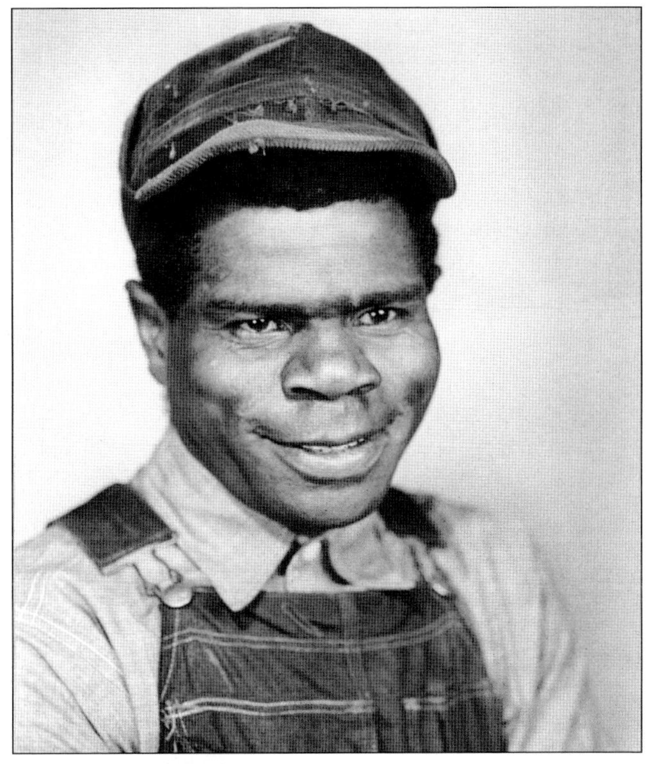

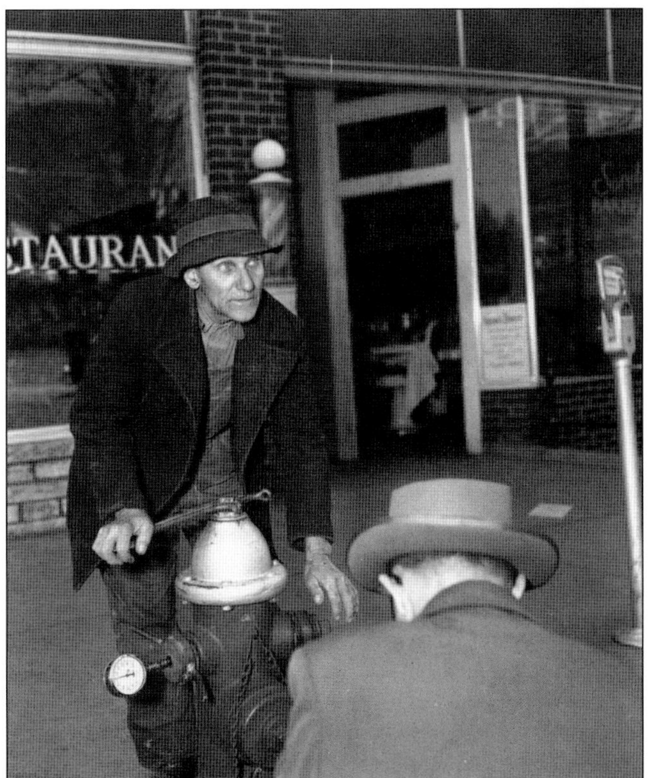

In this image, Abner Charles Shoemake (1883–1958), Boone's city water superintendent for more than 30 years, checks the pressure on a fire hydrant while an unidentified man with his back to the camera assists. Mayor Gordon Winkler said of Shoemake upon his retirement, "The city has never had a better public official." Behind Shoemake are the K and M Gateway Restaurant and the Sanitary Barbershop in the Hodges Building.

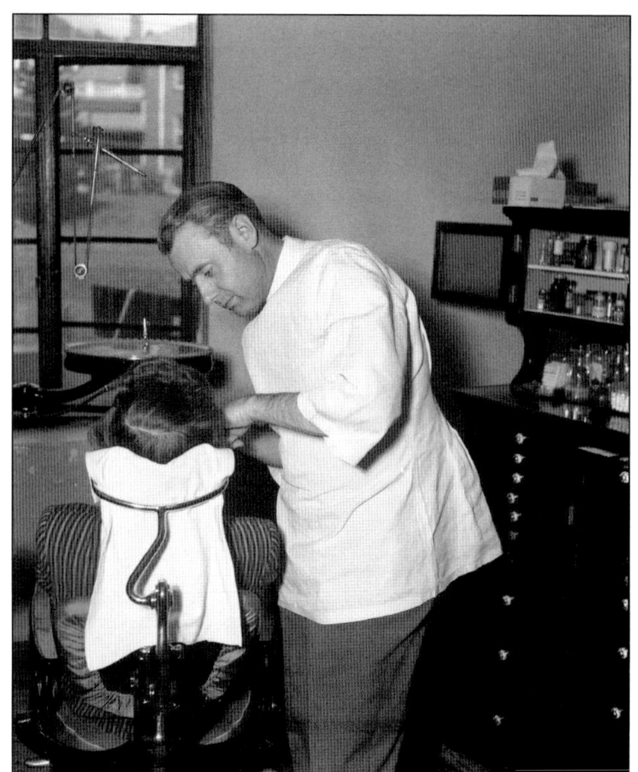

Dr. E.T. Glenn operated a dentist practice out of the second-floor rooms in the Appalachian Theatre along with his brother in law Dr. Jack D. Lawrence (1920–2017). Jack's brother Dr. Charles Ray Lawrence (1912–1998) was an optometrist in the same office space. In this photograph, Glenn is examining a patient who may have been staring at the Daniel Boone Hotel through the window to take her mind off of the exam.

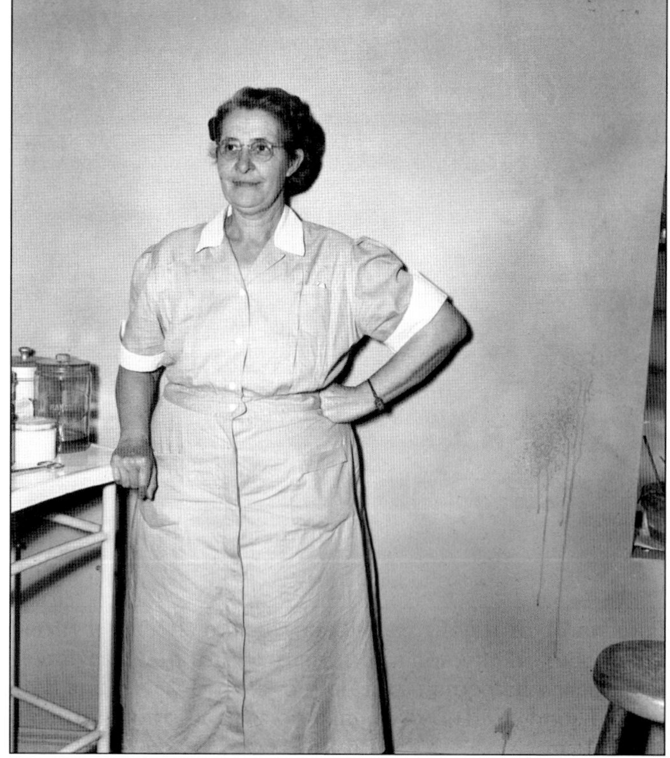

Nurse Edith Hampton poses in an examining room in this image taken at an unidentified clinic or medical office. At the time this picture was taken, Watauga Hospital was raising funds to build modern nurses' residences and add equipment. In order to provide sufficient nursing staff, the hospital often hired people from out of town and rented apartments for them in Boone.

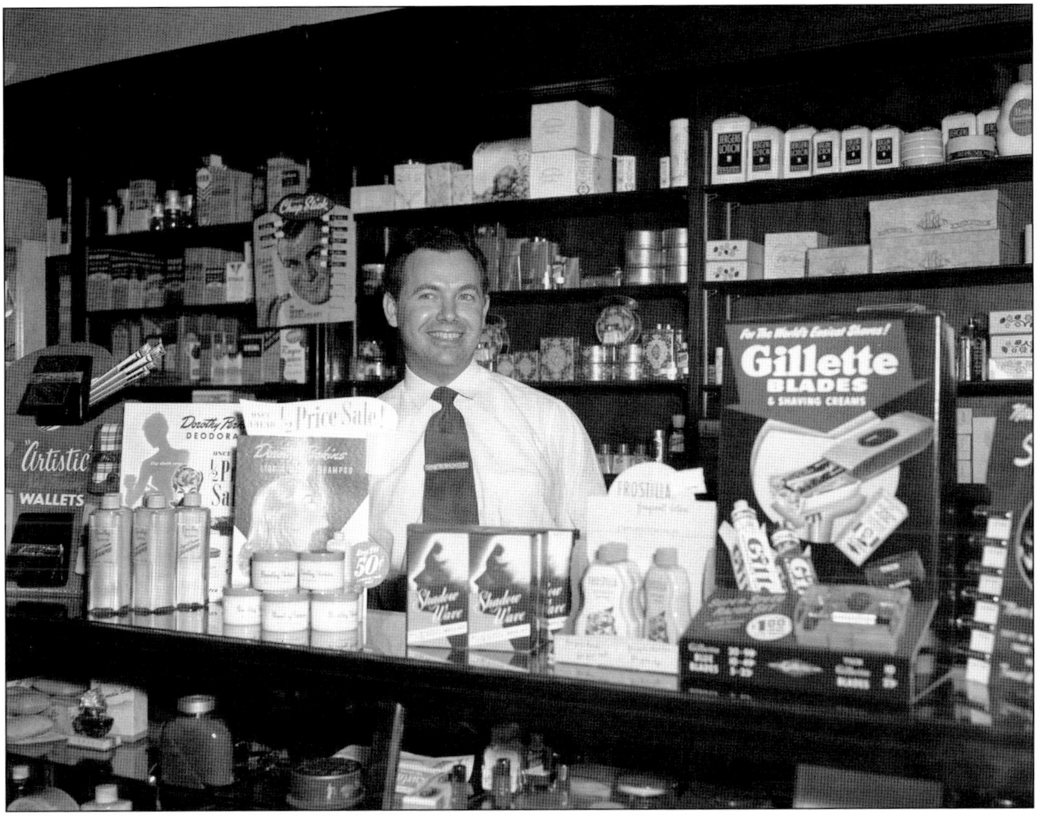

In the time when Blair was taking these photographs, the Carolina Pharmacy was located on King Street near its intersection with Appalachian Street, and the pharmacy's hot doughnuts were a popular local treat. This is Jack Glenwood Mock (1915–1997), whose father, Charles Henry Mock (1886–1977), was the main pharmacist. Jack was active in the local Lions Club and the *Echoes of the Blue Ridge* pageant.

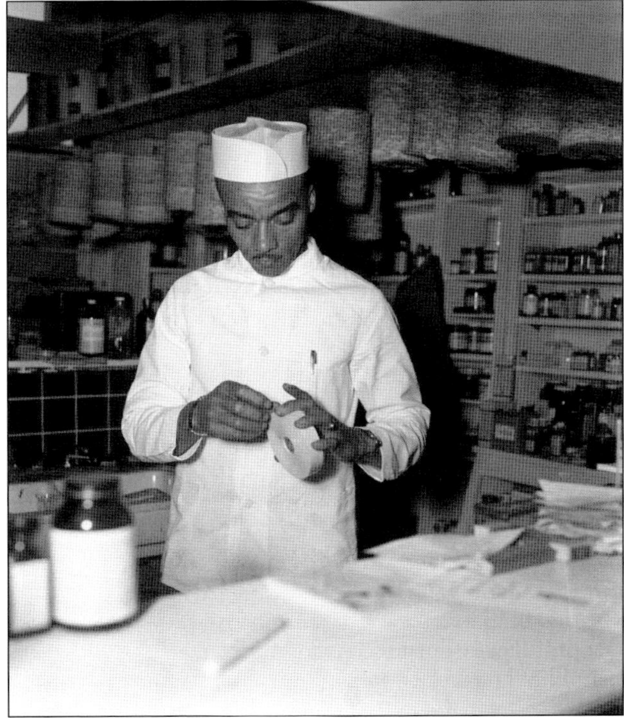

Shown in 1952 preparing prescriptions at the Boone Drug Company on King Street, Lee Voyd Murphy Whittington (1923–1998) worked with the pharmacy for a number of years after serving in the US Army during World War II. The large spindles in the background contain stacks of filled prescription forms.

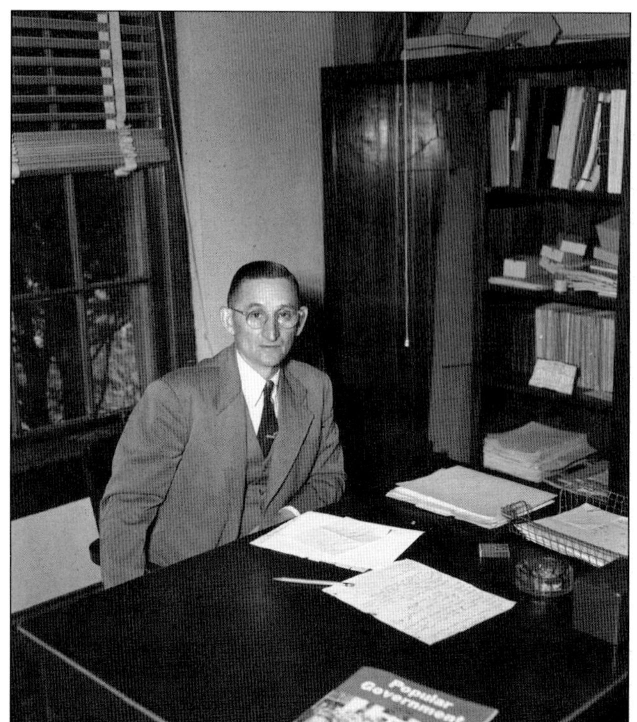

David Patterson Mast (1901–1994) worked for many years as the director of Watauga County Social Services, then known as the welfare department. In this image, Mast is seated at his desk in what is likely the Watauga County Administration Building, the native stone building on North Water Street that was completed using WPA funds in 1939.

Dr. Mary Michael not only ran the Alleghany-Ashe-Watauga District health office in the 1950s, but she also was a major figure in the Boone Business and Professional Women's Club. Dr. Michael implemented vast improvements in public health screening during the 1950s, particularly among children, in the wake of major outbreaks of polio and tuberculosis.

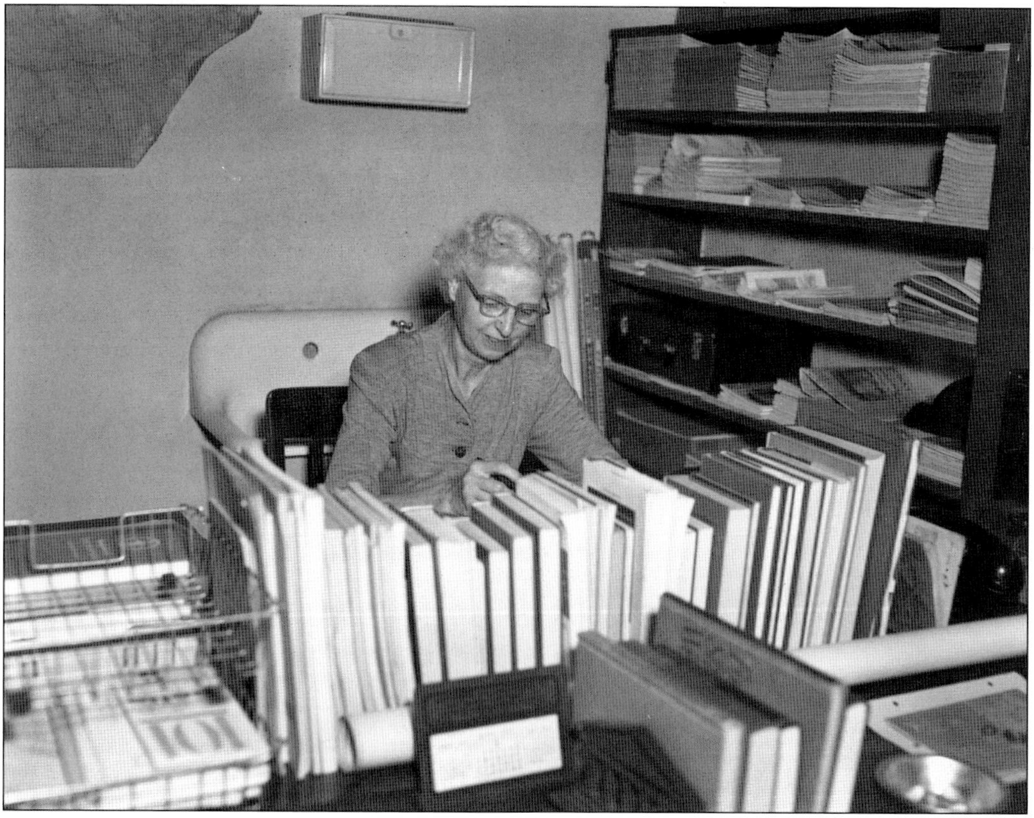

In this image, an unidentified Boone police officer stands next to a parking meter—a feature of downtown Boone's landscape for many decades. The officer is just outside Palmer Blair's photography studio in the R.T. Greer Building on Depot Street, which is now the home of Black Cat Burrito. The west side of the Crest Five and Ten is to the left.

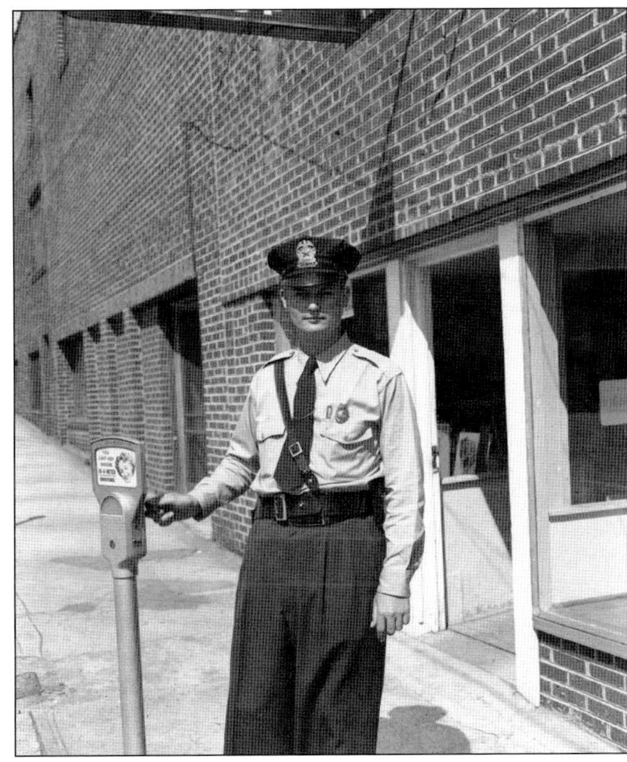

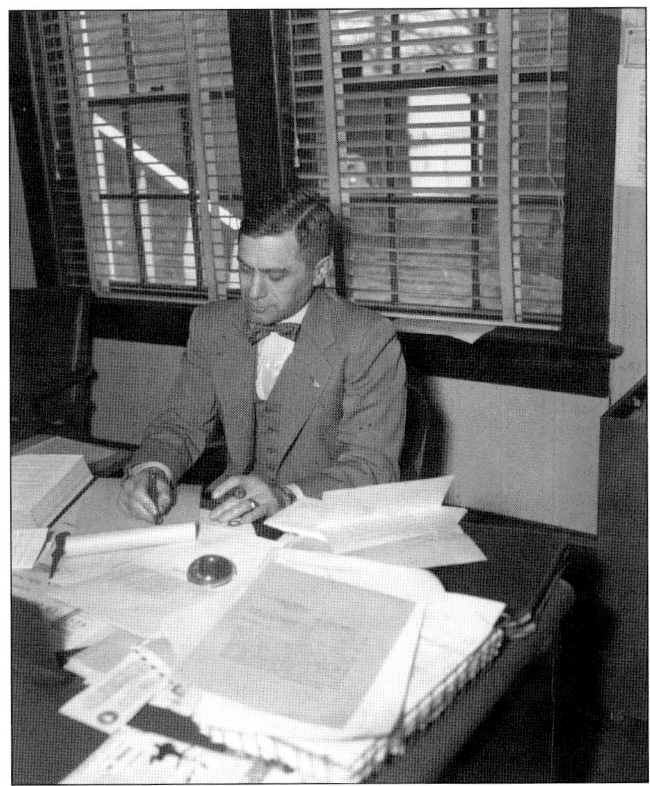

Blowing Rock native Wade Brown is pictured in the law office he built on King Street in 1938. Brown was one of three charter members of the Boone Area Chamber of Commerce. He was elected to the state senate in 1947 and the state house in 1951 before serving as Boone's mayor from 1961 to 1967. He was also a key figure in many of the tourism-based initiatives of the 1950s.

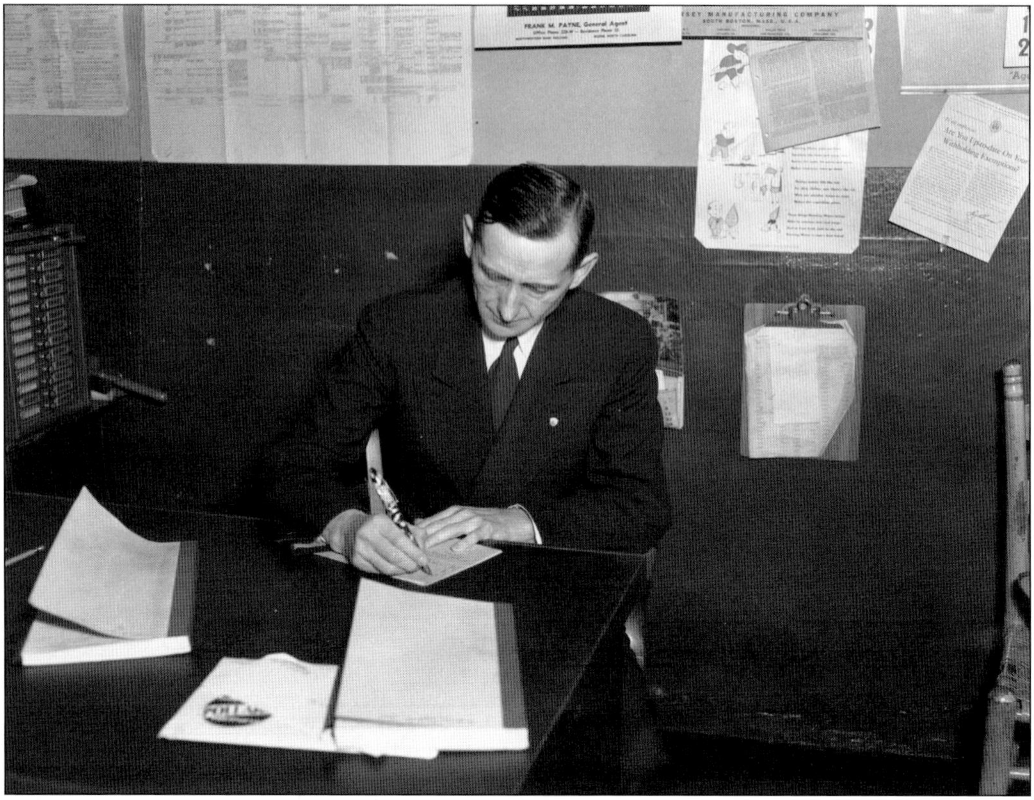

Mayor Gordon Henry Winkler (1903–1981) is shown signing papers at a desk in the city hall (although "city" is technically a misnomer, since Boone was incorporated as a town) located in the former Watauga Motor Company Building on Depot Street. Winkler served for a total of 22 years as mayor—from 1943 to 1959 and 1969 to 1975—and was a key figure in Boone's economic development.

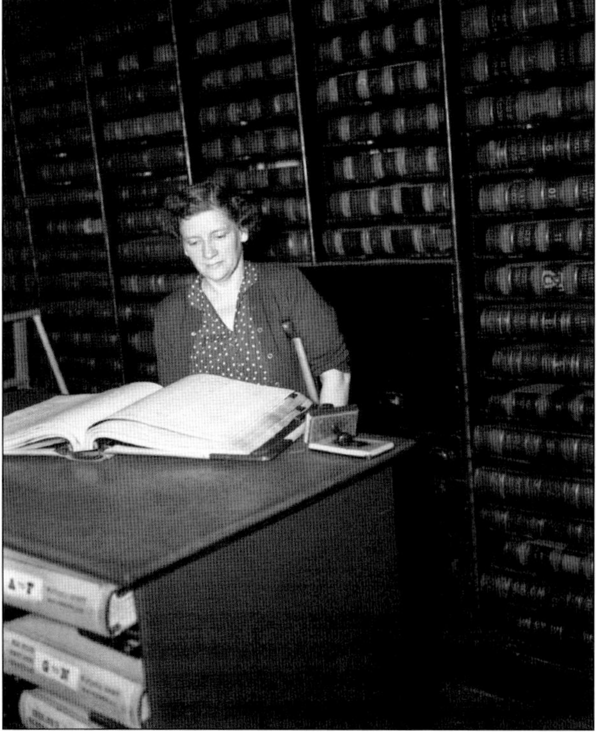

Helen Elizabeth Underdown (1906–1978) was a Blowing Rock native who attended Appalachian State Teachers College and served for many years as Watauga County's register of deeds. In this image, Underdown reviews an index book while standing in the 1905 courthouse room where the county's deed books were stored. An 1873 fire destroyed the first county courthouse and most early county deeds.

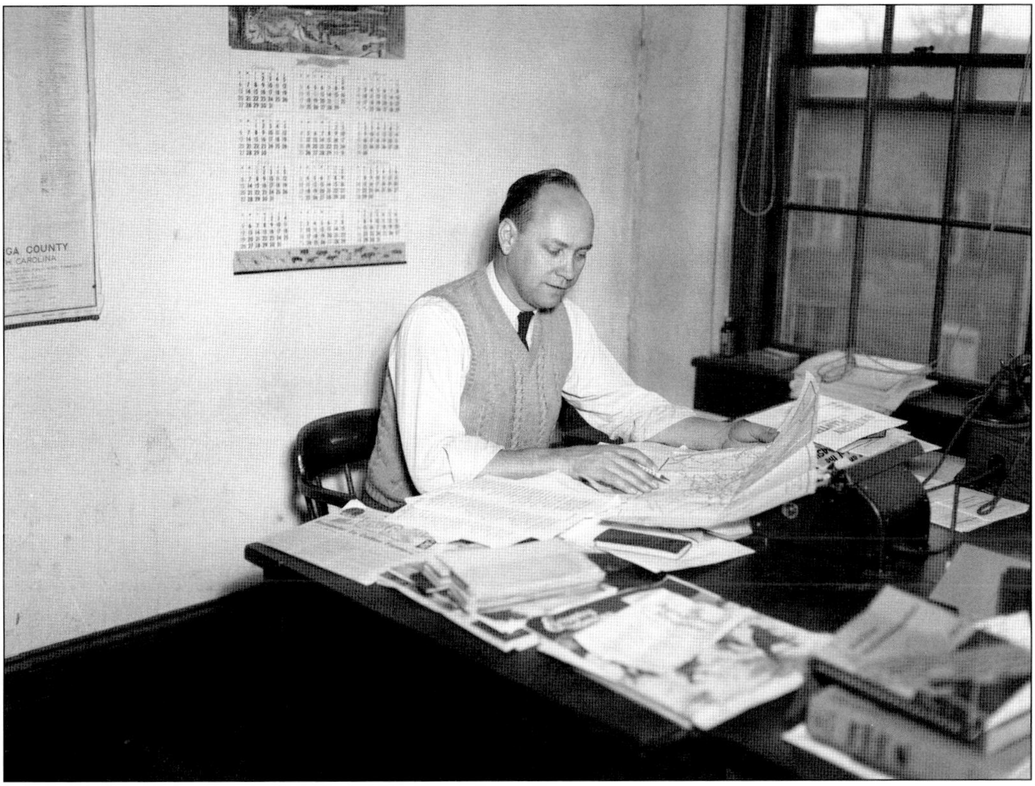

Lake Ernest "L.E." Tuckwiller (1908–1980) was a West Virginia native who was named Watauga County's assistant county farm agent in 1943. He served in various agricultural extension roles for decades thereafter. In this image, Tuckwiller reviews a county map from his office in the Watauga County Administration Building. The building outside his window is likely the rear of the 1875 courthouse.

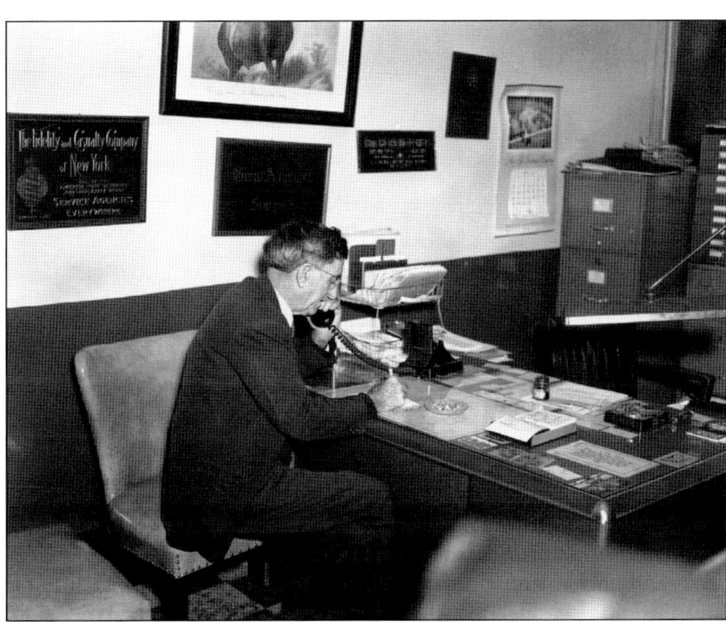

Columbus Monroe "Rorie" Critcher (1872–1960) is believed to be the man shown sitting at a desk in the Coe Realty office in the Appalachian Theatre building. A former sheriff and county treasurer, Critcher was best known for a series of businesses he owned in the county and downtown Boone. In 1952, Critcher was a principal at Tri-County Realty, which rented space in the Coe Realty office.

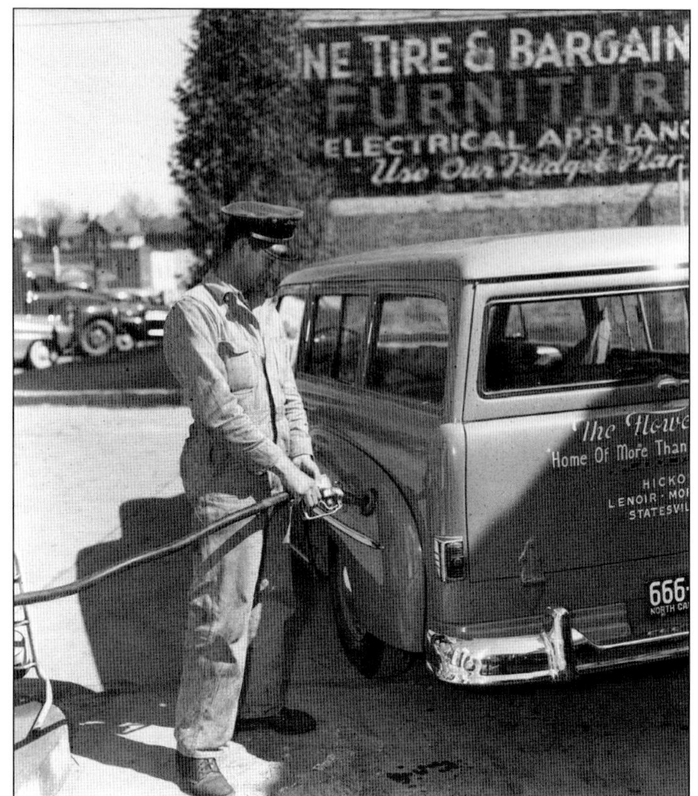

This image of Earl Thomas Jones (1922–1979) shows him pumping gas at the Sinclair service station in the heart of downtown, just west of the Boone Tire and Bargain Store. Jones owned the Sinclair operation in the early 1950s. A second Sinclair station was added on East King Street in the mid-1950s. The downtown location was converted into a new town hall in 1962.

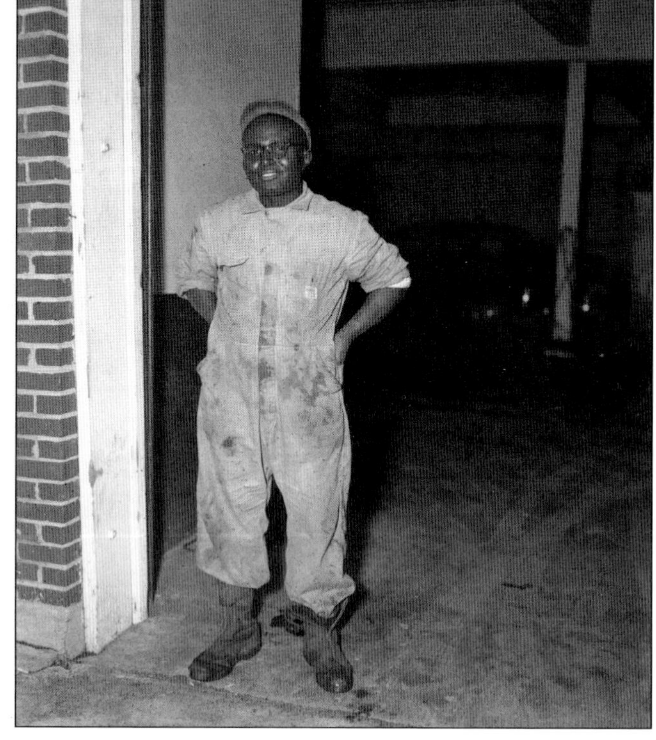

Rev. Arthur Will Stowe (1914–1996) served as minister at the Boone Chapel in the Junaluska community in the late 1930s, but he also worked as a mechanic at the Winkler Motor Company in the early 1950s. He is pictured standing in the garage bay of Winkler Motors. Stowe also served on the Watauga Consolidated School committee in the 1950s.

Thomas William Staple Collins (1915–1965) was the owner of Collins Body Shop, at the intersection of Winkler's Creek and Blowing Rock Roads. He was also a member of the Boone Volunteer Fire Department in the 1940s and operated a used-car dealership in the 1960s. He was killed in 1965 in a head-on collision near Charleston, West Virginia.

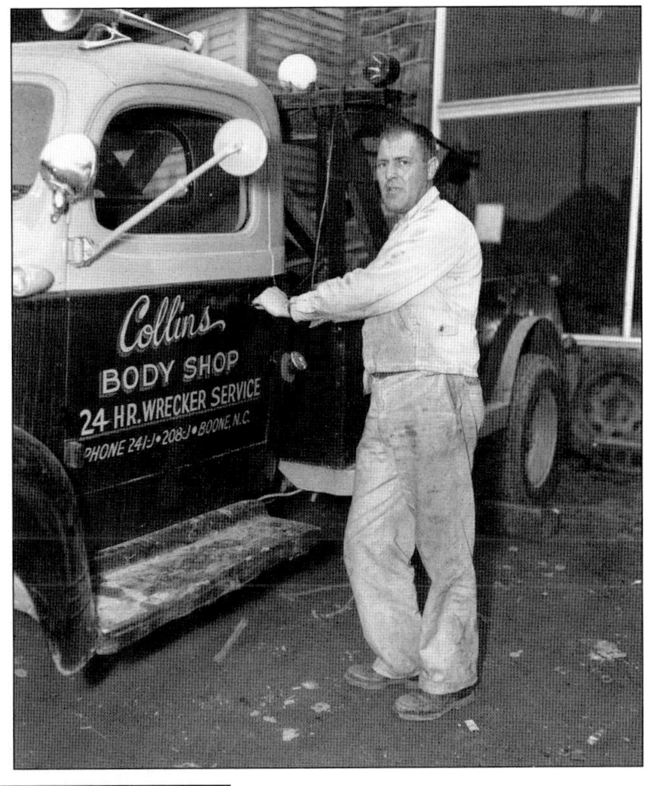

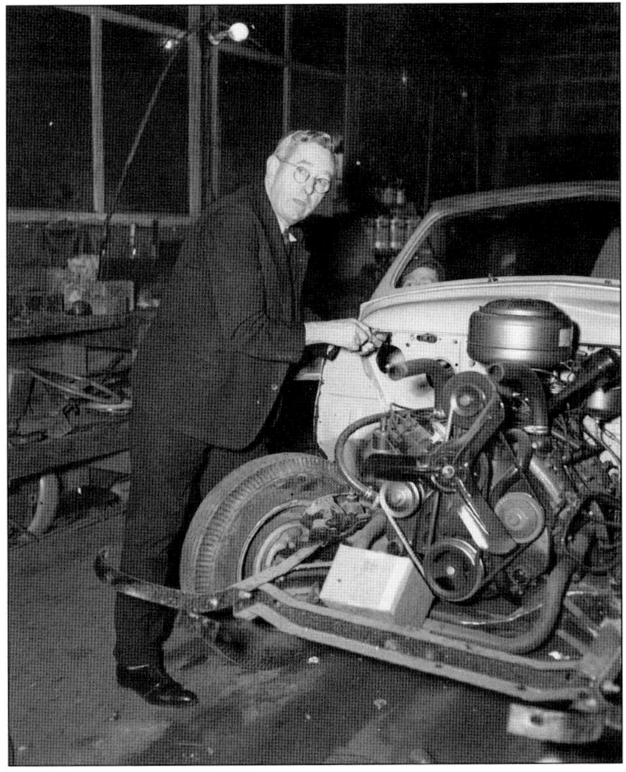

Austin Enoch South (1892–1965) is shown working on a car engine in the Boone Body Shop, where he was part owner. South was a major political and business figure in Boone, serving as Watauga County clerk of court from 1926 to 1946 and again from 1953 to 1962. The Boone Body Shop was on King Street opposite the 1875 courthouse and just west of the Sebastian Building.

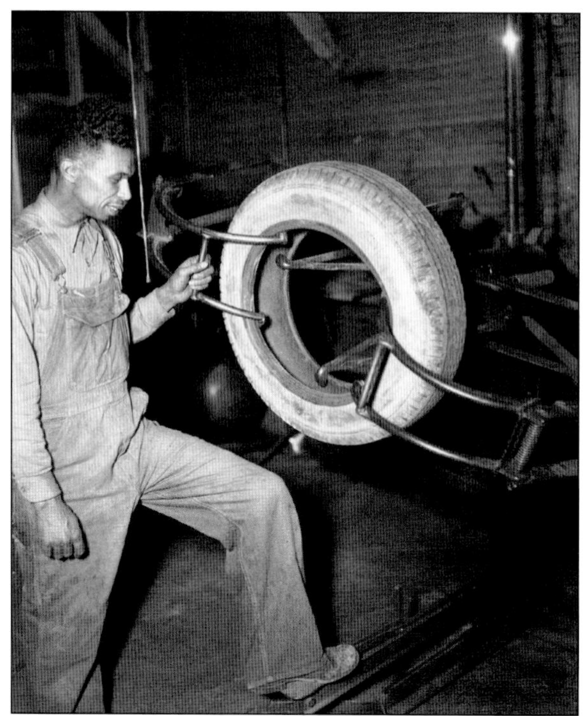

Neal Grimes (1914–1998) was a Junaluska resident and a deacon at the Mennonite Brethren Church, but he is shown working at Swofford Tire Company (later Goodyear Tire), on King Street opposite the *Watauga Democrat* office. Grimes worked at the tire company for 25 years and later worked for Carolina Tire and Kmart.

John Parlier, proprietor of the Depot Street cabstand John's Cabs, posed for this photograph while on his call box next to the Crest Five and Ten. Parlier operated the cabstand from at least the early 1940s, employing several drivers. He later ran the Co-Ed Snack Bar on Blowing Rock Road near the Appalachian State Teachers College campus in 1953, and the Horn Café at Greasy Corners.

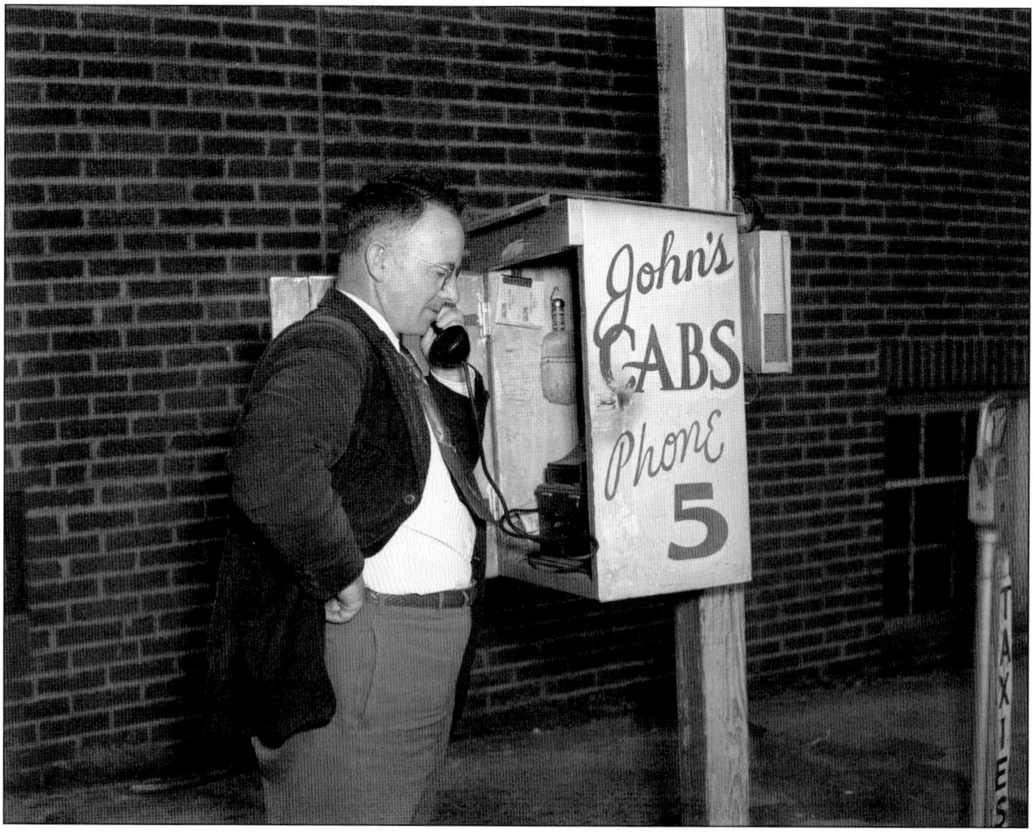

In addition to running the Blue Ridge Tourist Court in Perkinsville, Estel G. Wagner also invested in numerous other businesses around town. In February 1952, Wagner purchased the Murray Esso station at the corner of Hardin and Howard Streets, where he is shown operating the register. Wagner was later Boone's first real estate broker and a leader with *Horn in the West* and at the Boone Golf Course.

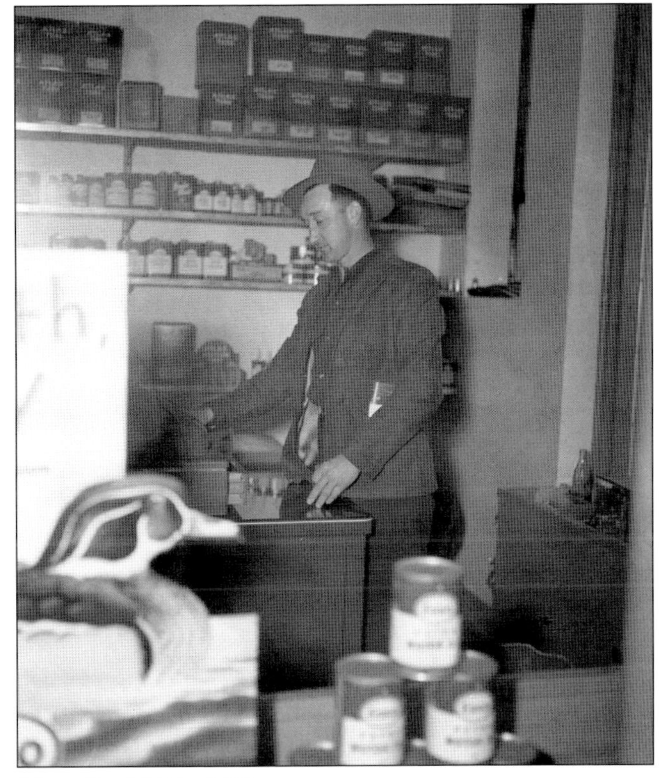

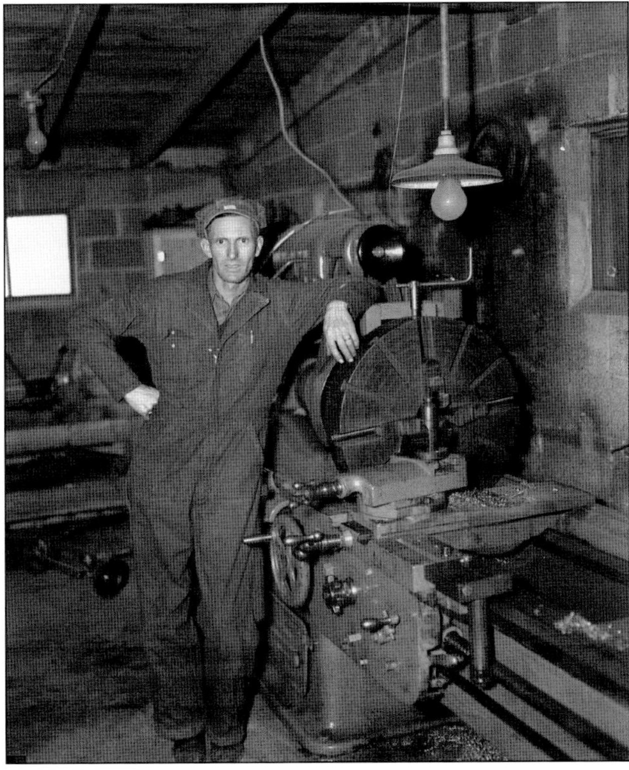

Frank Luther Triplett (1917–2003), pictured in his shop, was a World War II veteran and the principal at Triplett's Garage and Machine Shop on West Jefferson Highway in Perkinsville, but he also raced stock cars in North Wilkesboro in the pre-NASCAR days and served as a leader in local Boy Scout groups.

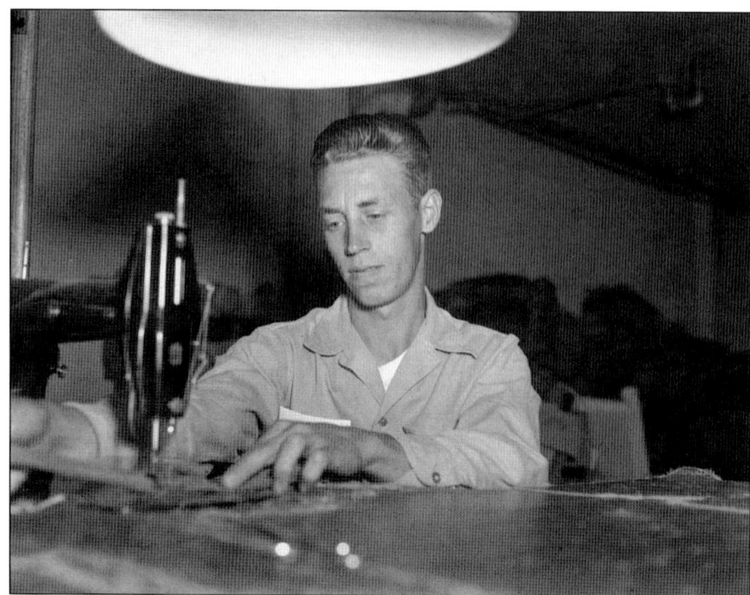

Shown working his upholstery sewing machine in 1952 is Kenneth Yount Moretz (1924–1987), who began working at Moretz Upholstering in 1946. In October 1952, Kenneth and Samuel Moretz purchased the business from H.L. Moretz and changed the name to Boone Upholstering Shop. It was on the west side of lower Depot Street behind the Duncan Motors Company building.

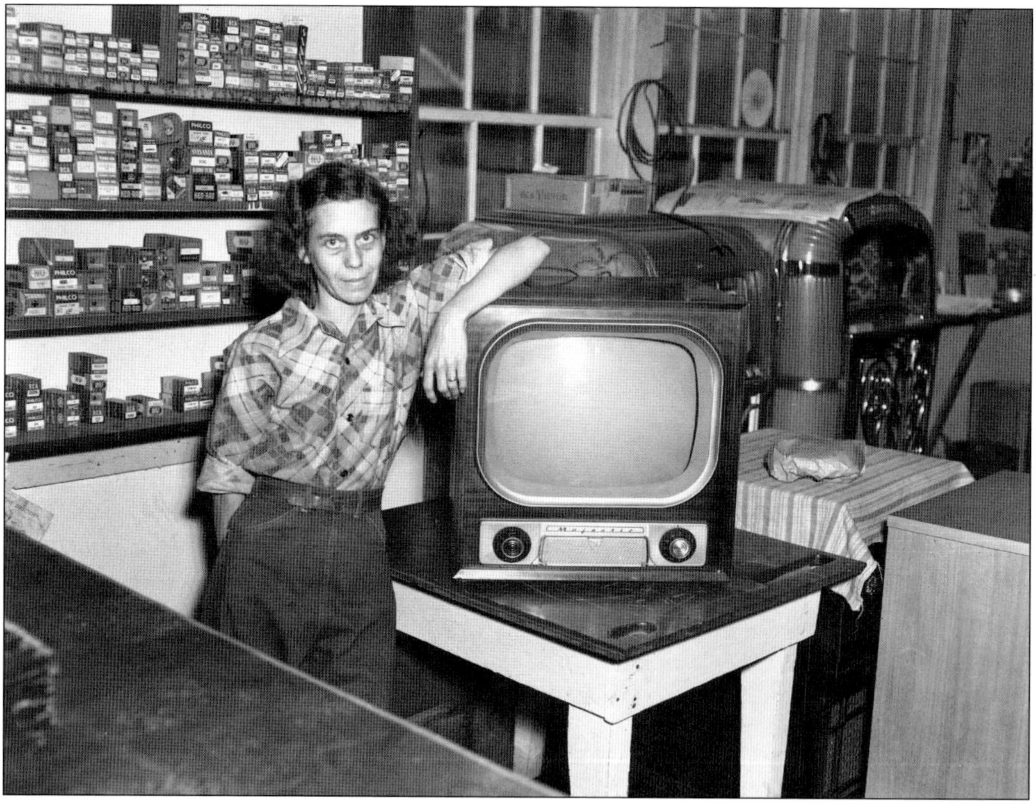

Terris Wilma Crumley Dacus (1915–2003) is posing in the Dacus Radio Shop on Howard Street, behind the Appalachian Theatre in the former Woodcraft Novelty Company building. She and her husband, Kermit Irwin Dacus (1908–1983), ran the shop in several locations around town through the 1940s and 1950s. Federal authorities busted Kermit for running a bootleg radio show out of the theater in 1943.

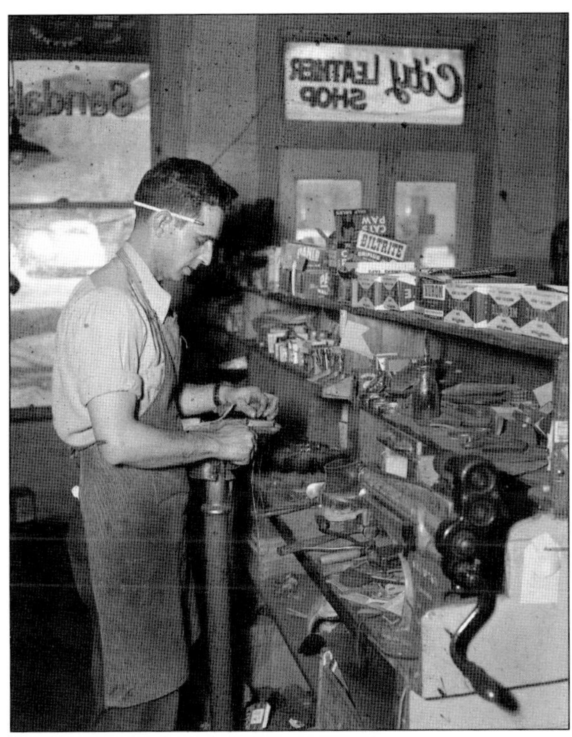

Harold Walter Jones (1925–1968), son of proprietor Will Harrison Jones (1898–1966), sews a new sole in the City Shoe Shop, located in the former post office between the *Watauga Democrat* building and the Rivers Old Home Place. Despite the name over the transom ("City Leather Shop"), Jones consistently advertised his business using the alternate name. The Jones and Day Bargain Store, a secondhand clothing shop, was also located in this space.

William Carl Walker (1883–1960) opened Walker's Jewelry in the 1875 courthouse in 1923 before moving to the west end of the Frank Linney Block in 1925; he remained in business there until his death. He served on the local board of education for decades and was an influential force in the Democratic Party. He went by the nicknames "Pope," "Hoover," or "Calvin," depending on his audience.

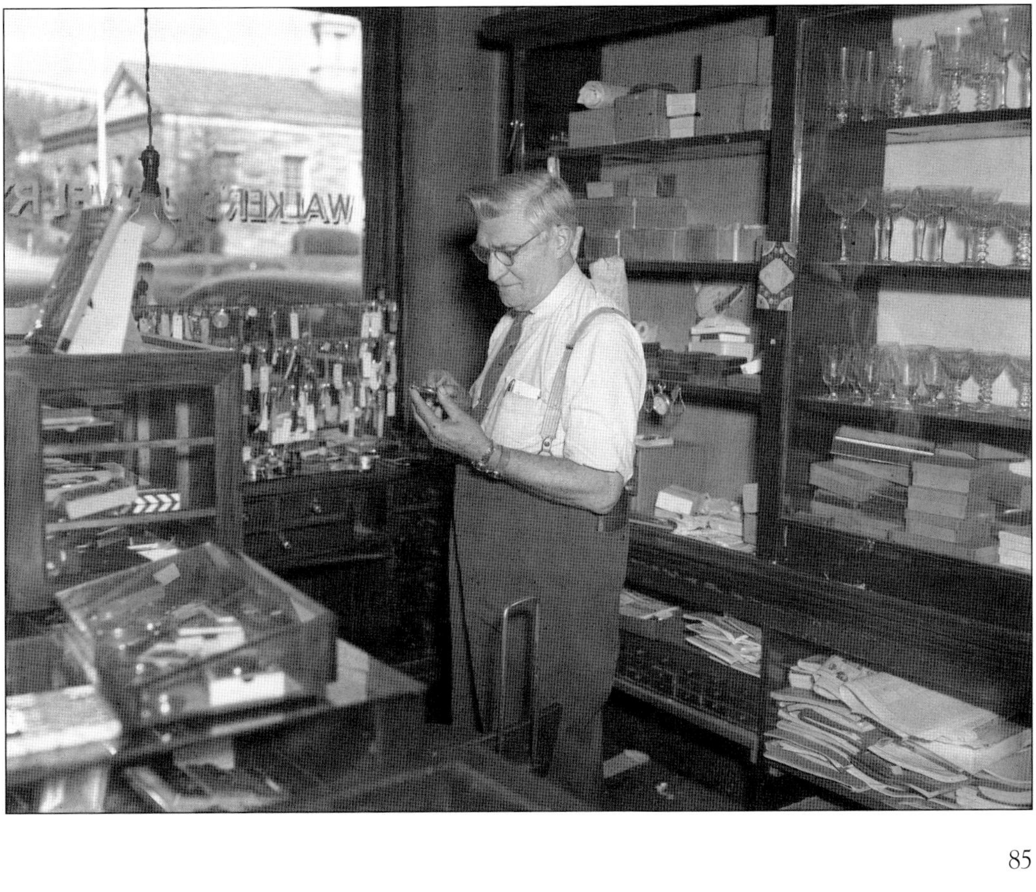

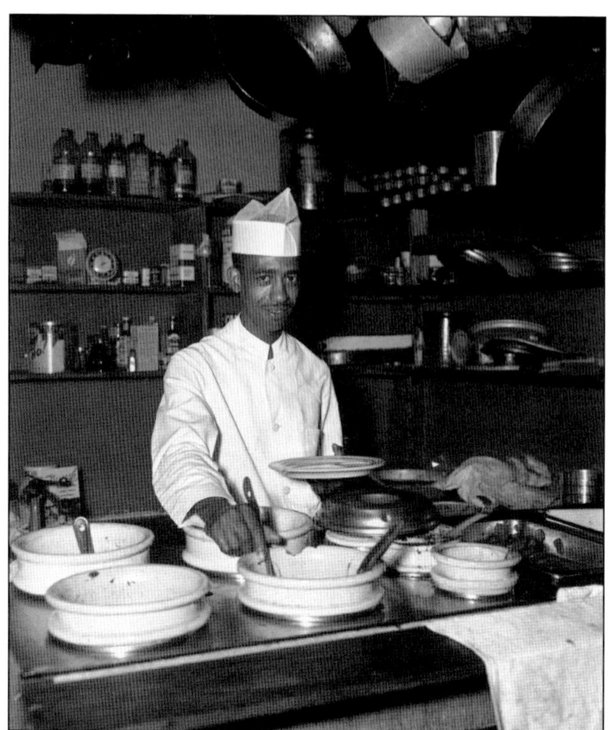

James Radford McQueen Sr. (1923–2002) was a Mountain City native who moved to the Junaluska community when he was four years old. He worked as a butcher before serving in the US Navy during World War II. After the war, he cooked—as shown in this image taken at either the Daniel Boone Hotel or Town House Restaurant. He ended his career supervising the Boone Sanitation Department.

Regina "Jean" Lawrence Greene (1920–2002) ran this small café, Kay's Lunches, with her husband, Clyde Smith Greene (1921–1995), in the southern portion of the R.T. Greer Building where Black Cat Burrito is now. A favorite hangout for Appalachian High School kids in the 1950s, the restaurant was named for the Greenes' daughter, Barbara Kay Greene Stacy (born 1947).

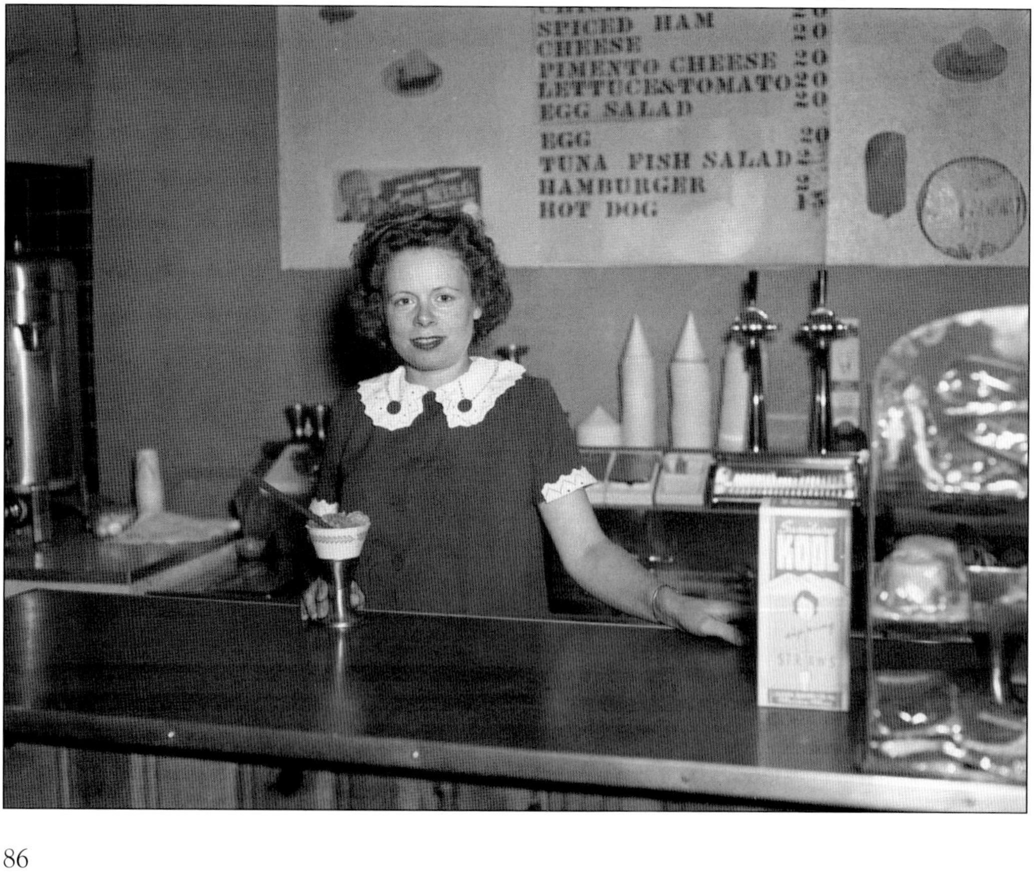

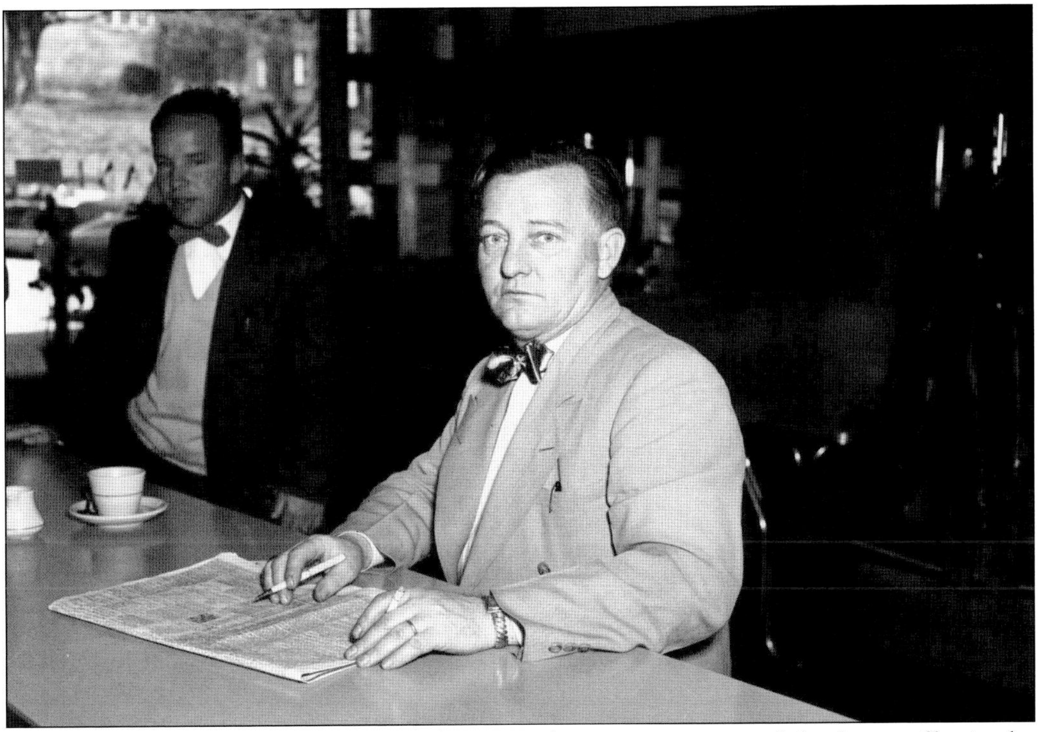

Howard Jones Cottrell (1907–1983) is shown reading a newspaper and drinking coffee in the Skyline Café, his restaurant in the Qualls Block, just months before the business was destroyed by a fire on Christmas Day. Cottrell was also the manager of the Appalachian State bookstore from 1938 until his retirement in 1971. His twin brother, Walter Raleigh Cottrell (1907–1977), was a frequent business partner of his.

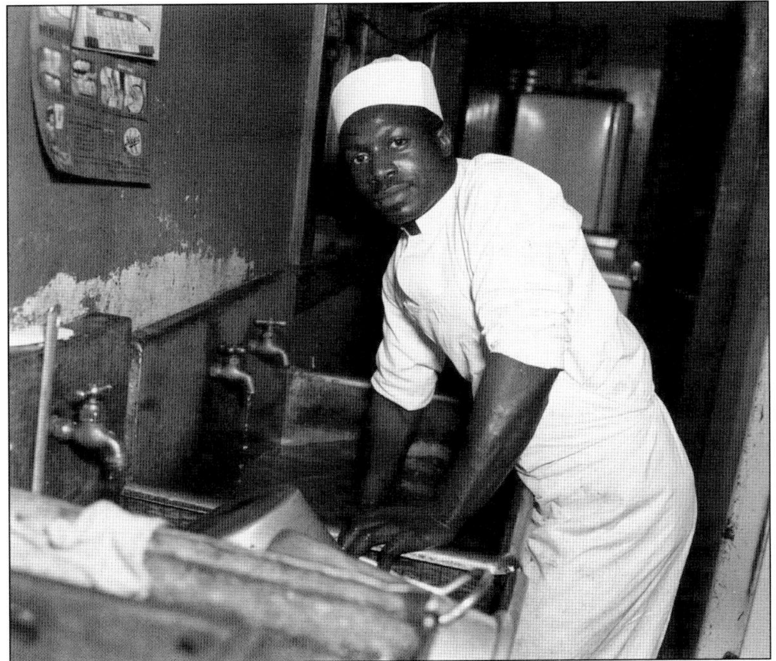

Robert Hagler Jr. (1923–1999), pictured washing dishes in an unidentified restaurant in Boone, was a Junaluska resident. In his teens, he worked as a laborer for WPA projects in town, and in later years, he worked on the Watauga Dam at Mountain City, as a mechanic at Andrews Chevrolet on North Depot Street, and as a butcher at the Jones Hollow Abattoir on Bamboo Road.

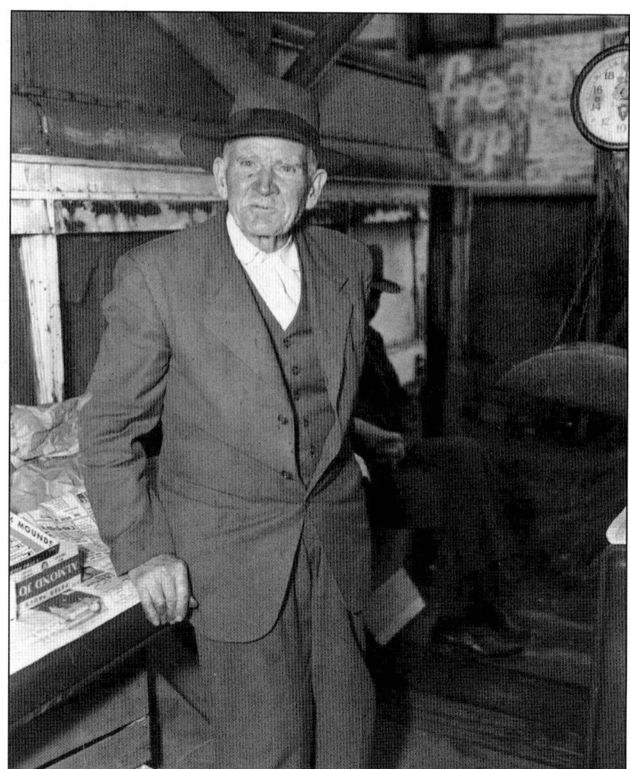

James Sanford Lyons (1873–1964) owned the old bus shell that provided some shelter at his seasonal produce stand at the southwest corner of King and Appalachian Streets. He opened the stand in 1929, but after Estel Wagner bought the lot in 1956, Lyons briefly tried selling produce from the arched alcoves of the closed Pastime Theatre.

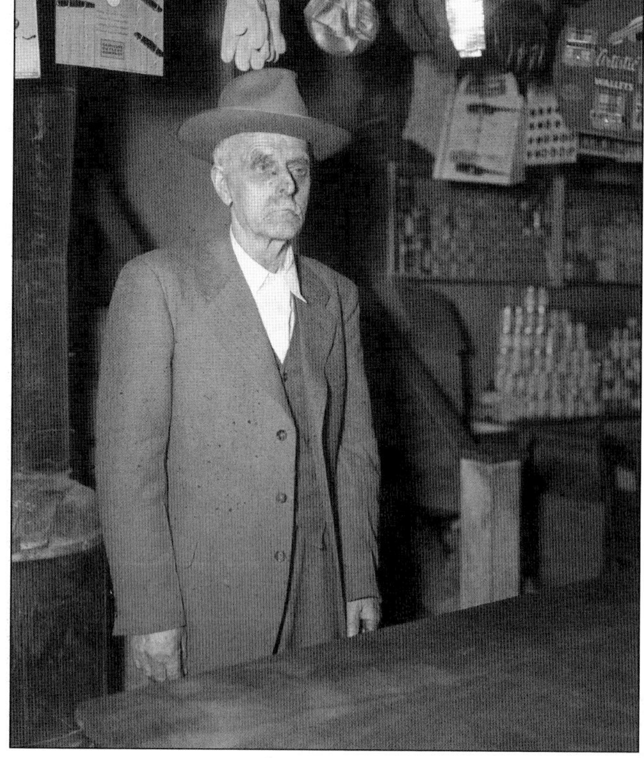

This resolute soul is Joseph R. "Idaho" Hendrix (1874–1975), affectionately known as "Ide." He worked in or owned a number of general stores over the course of his lifetime. In this image, he stands in the former Smithey's building opposite the Carolina Pharmacy, then known as the Jones and Brown Grocery. As Hendrix's hearing failed, locals remember him using a large horn to be able to understand his customers.

In 1952, Azalee Hampton Cook (later Stockard; 1925–2012) was working as a butcher at the Dixie Store (later Winn-Dixie) when it was next to the Carolina Pharmacy on King Street. In later years, she worked as a nurse for more than two decades. The old Dixie Store currently houses Macado's Restaurant.

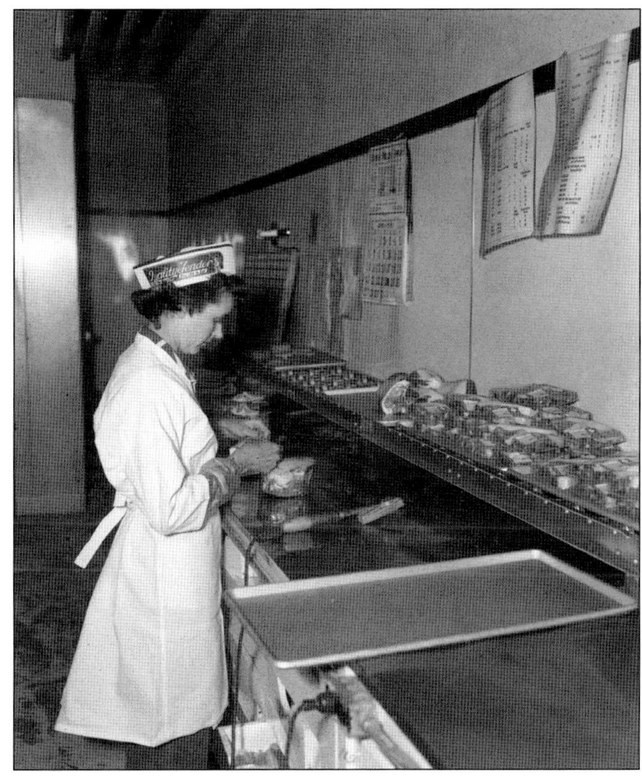

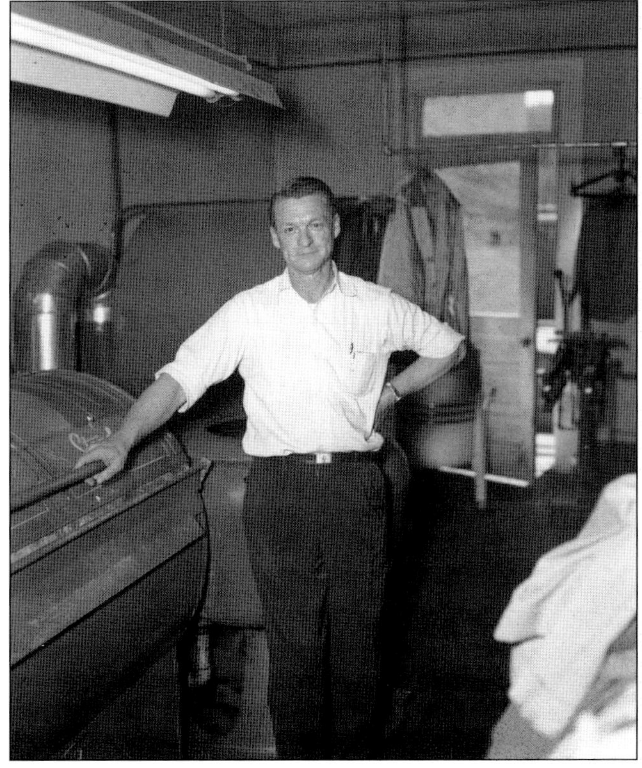

When this photograph was taken in 1952, Charles Olen Younce (1905–1955) owned and operated the Hi-Land Dry Cleaners, on King Street between Newton's Department Store and the *Watauga Democrat*, with his son Paul. The elder Younce died just three years later from a heart attack. Today, the Hi-Land Dry Cleaners space is home to the Mysterium Escape Room.

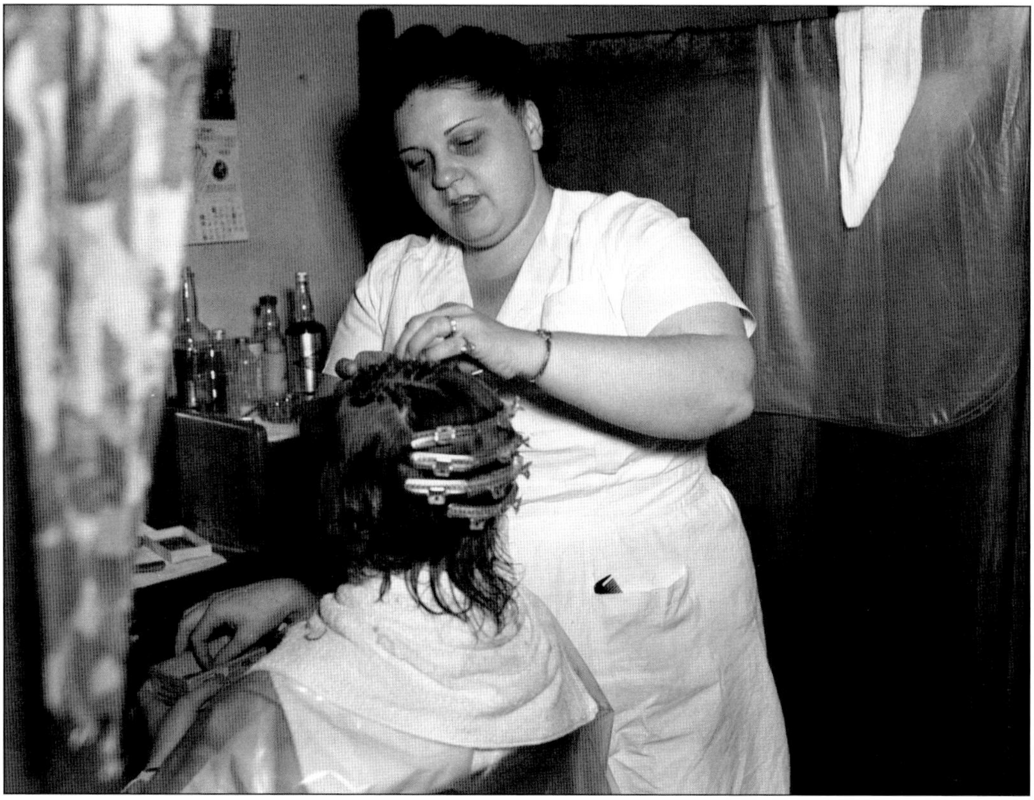

Among the many businesses packed into the Appalachian Theatre building was a small beauty salon, the Artistic Beauty Shop, which was tucked under the stairs leading to the second-floor offices. In this 1952 image, Vivian Peeler Brinkley (1917–1988) is working on a customer's hair while the customer holds a hairpin box.

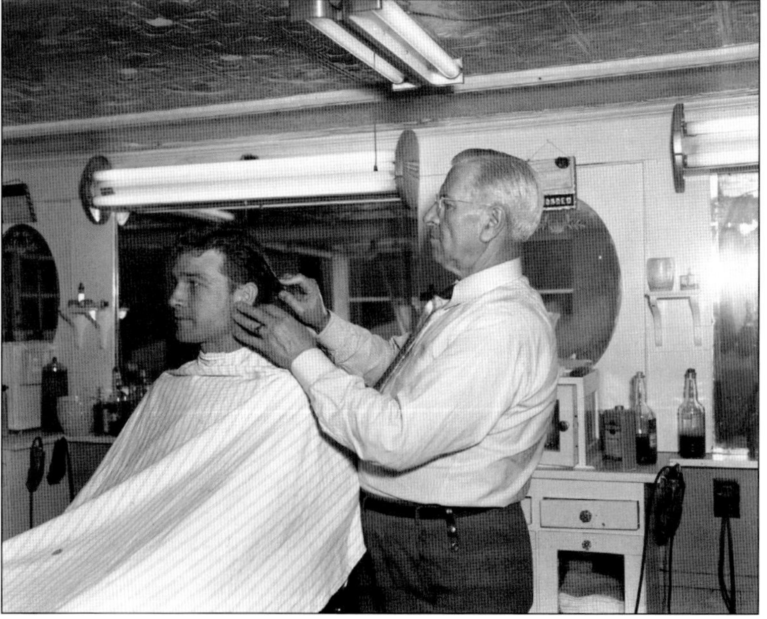

William Maston "Barber Bill" Hodges (1890–1962) trimmed hair at Shulls Mill during the lumber boom of the 1910s and set up his first barbershop at Boone in the Lovill Law Office near the southwest corner of King and Burrell Streets in 1921. Thereafter, he remained one of the most popular barbers in town, spending most of his career in his City Barber Shop under the Watauga County Bank.

This image shows James Perry Marsh (1924–2014; right) visiting with Stanley Austin Harris (1882–1976). Harris is credited with starting the Boy Scouts of America and organizing the first Black and Native American Boy Scout troops, and was active in many Boone initiatives during the 1940s and 1950s. Marsh was also active in community life for his entire career and was awarded the Order of the Long Leaf Pine.

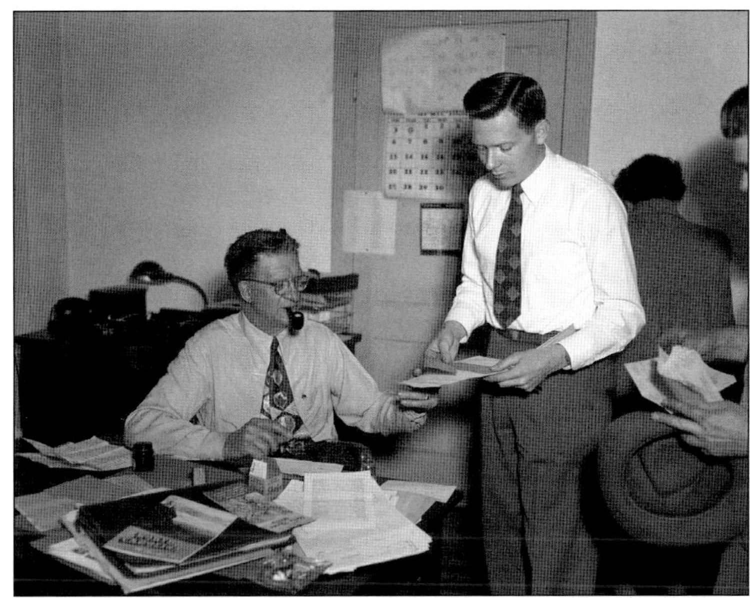

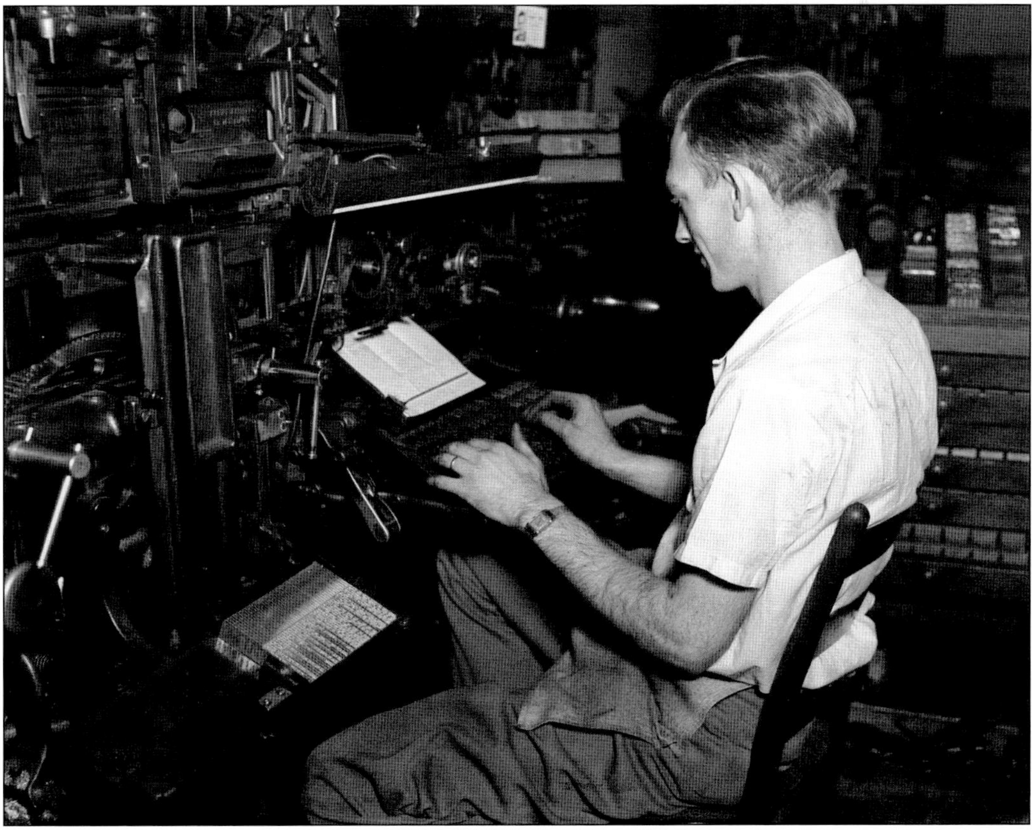

This fascinating image shows Charles Ernest "Ernie" Lewis (1923–1982) of the *Watauga Democrat* working at his linotype machine in 1952. Lewis, a World War II veteran, was later promoted to vice president of the Rivers Printing Company, which published the *Democrat*. Lewis's sister Bonnie Jean was married to *Democrat* publisher Rob C. Rivers Jr.

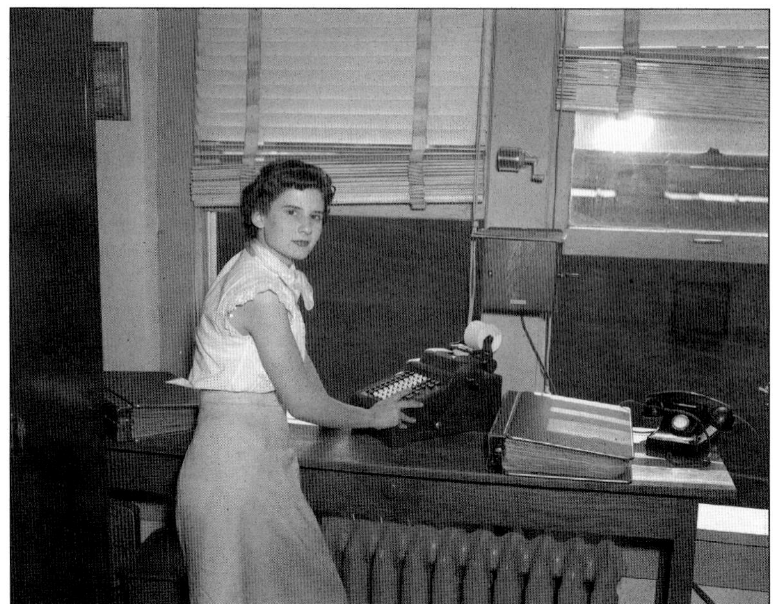

Elba McLura Cable Greene (1933–2004) is one of multiple women in the Workers of Boone series shown using office equipment in various clerical positions. Cable, a graduate of Cove Creek High School, had just joined the staff of Paul Winkler's Watauga Insurance Agency in the Watauga County Bank building when Blair took this picture.

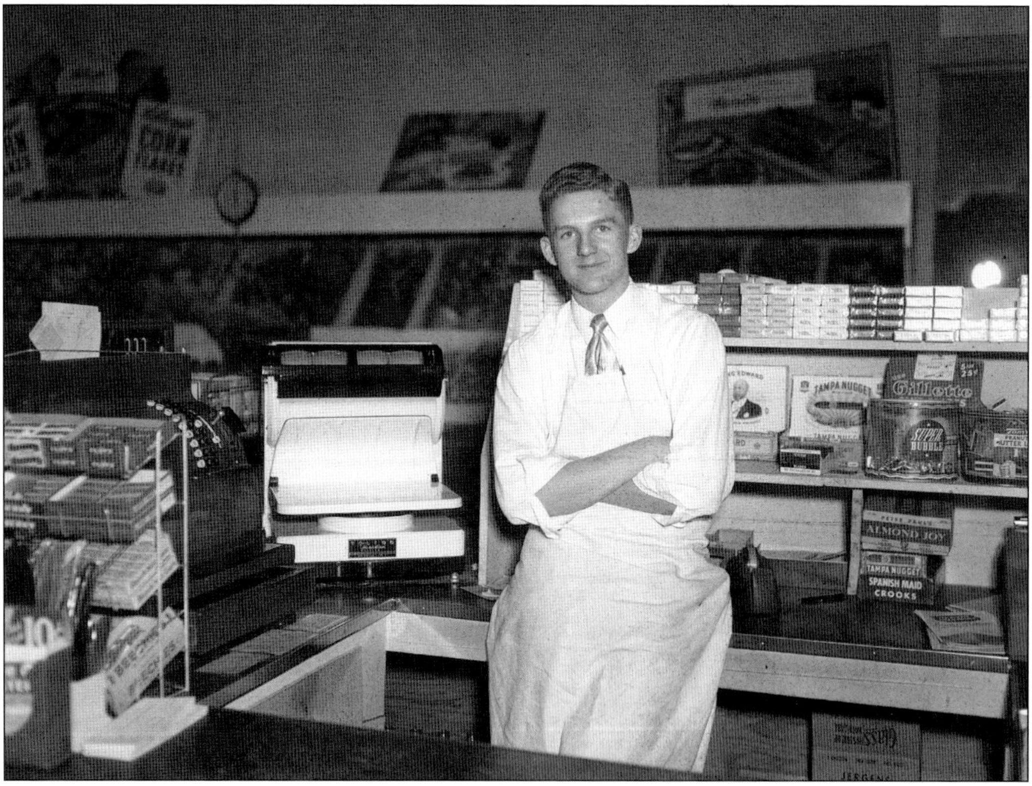

Dillard Glenn Hodges (1934–2013) is shown taking a short break from cashier duties at J.R. Craven's Boone Super Market in East Boone. Hodges went on to serve during the Korean Conflict, worked as plant manager in Boone for International Resistance Company (later TRW), and performed public service as the Watauga County clerk of superior court for 17 years. He was also a recipient of the Order of the Long Leaf Pine.

Five

Becoming a University Town 1960–1979

As the 1960s dawned, the Town of Boone and its residents enjoyed a mostly cordial and cooperative relationship with Appalachian State Teachers College. Strict rules at the college limited students' activities and movements, and residents generally appreciated the business and social opportunities afforded by having a respected college in the town. In the years that followed, however, cracks began to form in the town-gown relationship. The school's shift to university status in 1967 effectively doubled enrollment, and by 1979, enrollment at Appalachian State University had doubled again to about 9,500, nearly surpassing the 10,191 residents listed in the 1980 Census. Cultural shifts and college students' increasing demands for autonomy led to a much higher portion of students choosing to live off campus in cheaply built apartment complexes that began to spring up like weeds in downtown and on its periphery. A lack of strict zoning laws only compounded the problem and increasingly endangered Boone's established residential neighborhoods.

Zoning insufficiencies also allowed for the emergence of a new threat. Rampant, unrestricted development along the Blowing Rock Road, US Highway 421, and NC Highway 105 corridors—often in floodplains that were not yet subject to strict federal, state, or local oversight—led to a vast increase in impermeable surfaces such as parking lots in areas that had long absorbed water during heavy rains. As a result, flooding became a recurring and frequent issue. Meanwhile, continued increases in tourism only served to amplify cycles of environmental degradation, increased development, and surging vehicular traffic that overwhelmed local mountain roads. New developments on the periphery of Boone also began to undercut the stability of its downtown economy, where businesses often cut corners by employing ill-advised facelift schemes for their buildings instead of addressing maintenance and rehabilitation issues through a preservation-centered approach.

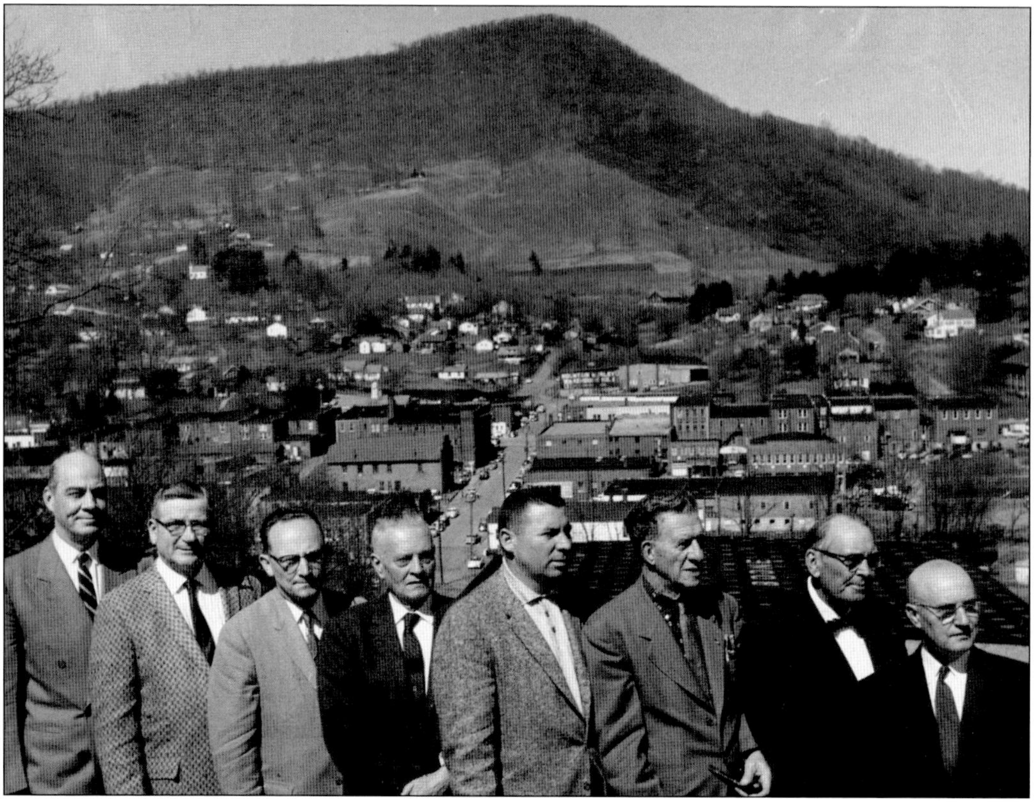

This 1960 image demonstrates the inextricable connections among Boone's businessmen and Appalachian State Teachers College (ASTC). From left to right are William Howard Plemmons, ASTC president; Glenn Andrews, Watauga Industries Inc.; Alfred Adams, Northwestern Bank; Dempsey Wilcox, Watauga Industries Inc.; Jerry Coe, Coe Insurance Agency; Stanley Harris, Northwest North Carolina Development Association; Watt Gragg, Watauga Industries Inc.; and Herman Wilcox, Boone Chamber of Commerce. (Alfred and Daisy Adams Collection.)

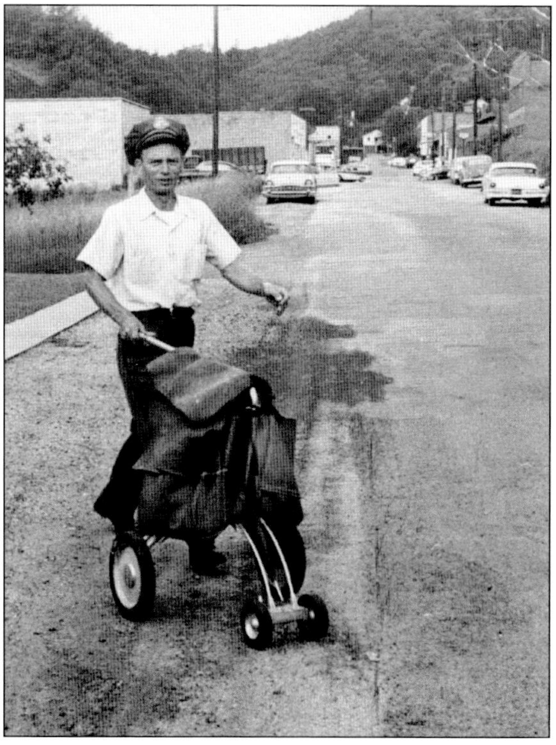

This c. 1960 photograph looking west on Howard Street shows postal carrier Von Hagaman as he delivers mail. At left is the new Goodnight Brothers Produce building (1958), with the original building (1944) in the distance, while the Winkler Motors Company Building built in 1946 (presently home to ECRS) is at right. (Von and Mickey Hagaman Collection.)

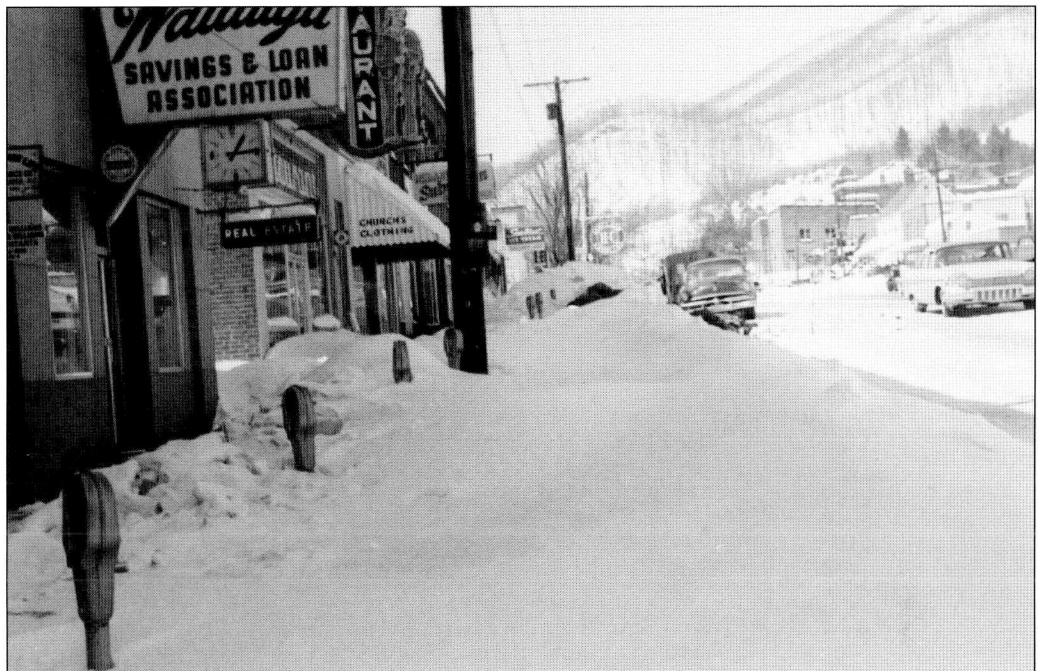

In this image taken in March 1960 looking west on King Street, snow covers the sidewalks of Boone nearly to the tops of the parking meters. The 1960 blizzard was actually a series of five major snowstorms and 17 total snow events over six weeks that produced nearly seven feet of snow and brought brutally cold temperatures to the area. (Glenn Thomas Collection.)

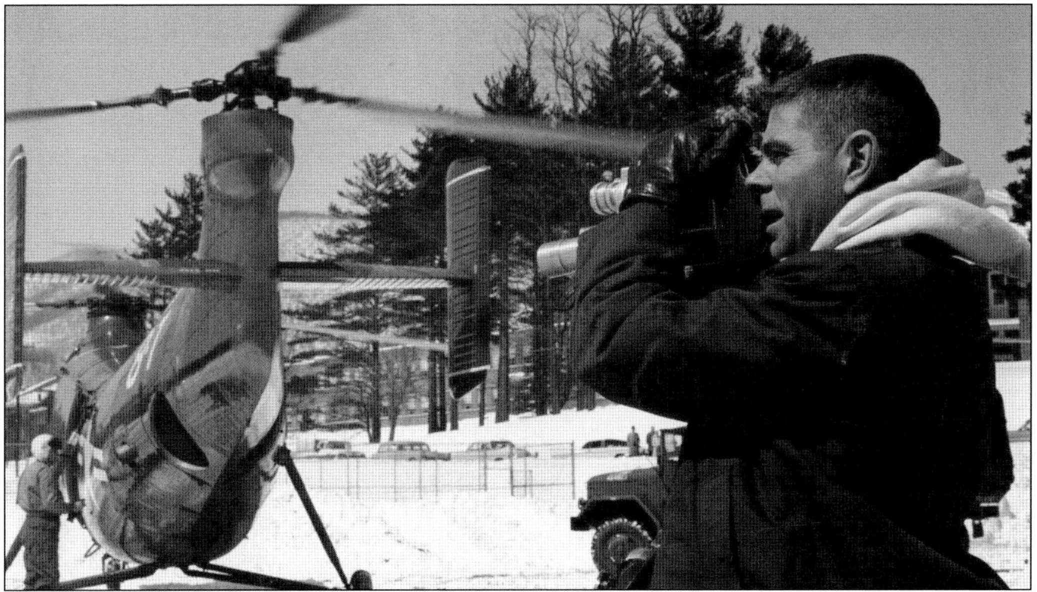

The March 1960 state of emergency prompted assistance from the Army and National Guard, which George Flowers filmed landing on the Appalachian State Teachers College campus. A local legend holds that when the National Guard showed up at one rural woman's house to render aid and asked if she had any food, she replied, "Well, I can spare a little, but I need the rest to get through the winter." (George Flowers Collection.)

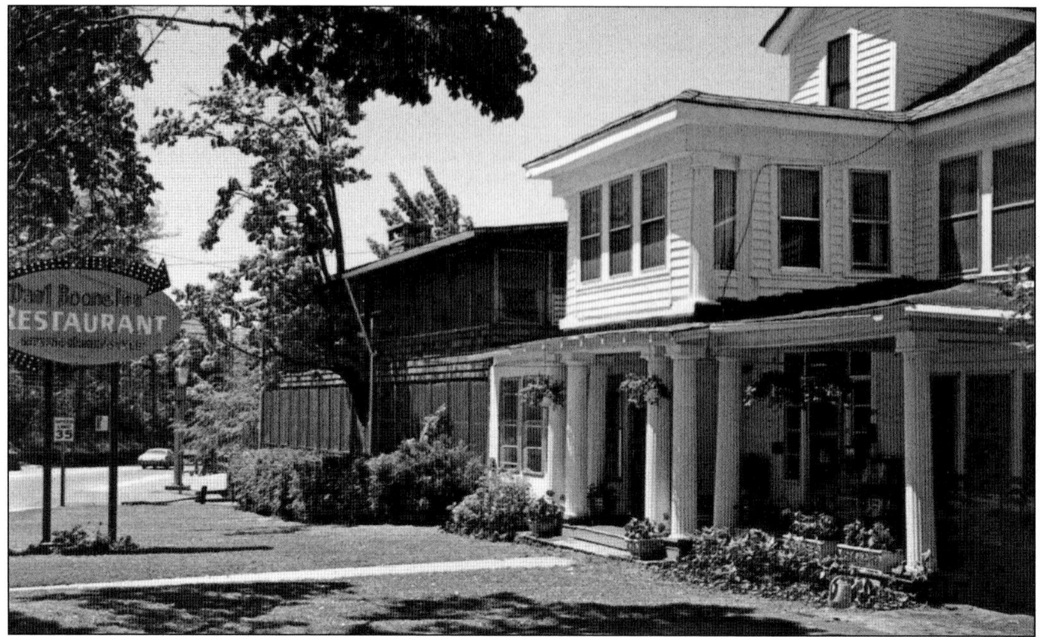

After a long time in use as a student rooming house in the 1950s, the former Dr. R.K. Bingham Home and Watauga Hospital transformed once again in 1959. That year, the Whitaker family opened a family-style restaurant called the Daniel Boone Inn and eventually added the large dining wing visible on this postcard. The landmark remains a popular culinary destination for tourists visiting Boone and the High Country. (Bobby Brendell Postcard Collection.)

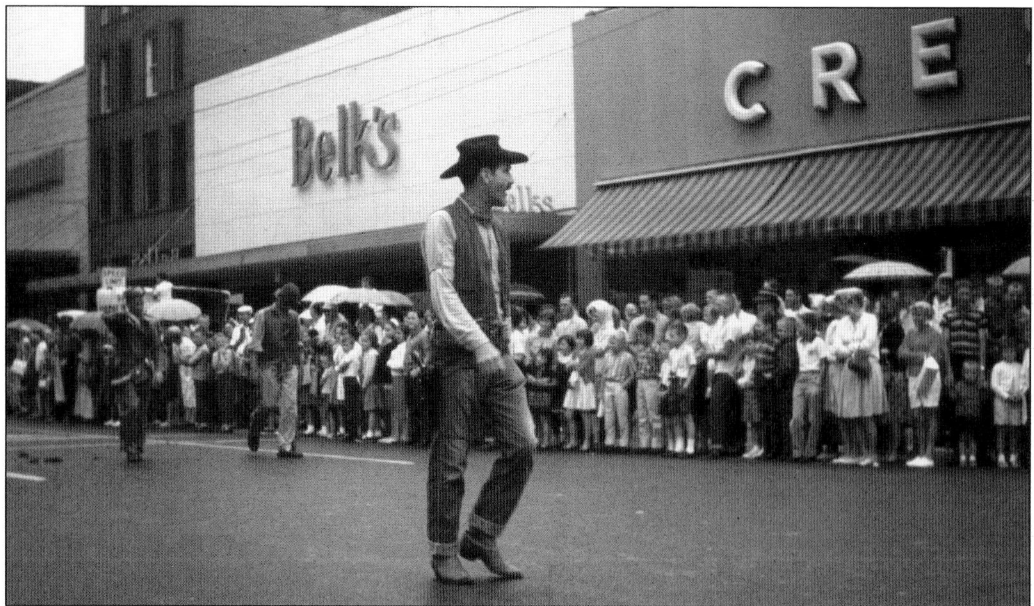

To commemorate the Carolina charter tercentenary, Boone Chamber of Commerce president Herman Wallace Wilcox (1903–1984) directed planning for a wagon train route from Ferguson to Boone along Daniel Boone's alleged 1773 route to Kentucky over the Blue Ridge. In this image, a cowboy walks past Belk's Department Store and the Crest Five and Ten during the 1964 Daniel Boone Wagon Train procession. (John Ward Family Collection.)

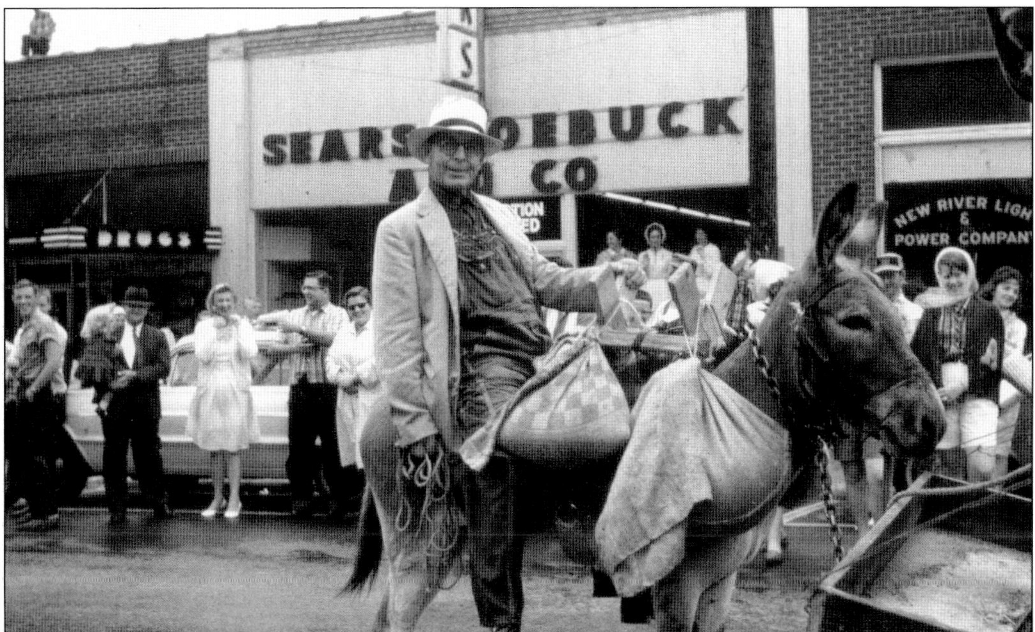

The Daniel Boone Wagon Train processions were an annual event for 10 years but stopped after 1973 as a result of waning interest. A brief revival in the 1980s failed to take root. In this image from the 1965 event, an unidentified man rides his donkey past the Carolina Pharmacy and Sears, Roebuck, and Co. in the former Dixie Store space. (Harlan Ledford Collection.)

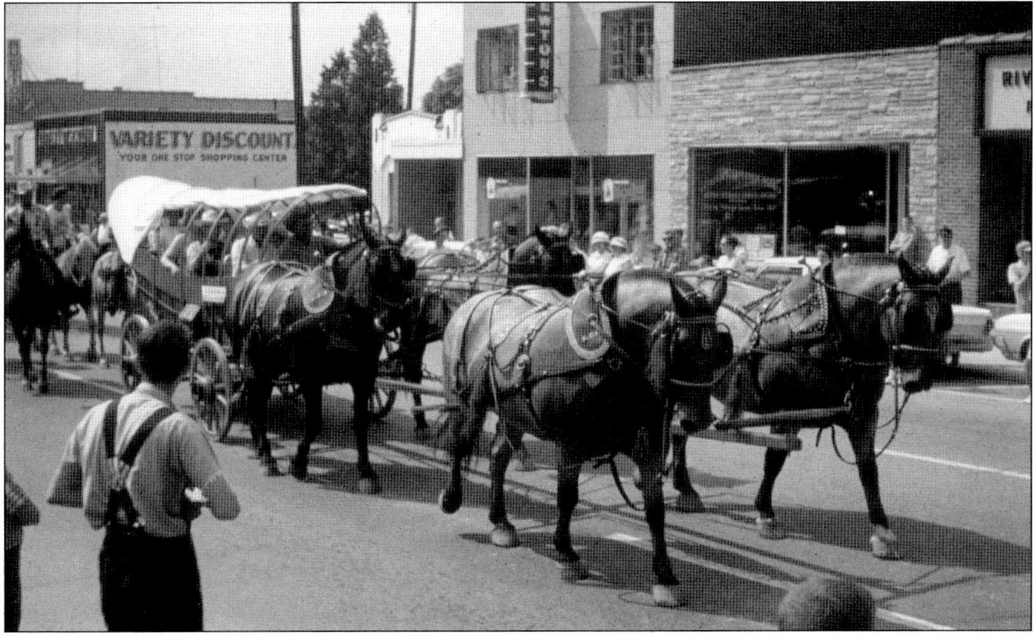

Historical inaccuracies were a feature rather than a bug of the Daniel Boone Wagon Train celebrations, as exemplified by this 19th century–inspired team of horses and a wagon in the 1967 procession. At center left is the former Sinclair service station, then being used as Boone's town hall. Newton's Department Store and its baby-blue structural glass front is at center. (John Ward Family Collection.)

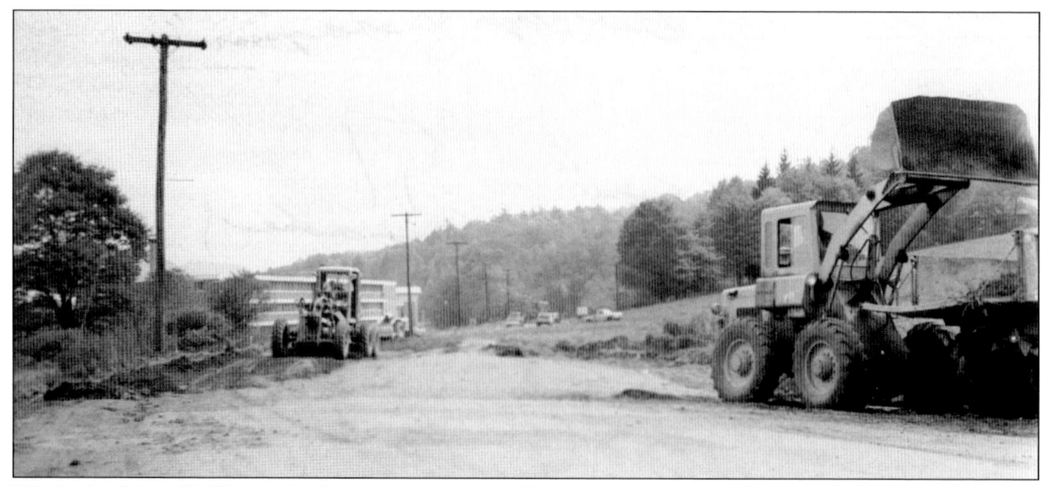

With the Linville River Railway gone and traffic issues compounding near campus, in 1968, town officials worked to create a Boone Thoroughfare by connecting Rivers Street along the old railbed with Faculty Street to the southeast, necessitating the demolition of the burley tobacco warehouse at lower Depot Street. In this image, earthmovers work to clear and widen the grade. Edward Duncan Hall is at left. (Historic Boone Collection.)

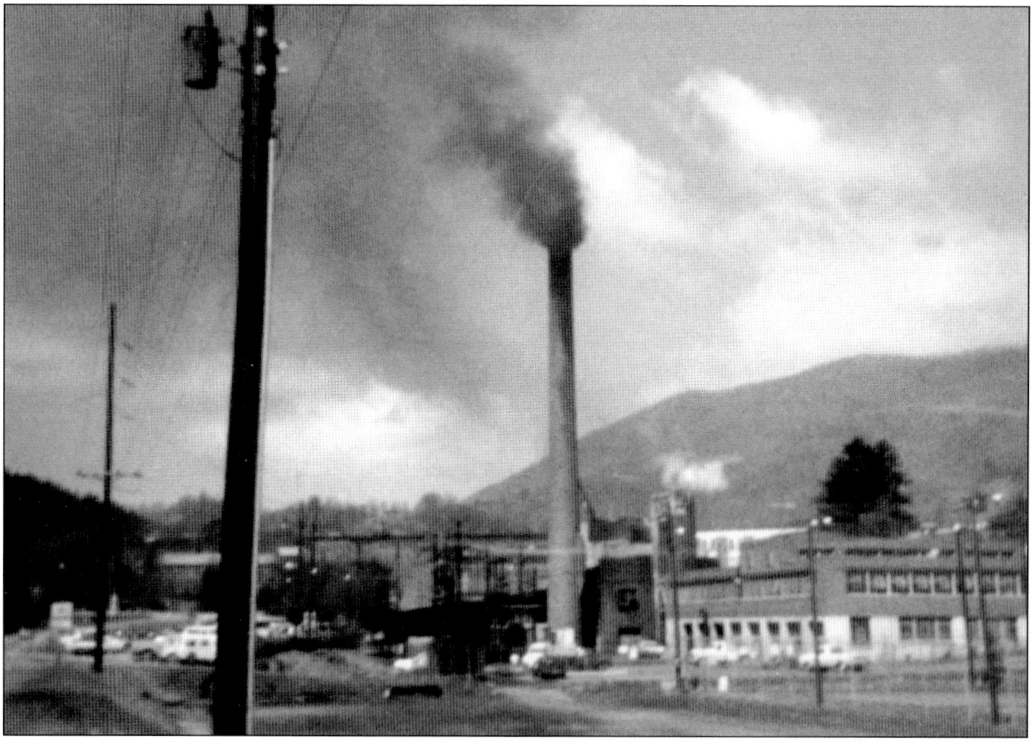

During the late 1960s and early 1970s, national attention on environmental issues captured the interest of Appalachian State University students and townsfolk alike. One target of concern was the coal-fired generator plant at ASU, which was built in 1924 and belched thick, black smoke for decades. In response to community pressure, the plant stopped using coal in 1973. (Rosalea Dorsey Collection.)

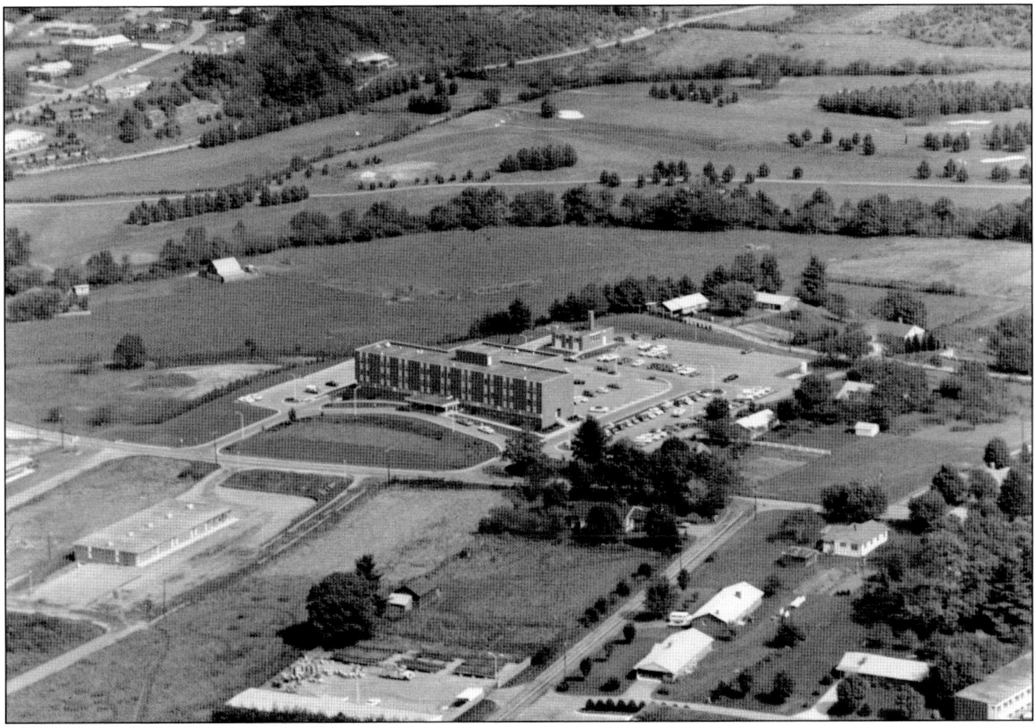

After decades of overcrowding and equipment deficiencies at the second Watauga Hospital, officials finally committed to the construction of a new hospital on Deerfield Road at the south end of Boone, not far from the historic Blair Farm. Built by C.P. Street Construction of Charlotte, the new 80-bed hospital—shown here in 1971—was dedicated in October 1967. (Henry Dewolf Aerial Surveys of Watauga County Collection.)

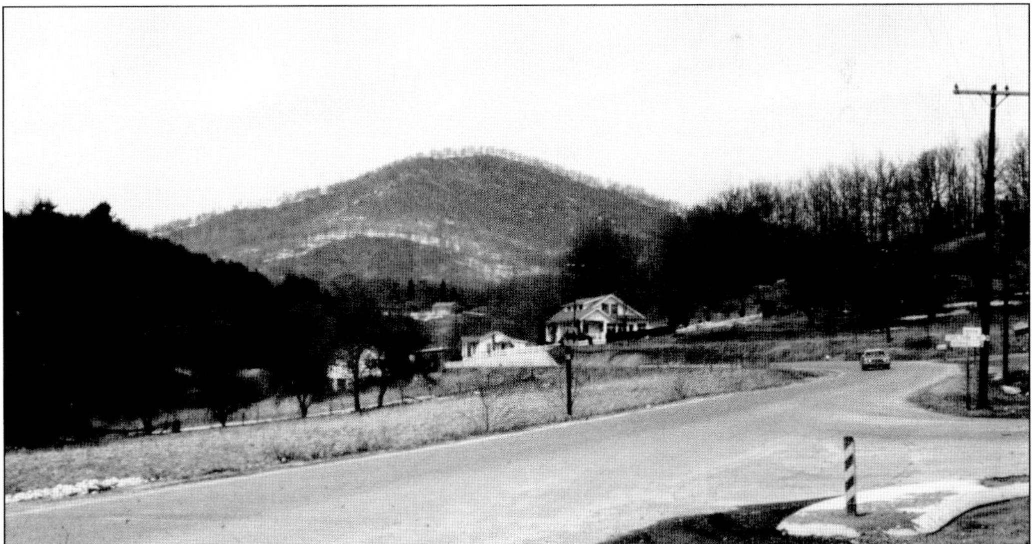

Despite the expansion of the university and the rapid growth of Boone in the 1960s, rural scenes were still common close to downtown. In this March 1969 image, a lone car on the two-lane road connecting Blowing Rock Road and East King Street makes its way past the intersection with State Farm Road. The Lorn Harrison House (at center right) still stands. (George Flowers Collection.)

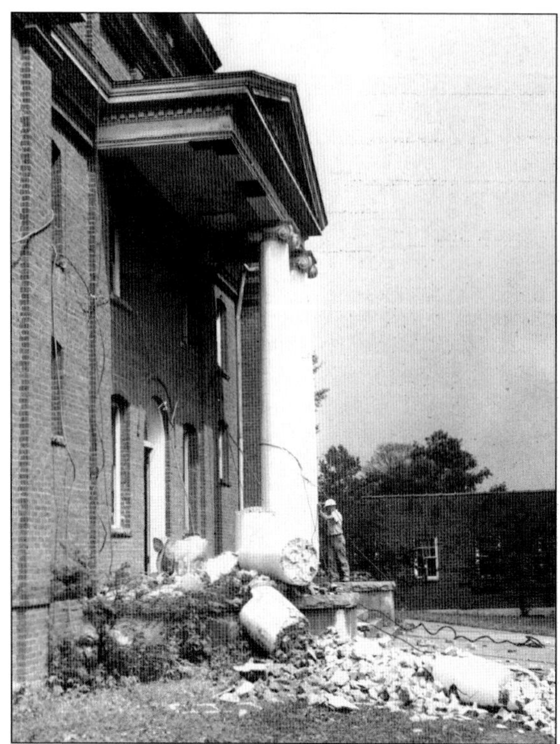

In 1967, citing issues of soft brick and a settling foundation, Watauga County officials moved forward with the demolition of the 1905 courthouse, with plans to erect a new courthouse on the same site. Salvaged brick from the courthouse was used to build a new home, located west of Boone, where the still-unsolved Durham family murders occurred in February 1972. (Henry Dewolf Aerial Surveys of Watauga County Collection.)

Construction on the new Watauga County Courthouse, designed by Clarence P. Coffey, was completed in 1968. One local critic described the new courthouse, pictured around 1971, as "the homely offspring of an illicit love affair between a supermarket and a burley warehouse." Citing the need for "improvements" after just 14 years, county officials completed an addition to the facade in 1982. (Henry Dewolf Aerial Surveys of Watauga County Collection.)

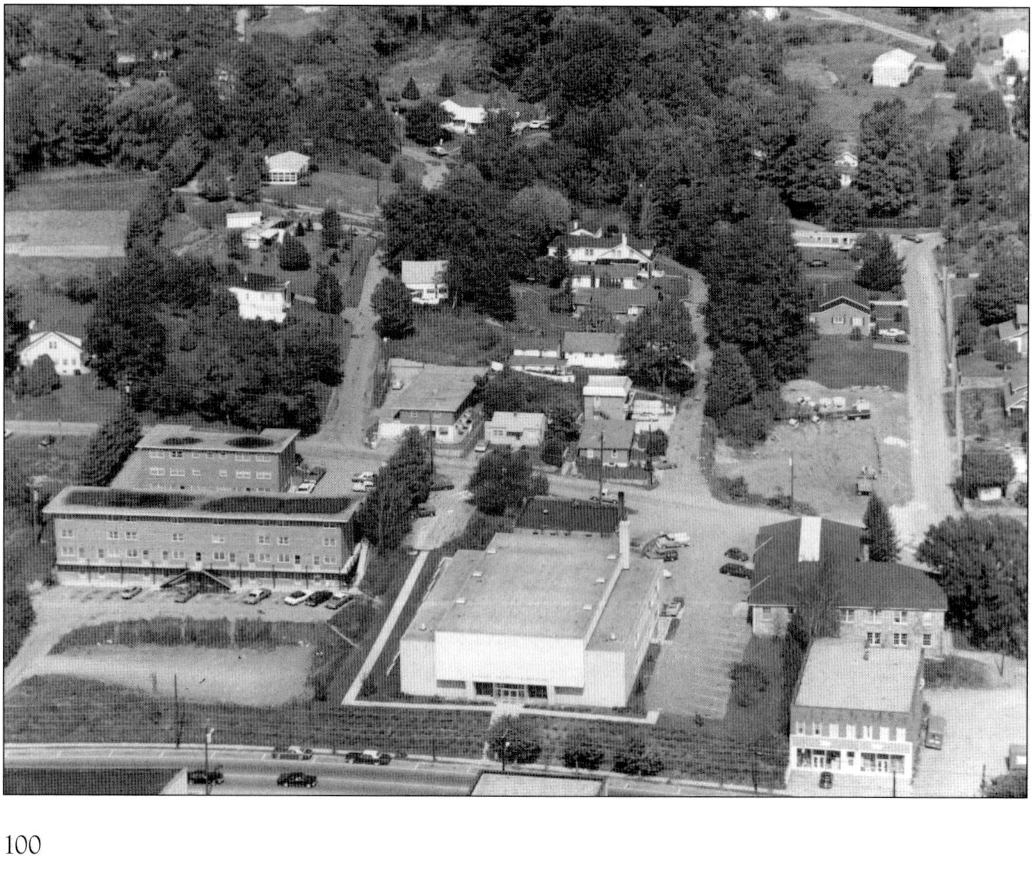

The threat of fire in the business district continued into the 1970s. In February 1970, an overnight fire badly gutted the John W. Hodges building on King Street, destroying the K and M Gateway Restaurant, the Sanitary Barbershop, and a small food store in the basement that was accessed via a sidewalk staircase. (Historic Boone Collection.)

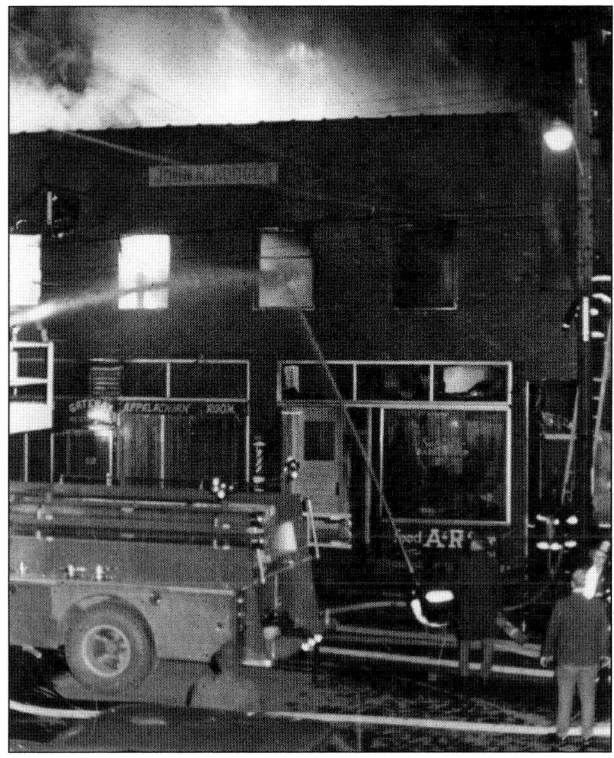

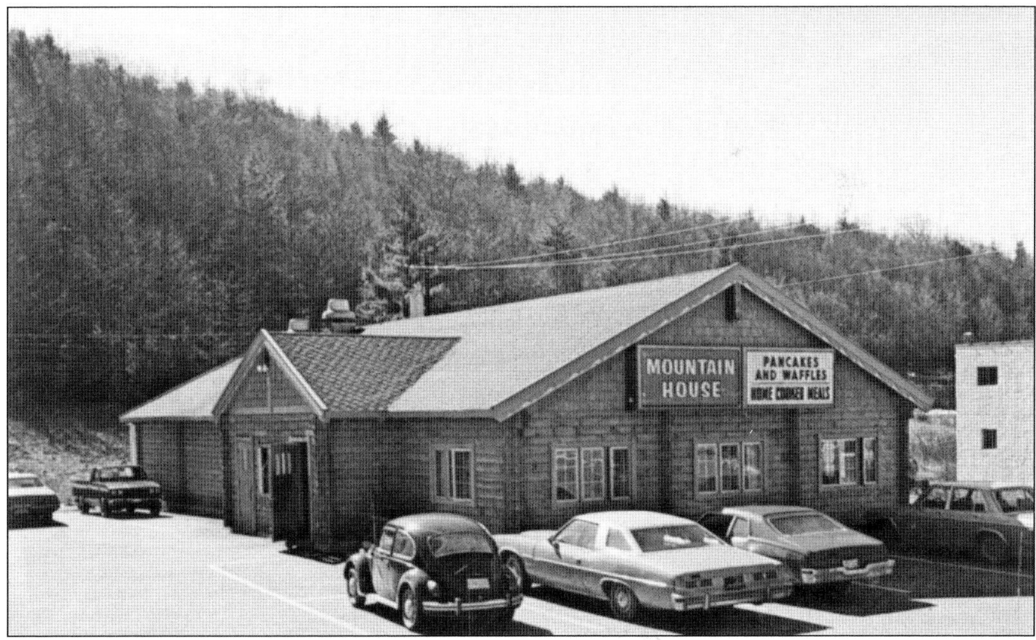

Throughout the 1970s, new businesses and construction continued to crop up along Blowing Rock Road to the south of town. This postcard shows the first location of Mountain House, a popular eatery operated by Beatrice Storie. A Walgreens now stands on the site. Mountain House moved to a couple of other locations and changed owners before it closed in the early 2010s. (Bobby Brendell Postcard Collection.)

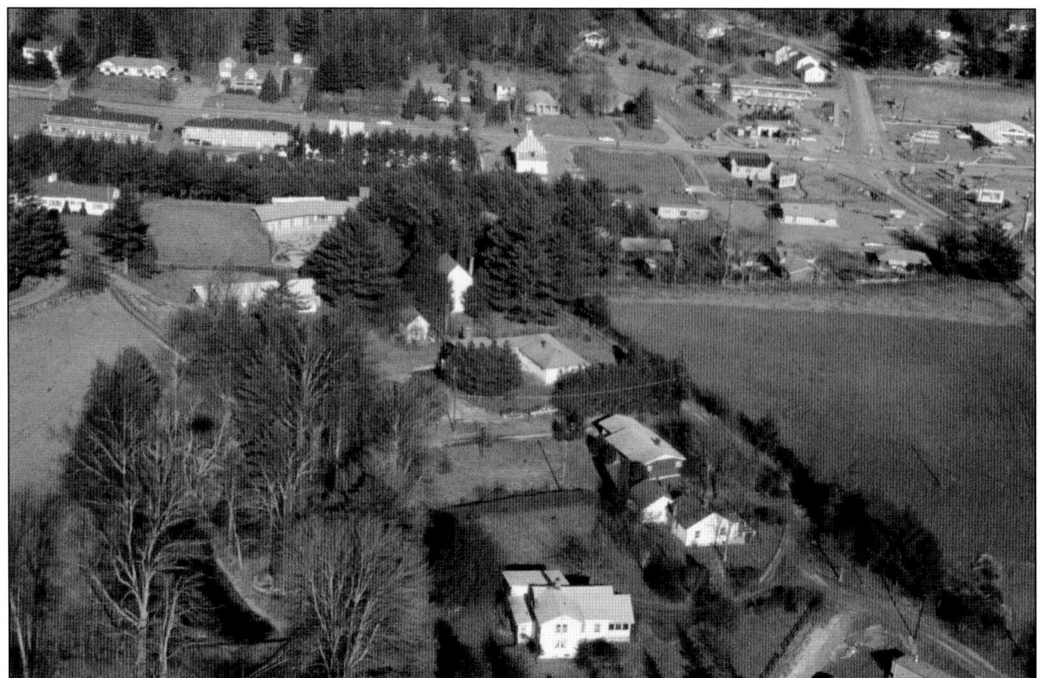

Blowing Rock Road sprawl unsettled some locals as a harbinger of things to come. This January 1971 image looking northeast shows businesses near the intersection of Blowing Rock Road and NC Highway 105 at upper right, while the houses along Wintergreen Lane and Flowers Drive are visible in the foreground. Buildings serving higher intensity commercial uses now stand on most of the Blowing Rock Road sites. (George Flowers Collection.)

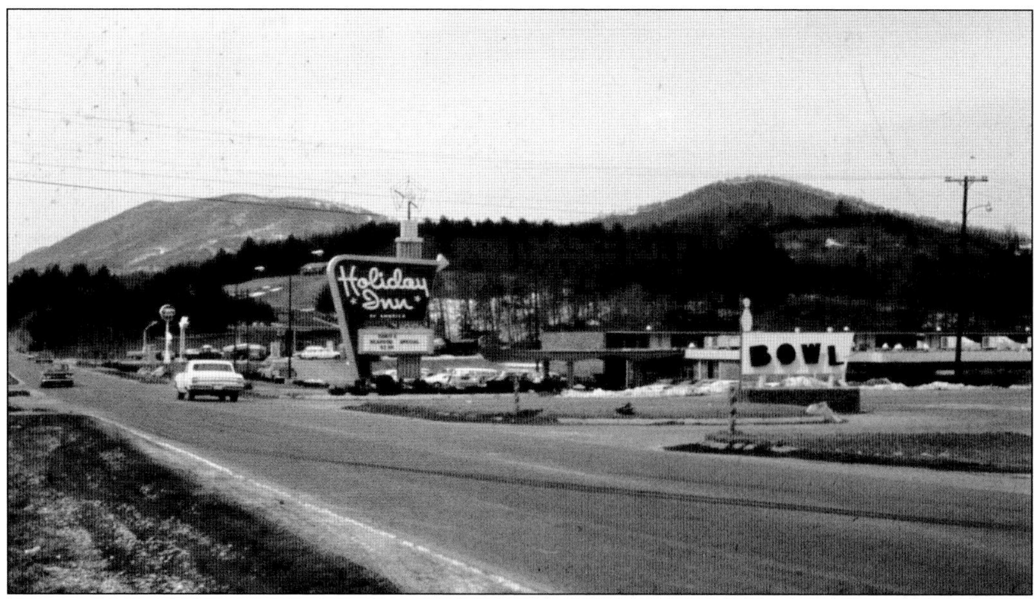

This March 1969 glimpse of Blowing Rock Road shows a Gulf station, the new Holiday Inn, and a sign for the local bowling alley on the northeast side of the road, all of which were close to where the Lowe's complex is today. Many old-time locals have fond memories of the Holiday Inn's Shrimparoo Buffet. (George Flowers Collection.)

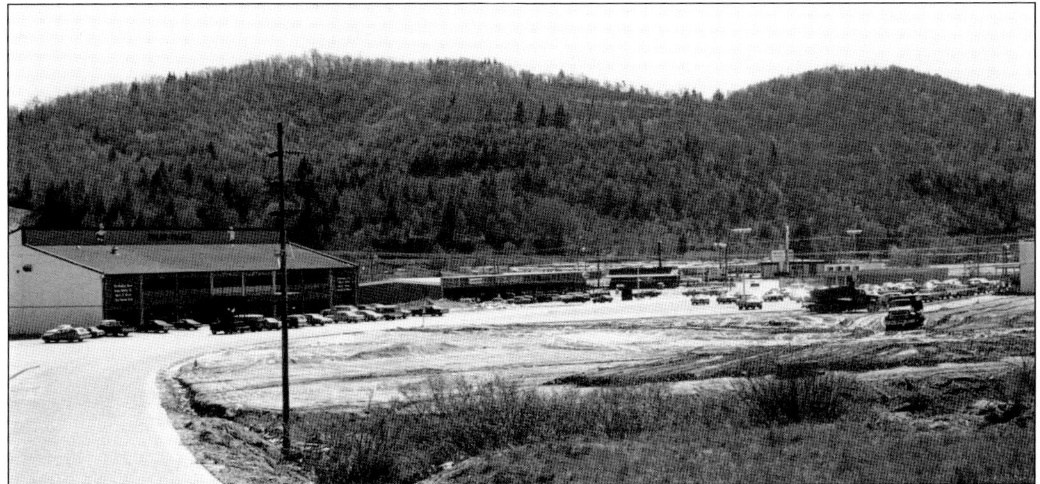

By the time of this image looking south along Boone Heights Drive in the mid-1970s, even more dramatic changes had occurred in the Blowing Rock Road area. Developers performed a considerable amount of grading to level the terrain on Boone Heights Drive. At left is the Polar Palace, a popular ice-skating rink located on what is now the site of the Broyhill Wellness Center. (George Flowers Collection.)

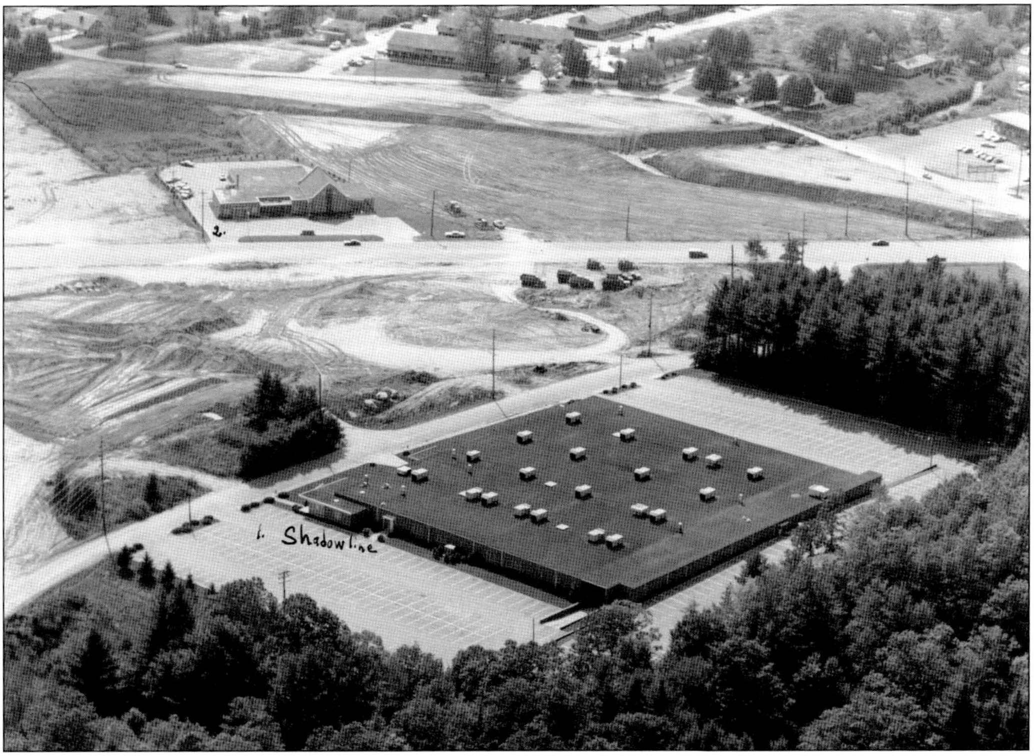

This c. 1971 low aerial image looking southwest shows the Shadowline plant just above the significant grading being completed for the eventual construction of the Shops at Shadowline retail center. The Reins-Sturdivant Funeral Home—currently town council chambers—is at upper left. The lack of any erosion-control measures is indicative of the lax environmental controls in the 1970s. (Henry Dewolf Aerial Surveys of Watauga County Collection.)

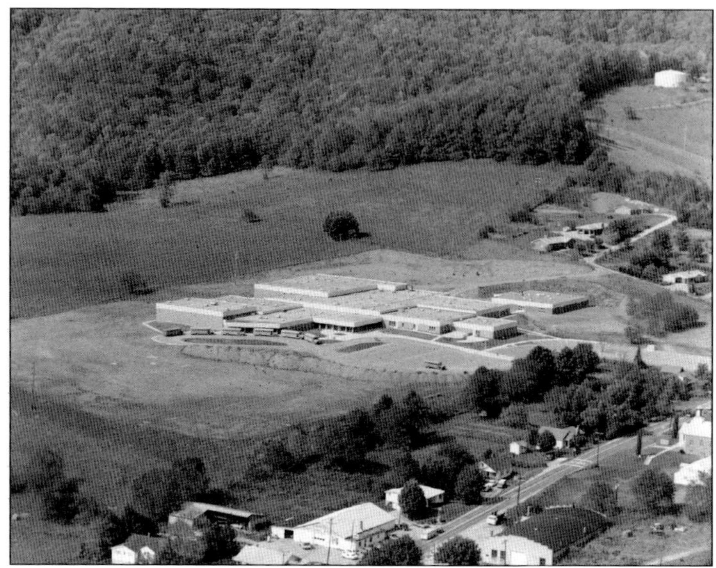

Hardin Park School, completed in the early 1970s on land in Perkinsville that was previously owned by the Farthing family, is visible in this c. 1971 image. New Market Boulevard had not yet been built, but Jefferson Highway (NC Highway 194) is visible at lower right, along with Coffey's Sportsman Center at lower center and Perkinsville Baptist Church at extreme lower right. (Henry Dewolf Aerial Surveys of Watauga County Collection.)

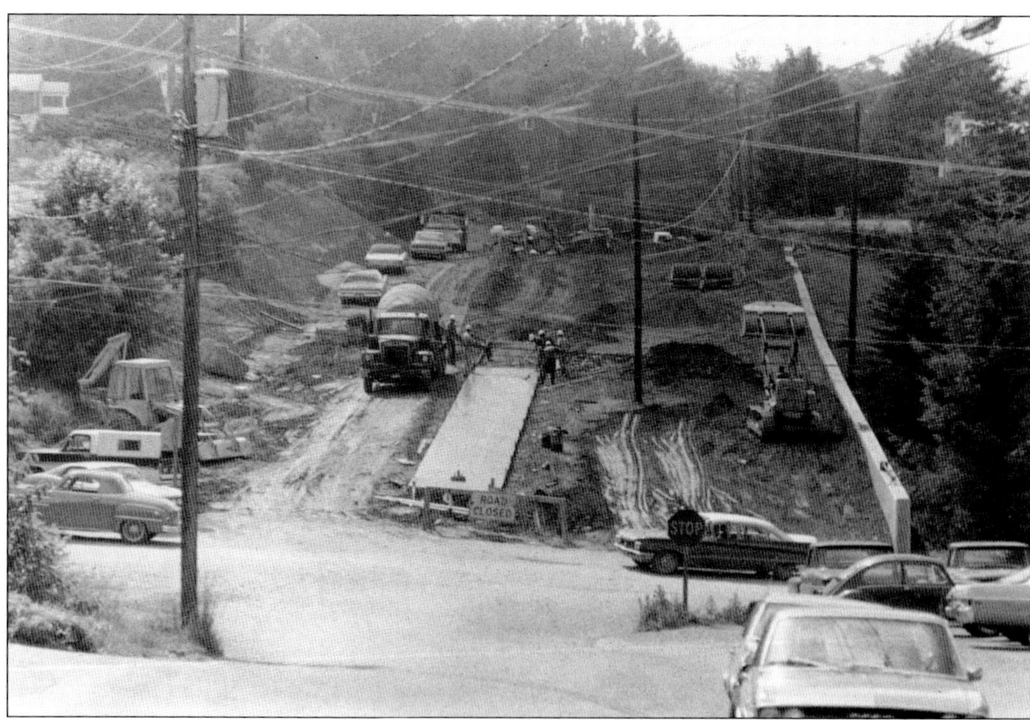

High tourist demand, rapid growth, and increased vehicle traffic meant greater demand for parking. This c. 1972 image looking east along Queen Street shows the widening effort intended to create a parking island in the center of the street. The A.E. and Roberta Hodges House (1940) on Grand Boulevard is at upper center, with the North Water Street crossing in the foreground. (Paul Armfield Coffey Collection.)

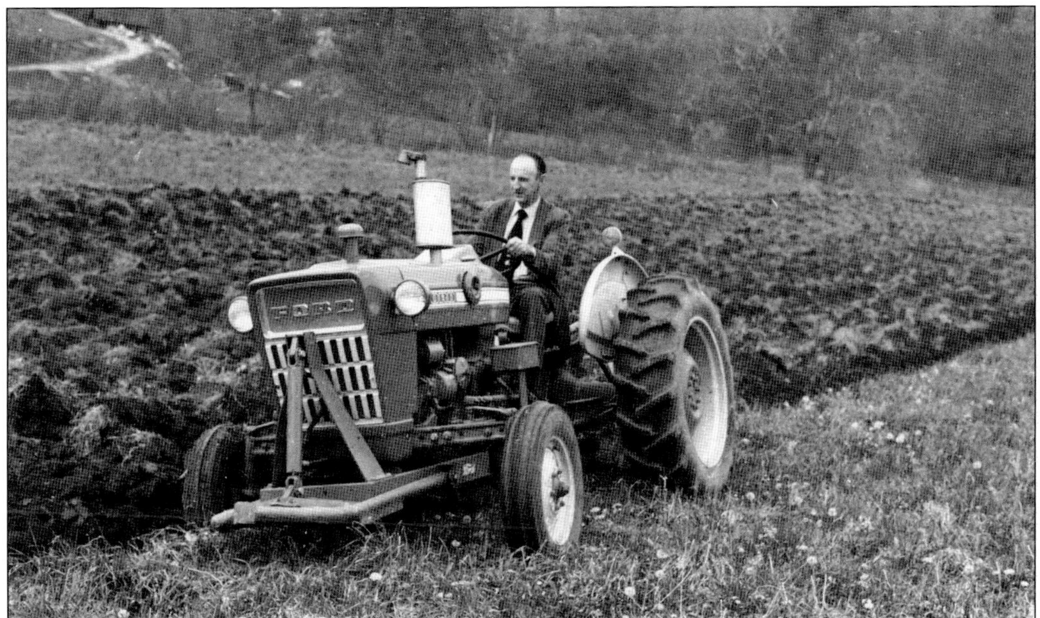

In this April 1974 image, Appalachian State University chancellor Dr. Herbert Walter Wey (1914–1999) is shown plowing up garden plots for faculty members on the university's 200-acre farm off State Farm Road. The farm was used for decades to supply food for students and faculty alike, but with the increased trucking-in of food, the university sought other uses for the farmland. Much of it is now used for recreation. (George Flowers Collection.)

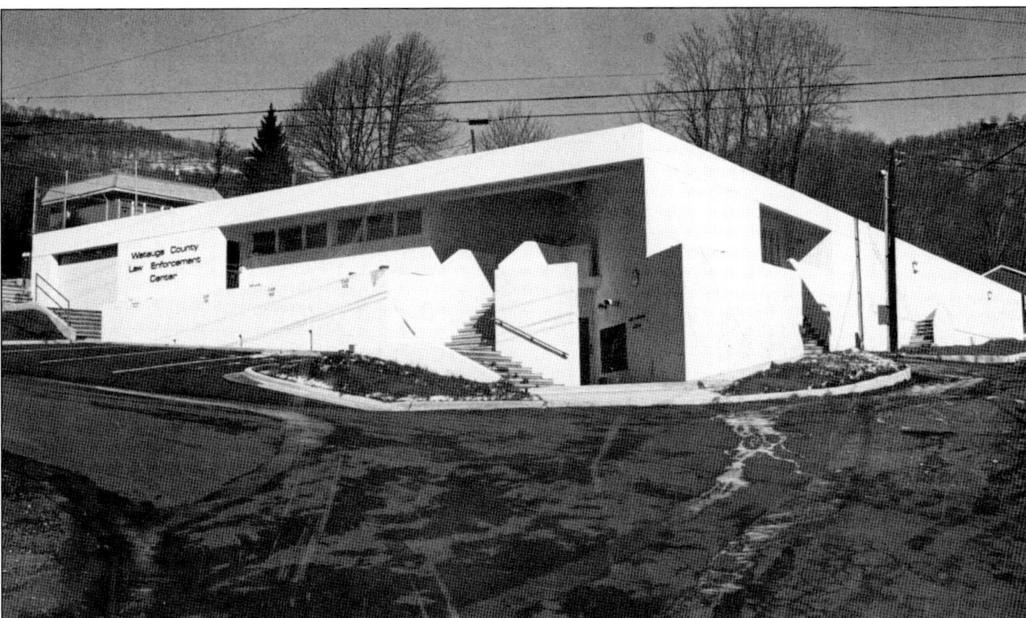

In November 1975, Watauga County completed this new law enforcement facility at the northwest corner of North Water and Queen Streets in downtown Boone, replacing the outdated 1927 jail behind the 1968 courthouse. When this facility, located adjacent to residential neighborhoods, was torn down in 2007 following construction of the Watauga County Detention Center west of Boone, the county unsuccessfully tried to erect a parking deck on the site. (George Flowers Collection.)

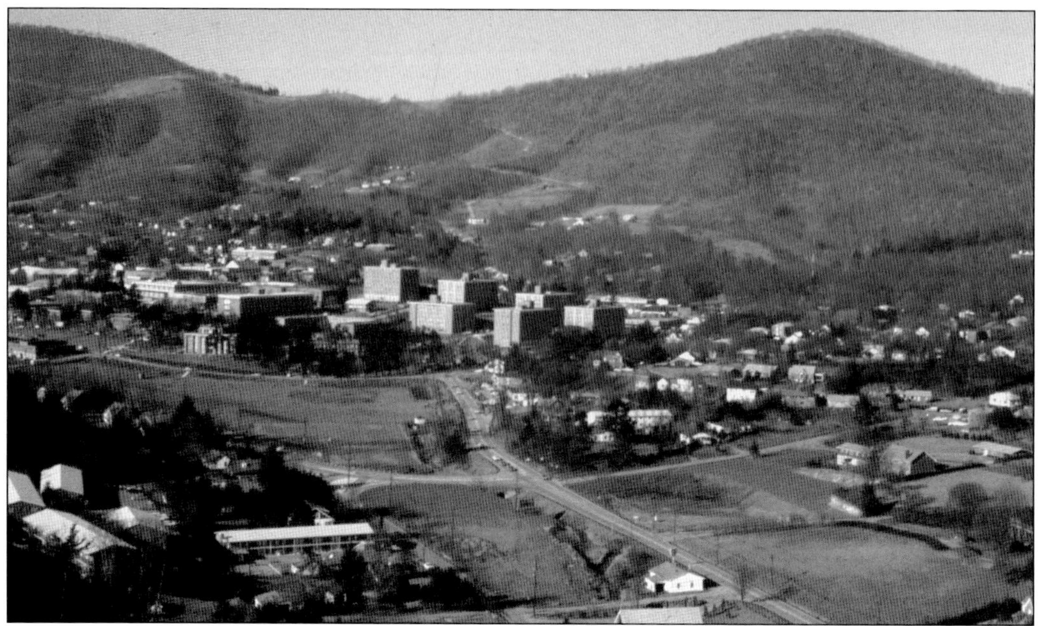

This January 1971 image shows Blowing Rock Road at lower right progressing toward Faculty Street and the Appalachian State University campus at center left. Boone Creek remained mostly daylighted, or uncovered, with few buildings in its floodplain. Only a few homes were perched on the ridgelines of Howard's Knob and Rich Mountain, while most of the forests cleared in the early 20th century had started to fill back in. (George Flowers Collection.)

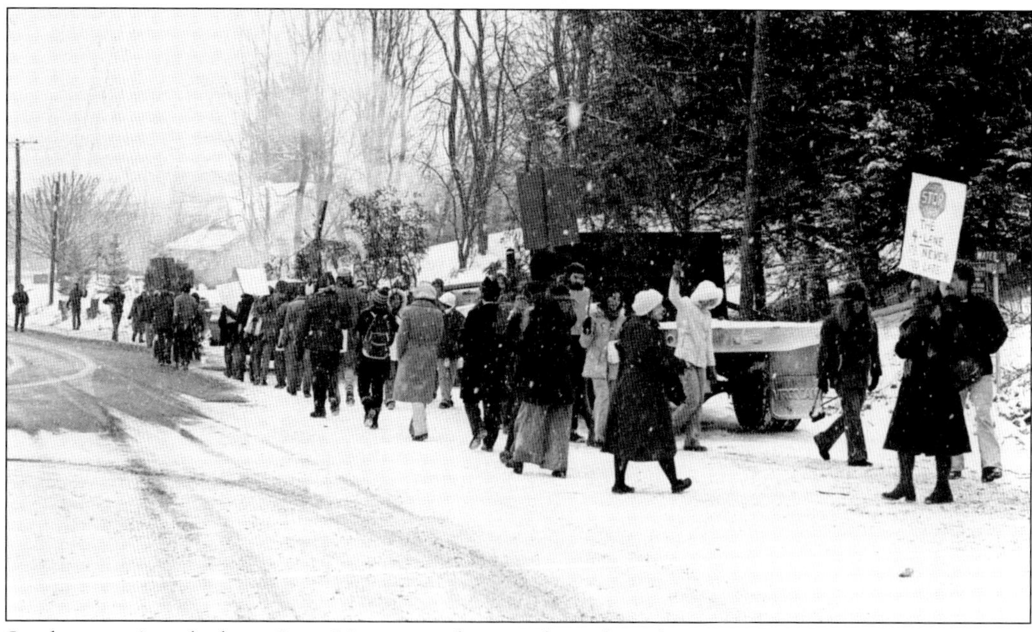

Students at Appalachian State University frequently took to the streets to protest environmental problems or demand action from the university. In this February 1977 photograph, students are picketing at the intersection of Burrell and Rivers Streets to protest the proposed widening of Rivers Street to four lanes and the cutting down of trees on campus and throughout Boone. (George Flowers Collection.)

Local mythology has long held that woolly worm banding is predictive of the forthcoming winter's precipitation and temperatures. To test the theory, as well as other weather superstitions, biology graduate student Rob Hunt (left, covered in the fuzzy critters) and junior biology major Phillip Timmons joined six other students in creating a Center for Woolly Worm Studies in October 1975. (George Flowers Collection.)

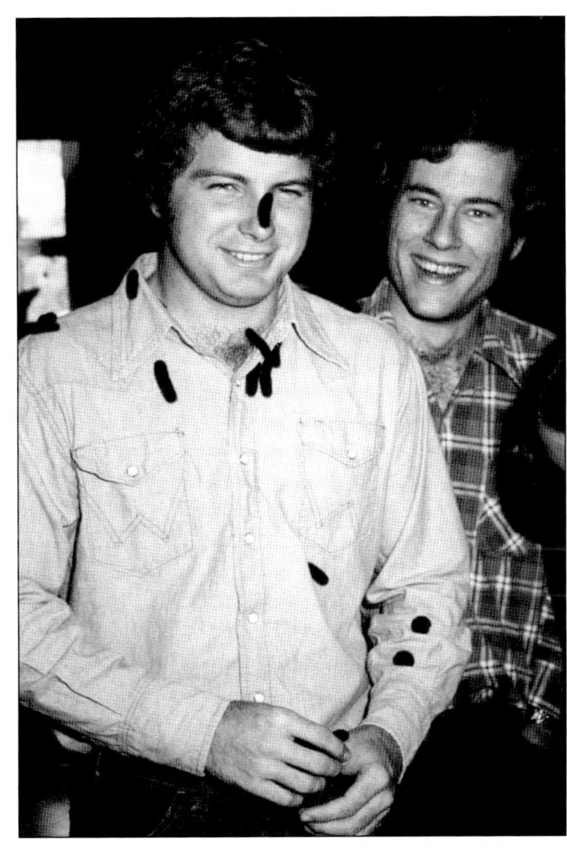

By the 1970s, many of the older agricultural industries in the Boone area were beginning to decline, and some farmers turned to Christmas trees to make profitable use of their land. Shown here are Edward Cole (left) and Guy Cockburn, winners of the National Christmas Tree Champion Contest at the National Christmas Tree Growers Convention held at Appalachian State University in August 1974. (George Flowers Collection.)

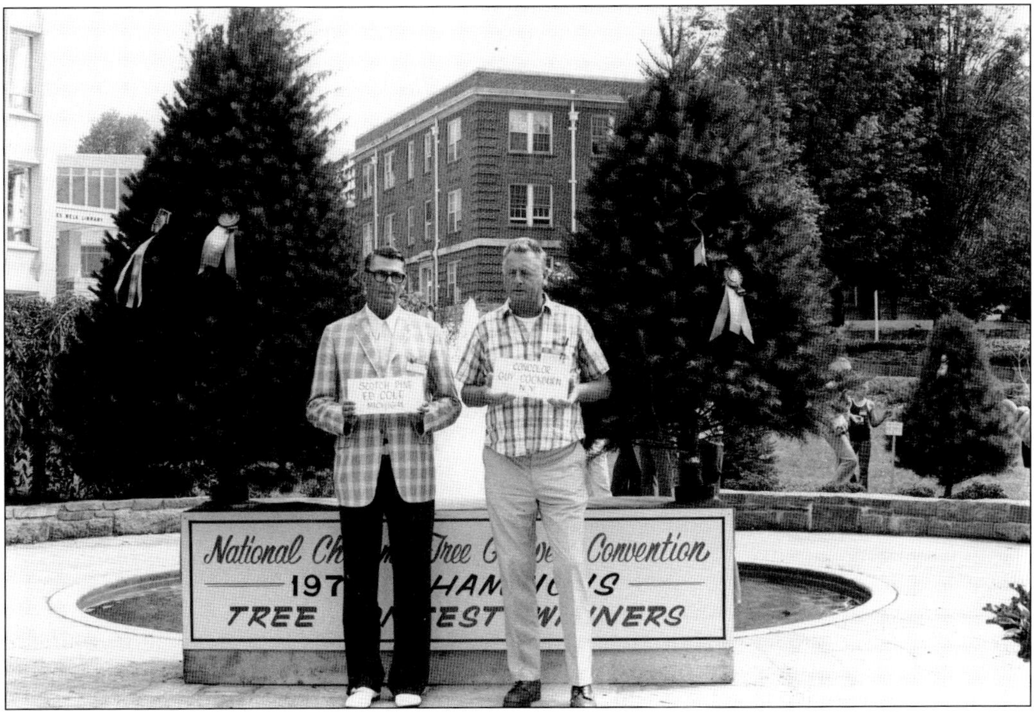

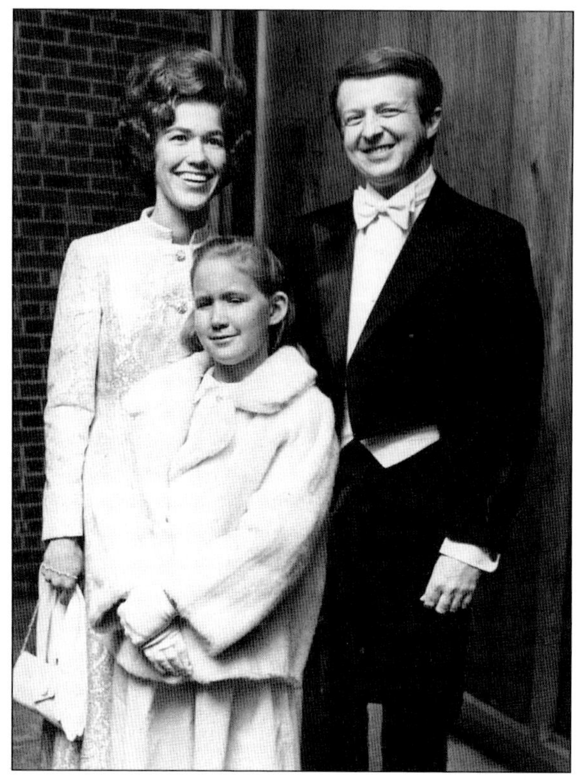

Boone has always produced its share of leaders who made their way off the mountain to shine on the state and national political stages. In 1972, James Eubert Holshouser Jr. (1934–2013), who grew up in a house on Grand Boulevard, was elected governor of North Carolina. He poses here around 1973 with his wife, Patricia Ann Hollingsworth Holshouser (1939–2006), and their daughter Ginny. (George Flowers Collection.)

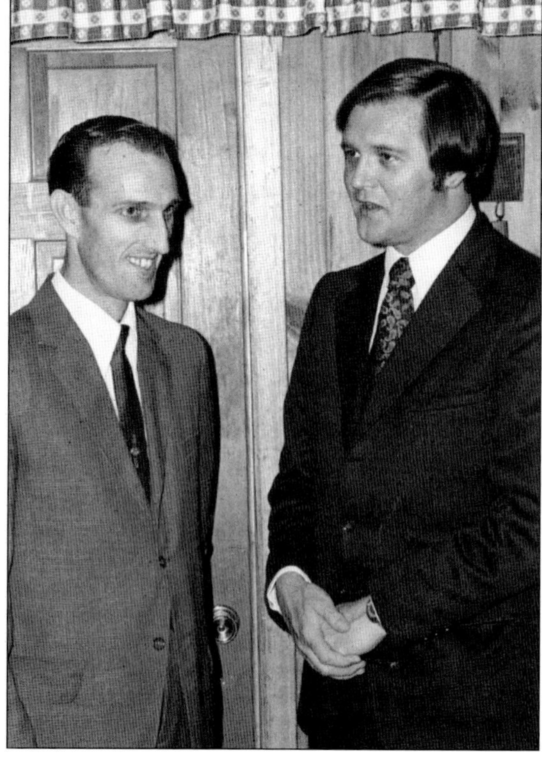

Another local boy made good is Rufus Lige Edmisten (right, born 1941), pictured in 1974 with Boone police lieutenant Arlie Wesley Isaacs (1940–2017). In 1973, Edmisten worked as deputy chief counsel for the Senate Watergate Committee and served the subpoena to the Nixon White House for the Watergate tapes. Edmisten also served as North Carolina's attorney general from 1975 to 1984 and North Carolina secretary of state from 1989 to 1996. (George Flowers Collection.)

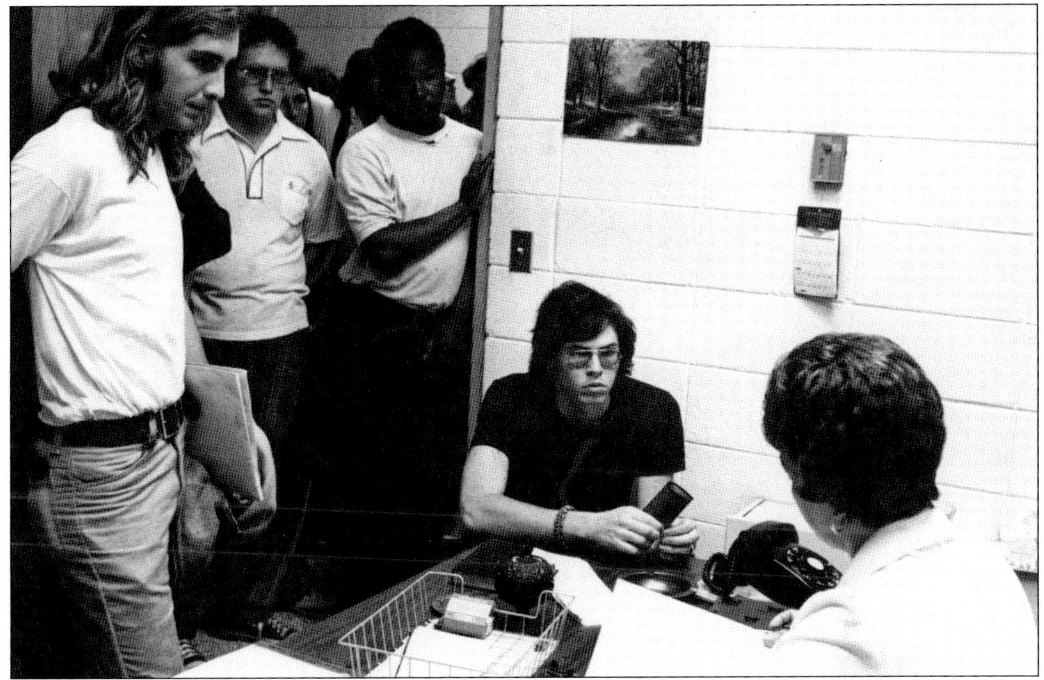

A longstanding conflict in Boone has focused on the voting rights of Appalachian State University students, many of whom are not originally from the area. Local authorities have often tried to disenfranchise these students. This image from May 1975 shows the climax of a protest march with 125 students heading to the Watauga County Courthouse, where Fred A. McGee Jr. (seated) was told he could not register. (George Flowers Collection.)

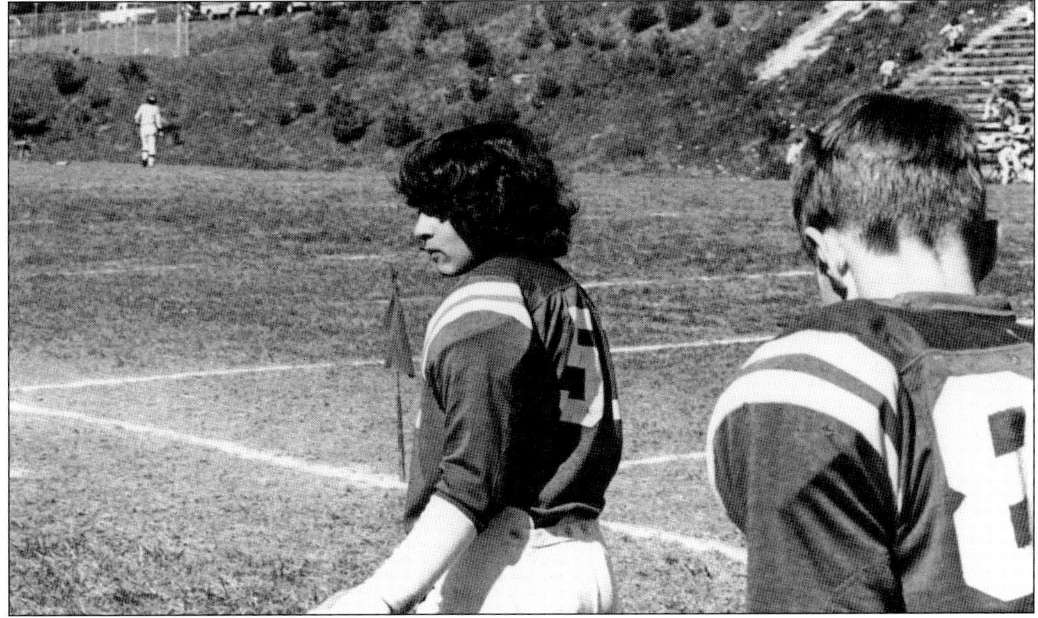

Boone has also had its share of trailblazers in the quest for equality, equity, and justice, many of whom have been young folks. Sophie Mahmoud (center, born 1962) was only 13 when she became the only female player in Boone's Midget Football League in October 1975. (George Flowers Collection.)

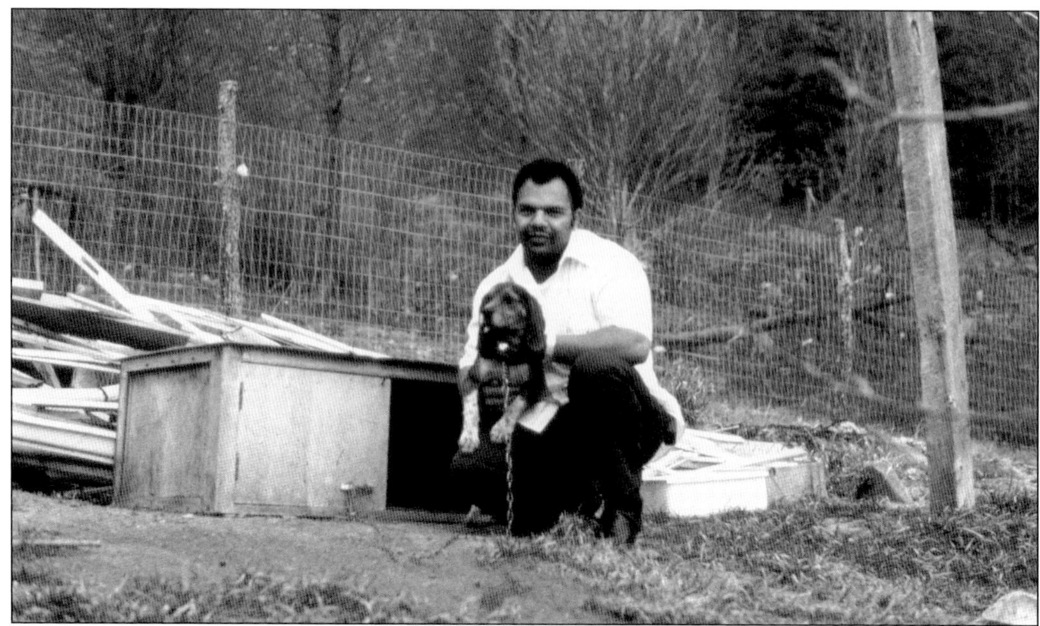

Grady Cecil Jackson (1947–1996) was born in Elk Park but moved to the Junaluska community as a small child. After high school, he worked at Appalachian State University's physical plant and in the grounds department. An avid hunter, Jackson kept beagles near Howard's Knob, but he also enjoyed photography. His 1970s photographs are an invaluable chronicle of Junaluska community life. (Cecil Jackson Slide Collection.)

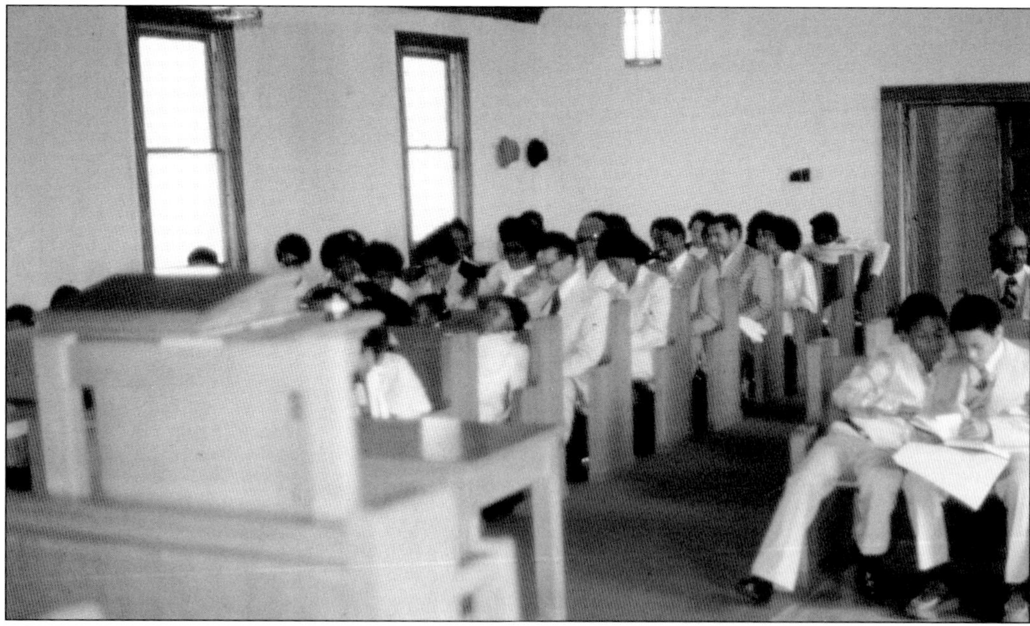

This 1979 image shows members of the Boone Mennonite Brethren Church in the sanctuary's pews. To the right are Cecil Jackson Jr. and Nathaniel Young, with James McQueen Sr. behind them. Other church members in this photograph include Lena Horton, Christy D. Fox, Sandra Hagler, Don Grimes, Magnolia W. Grimes, Neil Grimes, Robert Allison, Louise H. Goins, and Carrie W. Hagler. (Cecil Jackson Slide Collection.)

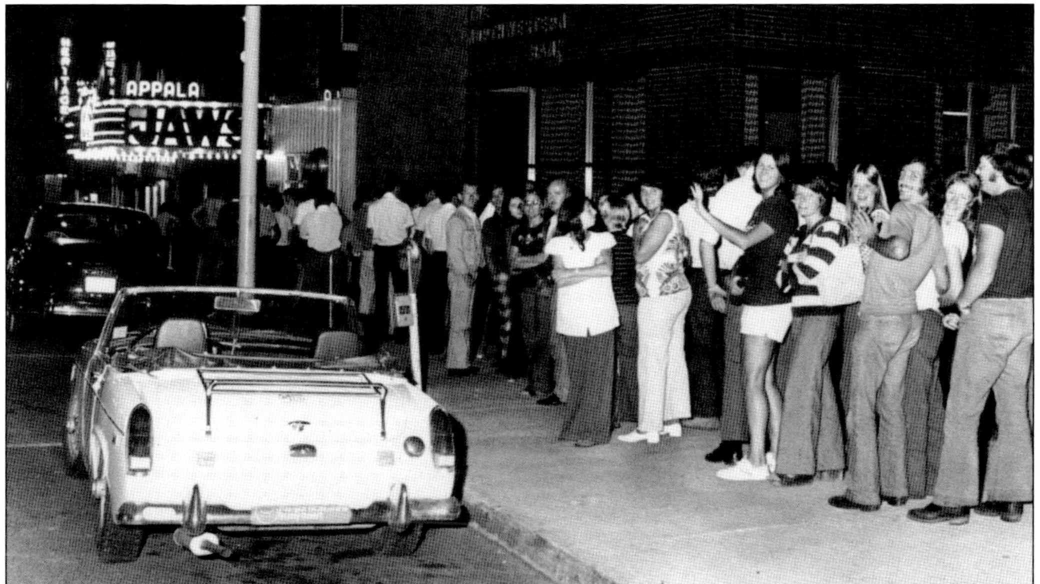

Students from Appalachian State University line the sidewalk in front of the Appalachian Theatre and the Northwestern Bank (now Town Hall) in August 1975 for the Boone premiere of *Jaws*. Town officials required the marquee's removal around 1980, and in 1982, the owners enclosed the balcony to create a twin screen. The theater struggled to compete with the multiplex in Perkinsville and closed in 2007. (Paul Armfield Coffey Collection.)

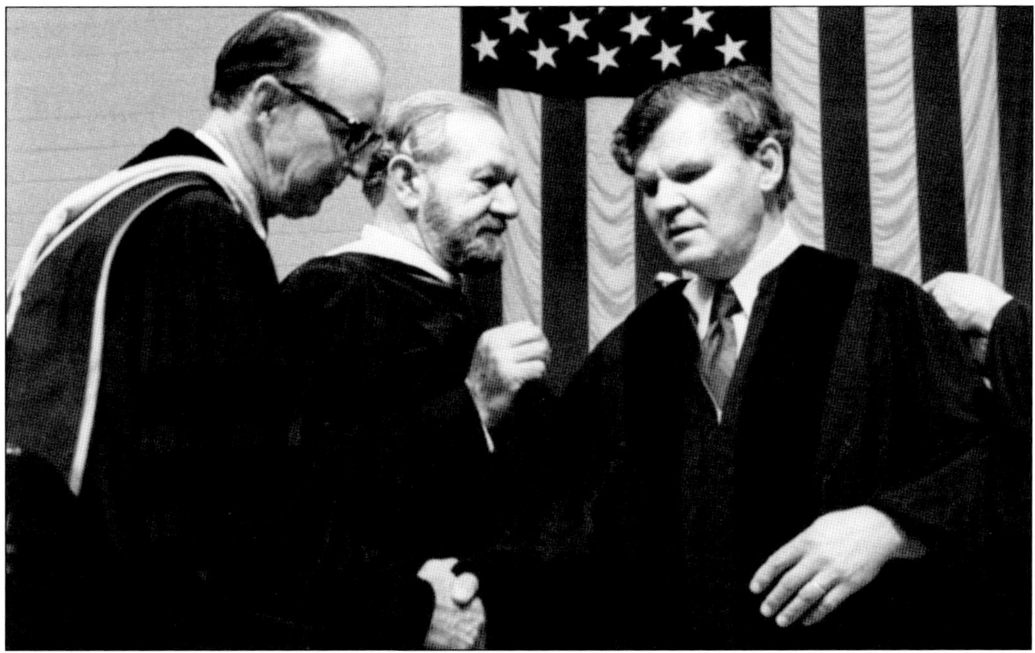

Doc Watson and his son Merle (1949–1985) had national reputations as folk musicians by the 1970s, and together, they recorded more than a dozen albums before Merle's tragic death in a tractor accident. Doc (right) is receiving an honorary degree from Appalachian State University chancellor Herbert Wey (left) and Dr. Rogers Whitener in 1973. Doc Watson Day has been celebrated in Boone every year on the third Friday in June since 2011. (George Flowers Collection.)

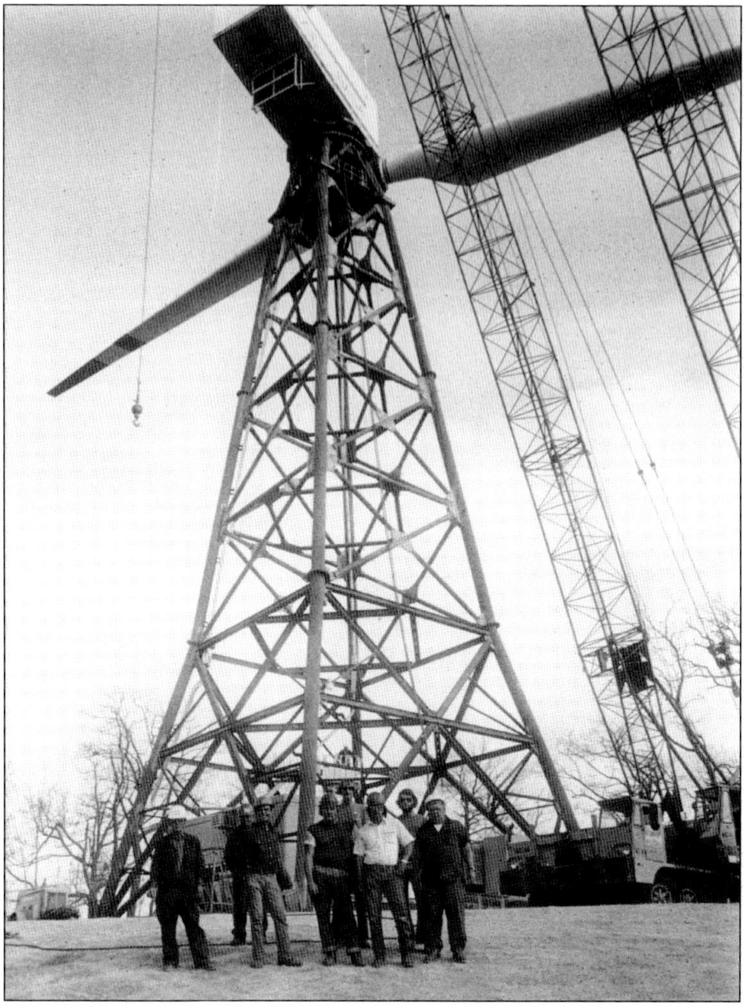

In 1979, this crew installed this experimental General Electric Mod-1 wind turbine on Howard's Knob on behalf of NASA and the US Department of Energy. Local excitement led to a mockumentary on a mythical cult known as the "Whooshies," and one savvy marketer sold cans of air allegedly pushed by the turbine. Mechanical problems plagued the turbine, and it was removed in 1983. (George Flowers Collection.)

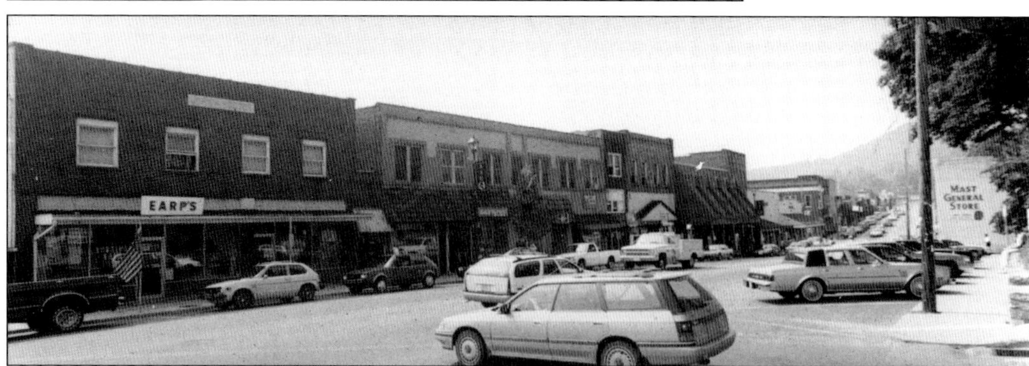

As the 1980s dawned, many of downtown Boone's historic buildings featured additions and inappropriate architectural treatments that obscured their original architecture and beauty. This picture taken at the King Street–Grand Boulevard intersection shows, from left to right, the Hodges Building, Qualls Library Building, Qualls Block, Perry and Winkler Building, H.W. Horton Building, and Boone Drug Company building with its new awning porch. (George Flowers Collection.)

Six

The Character of Boone

1980–Present

During the 1980s, many locals grimaced when developers demolished the Daniel Boone Hotel on King Street, then erected a sprawling condominium complex that dwarfed surrounding properties and eliminated one of Boone's most prized urban green spaces. Meanwhile, downtown merchants saw their prospects dinged with the 1981 opening of the Boone Mall, which offered plentiful parking and a climate-controlled shopping environment. To recapture clientele, some downtown merchants tried to transform downtown into a Disneyesque "mountain village" by appending shed roof porticos and out-of-character architectural treatments or by removing original treatments that had been judged to be passé. All of these changes made residents fear that Boone was losing its charming character.

Meanwhile, Appalachian State University enrollment continued to rise, eventually surpassing residential population levels in the 2010s. Desperate for land on which to build new dorms and classrooms, the university increasingly looked to downtown properties for expansion. To quell these pressures and mitigate uncontrolled development, Boone Town Council instituted stricter zoning measures, even establishing an extraterritorial planning jurisdiction (ETJ) in 1983 as a buffer between town lots with strict zoning and county lots with relatively lax zoning. After the North Carolina legislature revoked Boone's ETJ law in 2014, the Watauga County commissioners weighed in with their support for the move. This action, coupled with a 2013 decision by the Watauga County commissioners to change the method of sales tax distribution from per capita to ad valorem, resulted in multiple lawsuits between the county and town that remain unresolved as of this writing.

Despite this ongoing undercurrent of animosity among town, county, and gown, Boone has nevertheless moved forward in the past 10 years with measures to preserve its history and character. In 2014, the town took control of the historic Boone Cemetery, protecting it from ongoing university intrusions on the property. The Boone Historic Preservation Commission has also worked hard to start its own historical marker program and secure local historic landmark status for several buildings, and as of September 2021, the town was considering the establishment of a downtown Boone local historic district. Time will tell what the future brings to Boone.

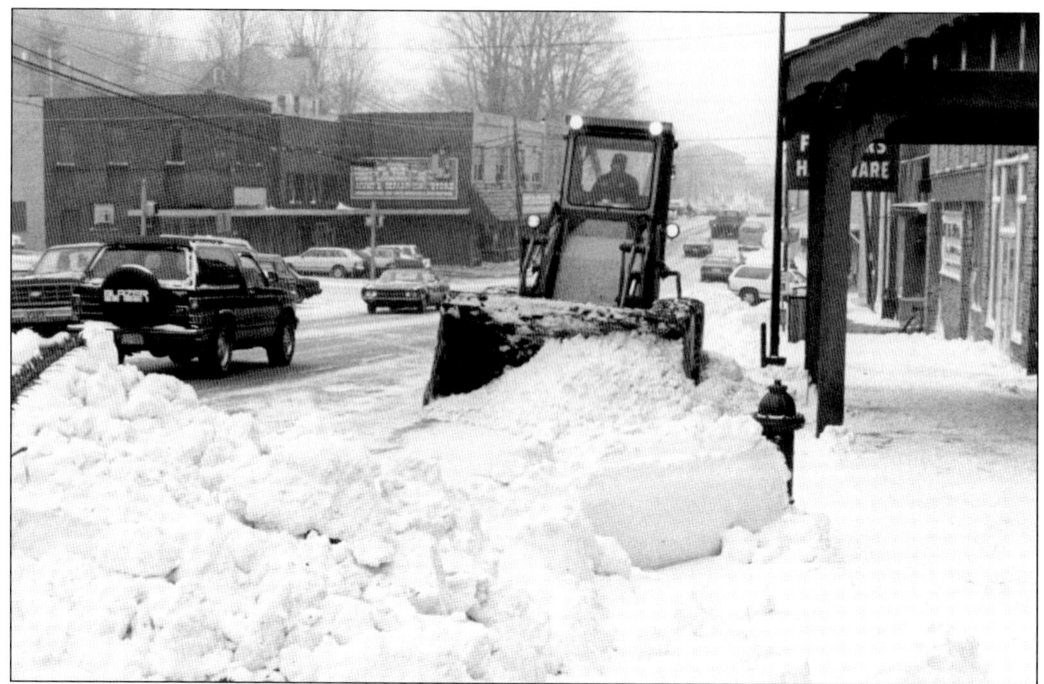

During the early 1980s, some locals began promoting an imagined "mountain village" theme for Boone's historic architecture, with shed-roof porches and awnings as a common treatment downtown. This 1986 image shows one such porch on the east end of the Frank A. Linney Block as a front loader removes the remains of a heavy snowfall from parking places on King Street. (George Flowers Collection.)

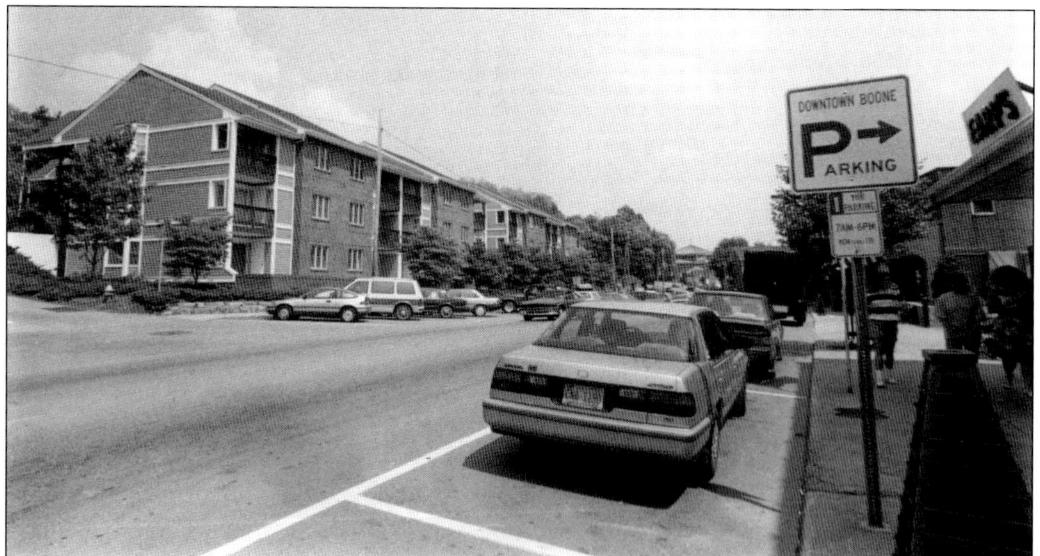

In the early 1980s, preservationists' efforts to save the Daniel Boone Hotel failed, and it was demolished for the Daniel Boone Condominiums (pictured) shortly after the hotel was listed in the National Register of Historic Places. By the 1980s, local merchants also urged the removal of parking meters to help stimulate downtown business lost to the Boone Mall and outlying shopping areas. (George Flowers Collection.)

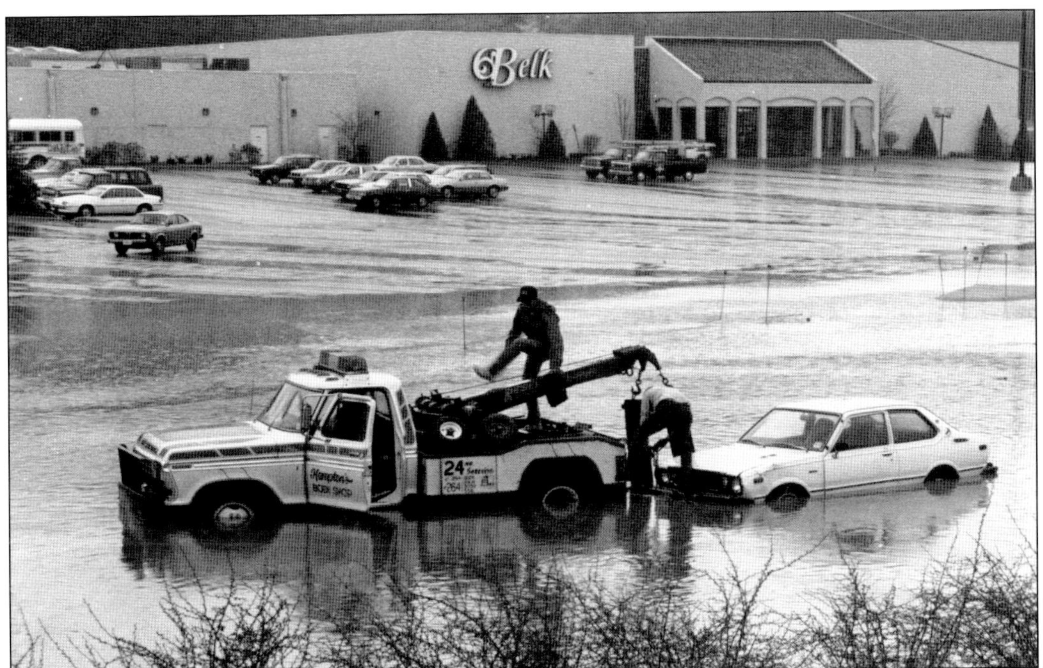

The Boone Mall opened just off Blowing Rock Road in March 1981 despite the fact that much of its parking lot sits in a floodplain at the confluence of Hodges, Winkler, and Boone Creeks. Many locals, like the driver of this car, learned in short order that parking on the northeast side of the mall can be risky during Boone's frequent heavy rain events. (George Flowers Collection.)

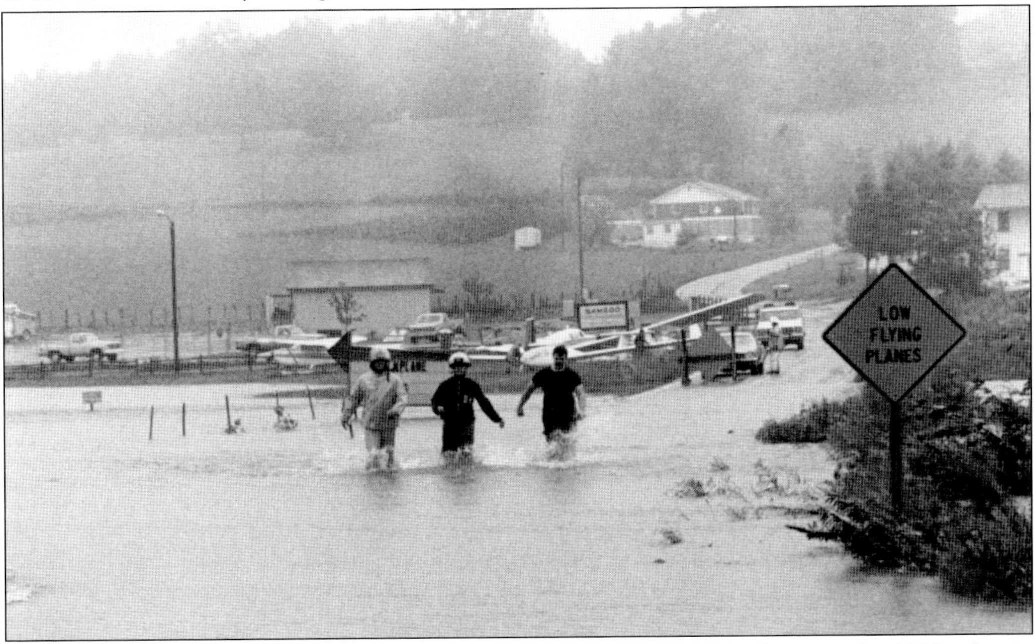

Other parts of Boone also began seeing heavy flooding on a frequent basis in the 1980s, due in part to impervious surfaces in new developments that increased runoff and overwhelmed streams in the Boone basin. In August 1985, flooding at the Boone Airport where Bamboo Road crosses the East Fork of the New River prompted officials to close the road. (George Flowers Collection.)

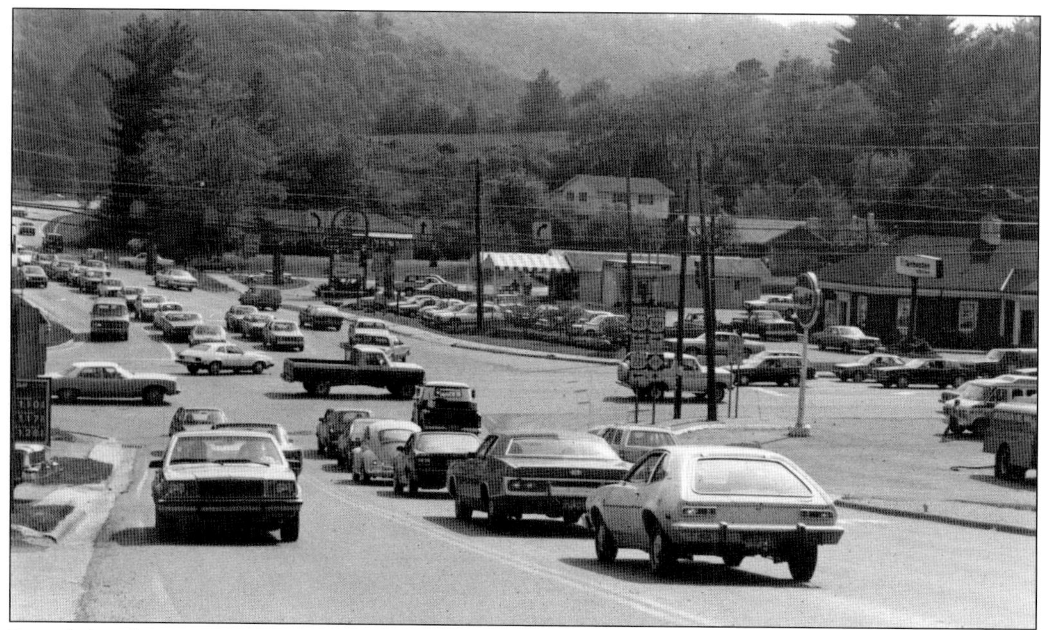

Rapid development of the Blowing Rock Road and NC Highway 105 corridors, coupled with increased mountain tourism, led to major traffic snarls throughout the 1980s. This May 1984 view looking southwest at the NC 105–US Highway 221/321 intersection shows lines of cars queued at the traffic signal. Despite later being widened to six lanes on NC 105 and five lanes on Blowing Rock Road, the intersection remains a bottleneck. (George Flowers Collection.)

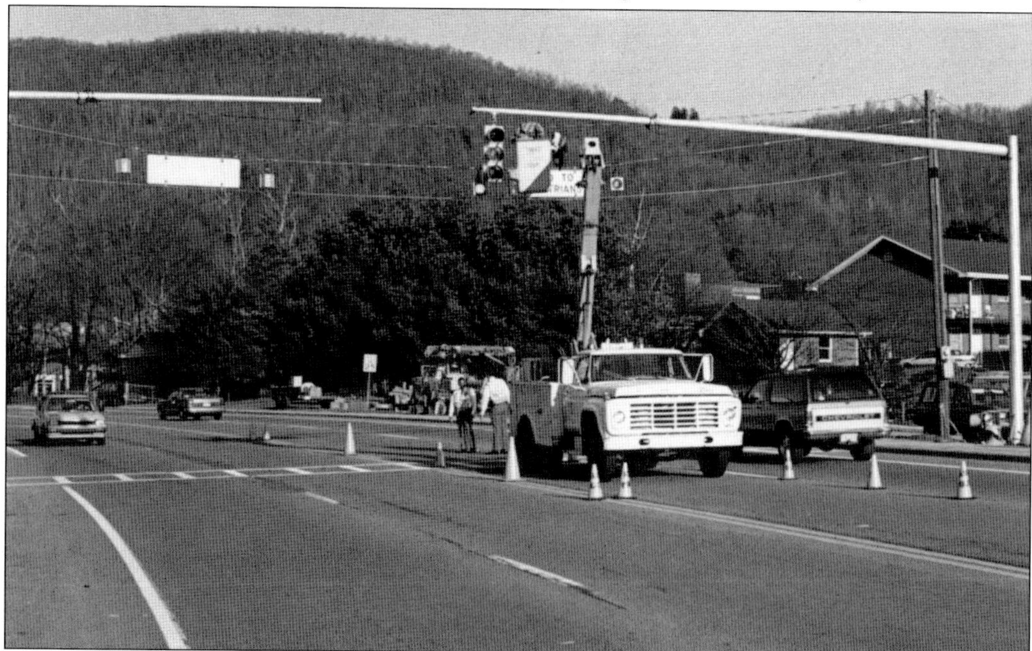

Appalachian State University students had opposed the widening of Rivers Street in the 1970s, and their fears were realized in 1994 when a car struck a professor as he crossed the street. Student protests led to the installation of these pedestrian signals in December 1994 in the hope of minimizing the risks for members of the campus community. (George Flowers Collection.)

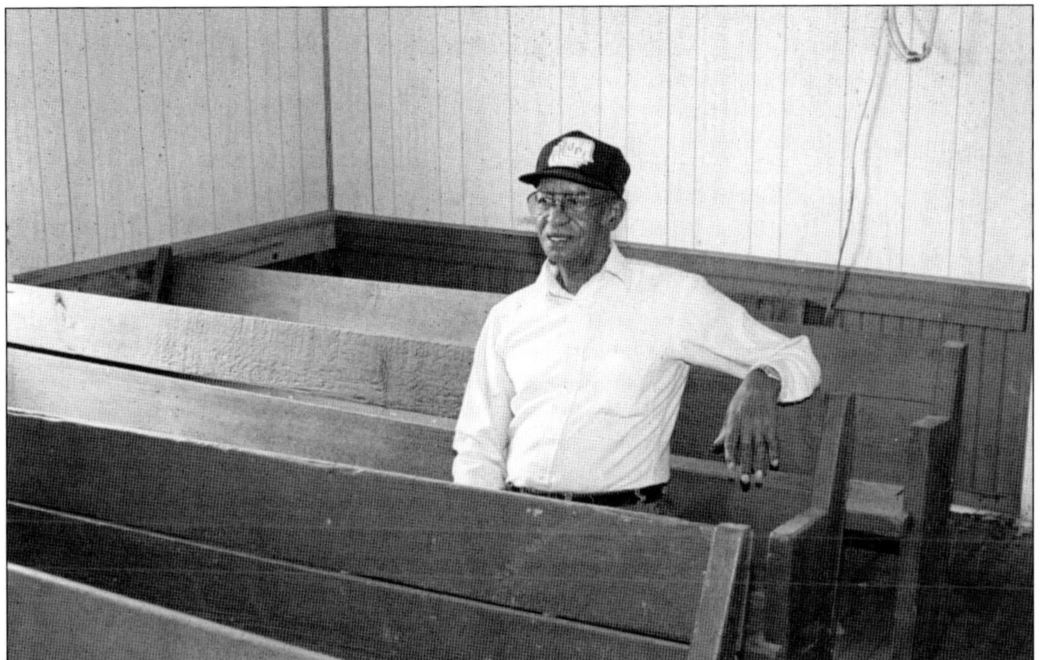

A 1932 lynching incident involving two members of the Horton family in Junaluska prompted a large out-migration of many members of the Boone Chapel, decimating the church and shifting the community's religious heart to Boone Mennonite Brethren. James McQueen, who had worshipped in Boone Chapel as a child, posed for this picture in the church in 1993, shortly before it was demolished in 1996. (George Flowers Collection.)

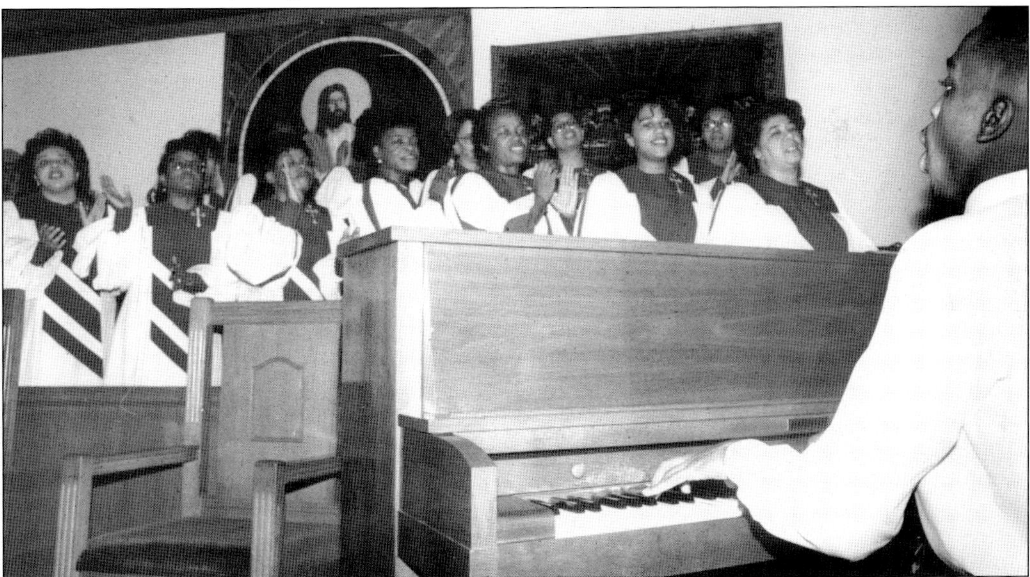

The Boone Mennonite Brethren Church remains the active and vibrant religious and social center of the Junaluska community. Pictured here are members of the Junaluska Gospel Choir performing during a service in the 1980s. While out-migration and gentrification remain serious threats to the Junaluska community, members of the Junaluska Heritage Association work hard to preserve the legacy of their community. (Paul Armfield Coffey Collection.)

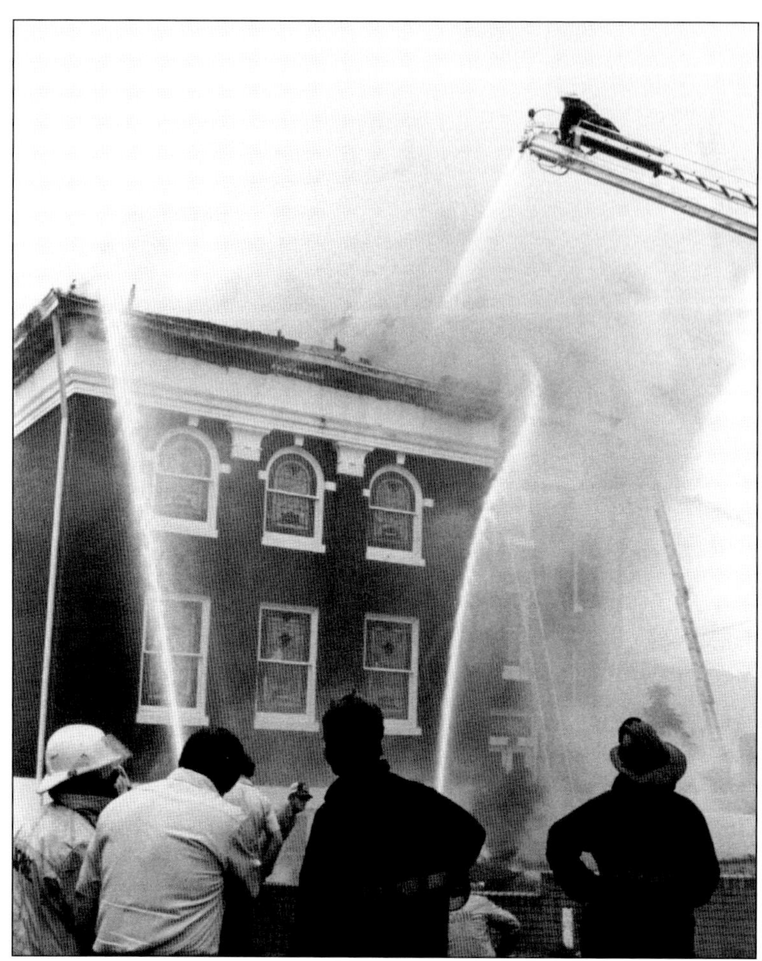

On July 1, 1981, a tar pot exploded during repairs to the Boone Methodist Church roof, sparking a fire that ultimately destroyed the landmark. The congregation rebuilt on the site and occupied the space from 1984 to 1992 before moving to a larger church with expanded parking on New Market Boulevard. The rebuilt church is now part of Appalachian State University's Turchin Center for the Visual Arts. (George Flowers Collection.)

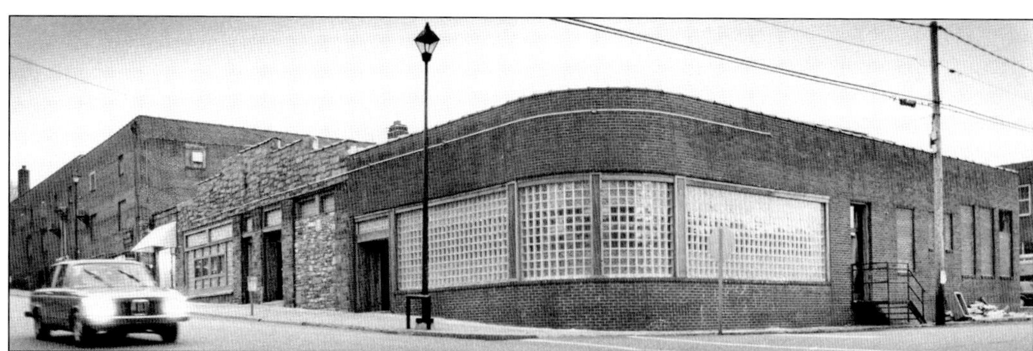

This October 1990 image shows the native stone Cook-Nichols Motor Company Building (1940) and the Winkler Motor Company Building (1947) at the corner of Depot and Howard Streets when they were both occupied by the Depot Street Music Hall. A July 1996 fire destroyed the Cook-Nichols building, leaving a gaping void now occupied by the Footsloggers courtyard and climbing tower. (Historic Boone Collection.)

Continued sprawl by Appalachian State University over the past three decades has been a constant source of conflict for the Boone community. Expansion along Church Street in 1995 forced the removal of the historic St. Luke's Episcopal Church to a lot on Councill Street. Frederick Carter Gilman (1907–1999), the church's oldest member, led the move as crucifer. (George Flowers Collection.)

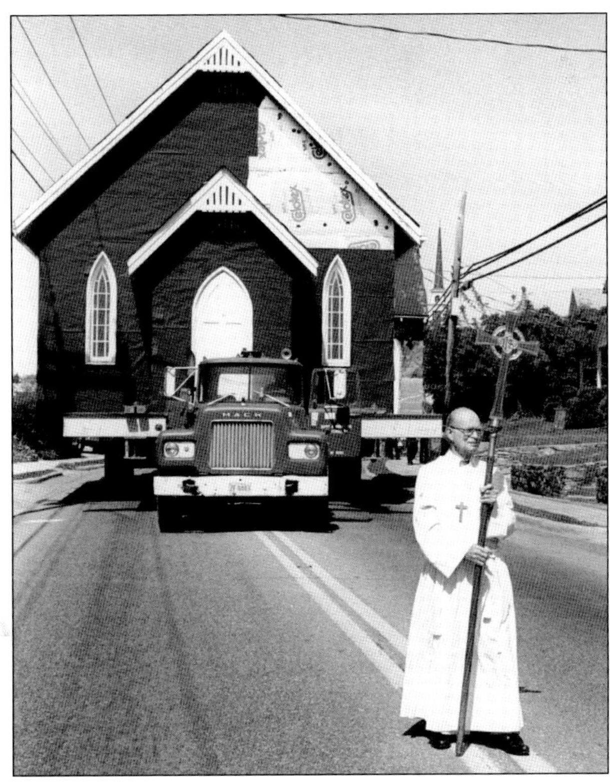

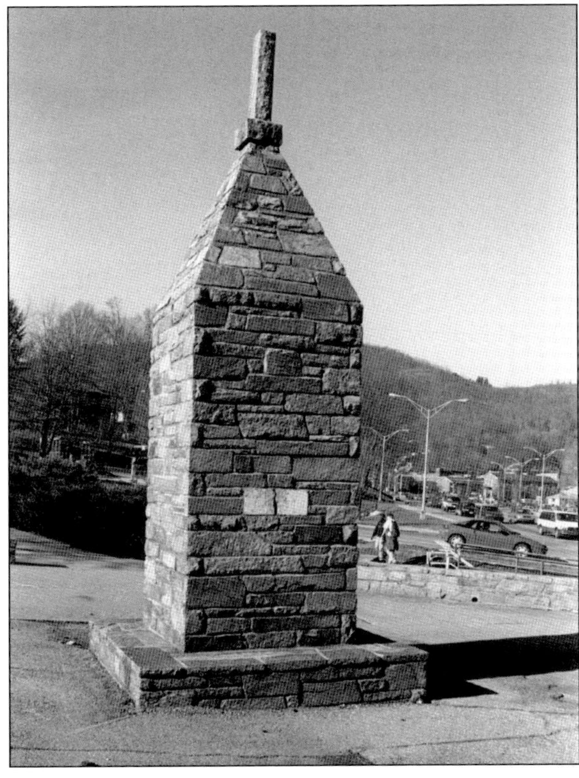

Following the demolition of the original Daniel Boone Monument in 1968, Appalachian State University erected a poorly executed replica at this location north of Justice Hall on Rivers Street. In 1994, ASU destroyed the second monument to make room for a new building that never materialized. Frustrated Town of Boone officials recovered the original plaques and built a third iteration near the Rivers House in 2005. (George Flowers Collection.)

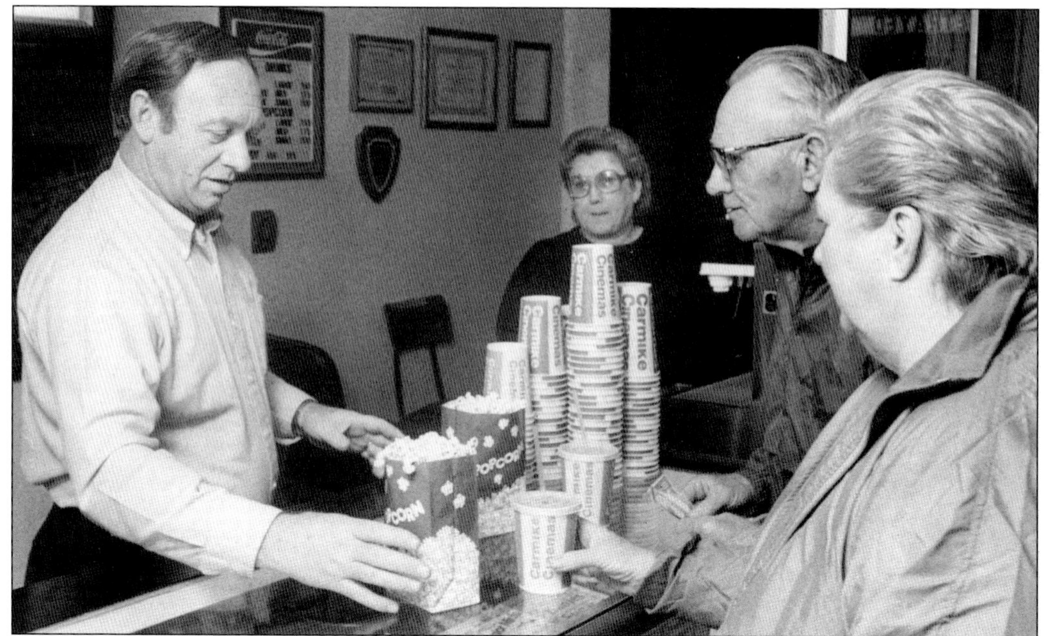

Following the conversion of the Appalachian Theatre on King Street into a twin cinema, Charles Jerry "C.J." Hayes (1936–2014) and his wife, Pauline Greene Hayes (1936–2019), continued to operate the theater they loved until Carmike Cinemas closed it and sold the building in 2007. C.J. and Pauline are pictured behind the counter at the concession stand in November 1988. (Paul Armfield Coffey Collection.)

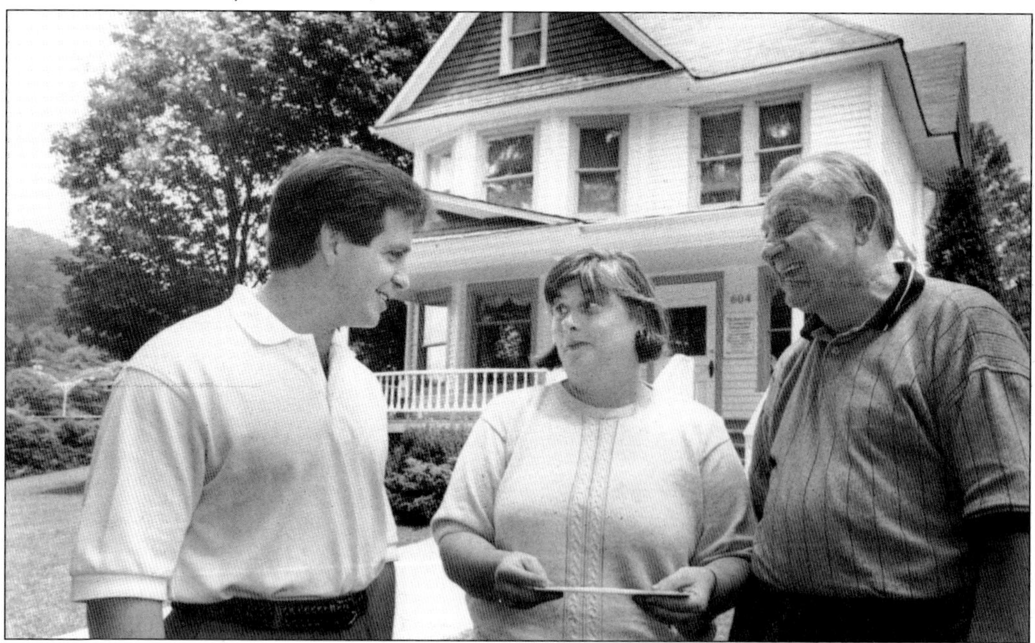

Mazie Jean Jones Levenson's (1914–2013) decision to sell the J. Walter Jones House on King Street to the Town of Boone in 1983 for use as a cultural and community center was a huge preservation win for Boone. Shown in front of the Jones House in the 1990s are Jim Maltba (left) with Kaye Edmisten (center) and Gene Reese from Historic Boone, a now-defunct group. (Historic Boone Collection.)

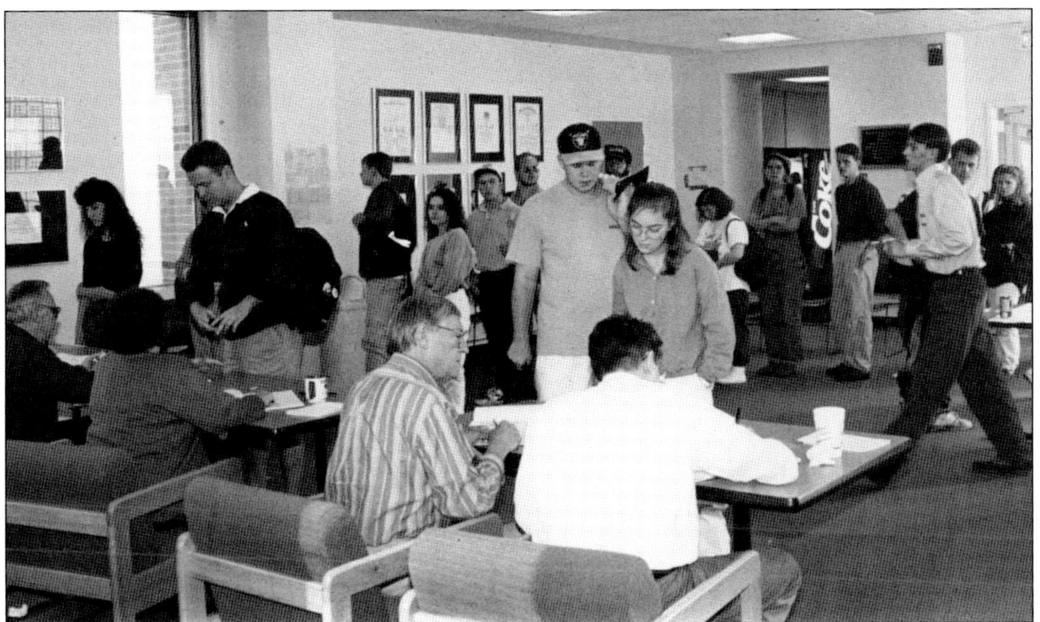

Election controversies still swirl every year over student voting and the placement of voting locations. This 1992 image shows voters lined up to cast ballots after local election officials moved Precinct No. 2's polling place from town hall to the John Walker Business School on the Appalachian State University campus. The move coincided with a dramatic increase in voting turnout. (George Flowers Collection.)

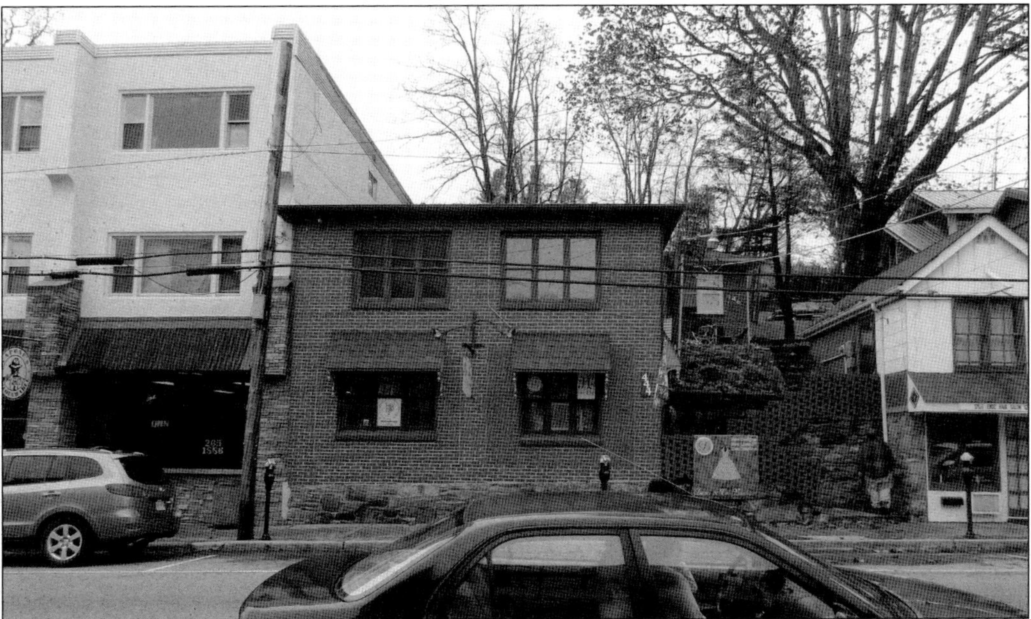

In the 1990s, a lack of affordable workforce housing in Boone, coupled with increasing demand for off-campus student housing, led to development throughout the community. Many landlords began converting their rentals, even in established residential neighborhoods, to a rent-by-the-bedroom model that drove up rental rates and put further pressure on the downtown area and Hippie Hill, which is pictured here in 2015. (Carolina Historical Consulting, LLC, Collection.)

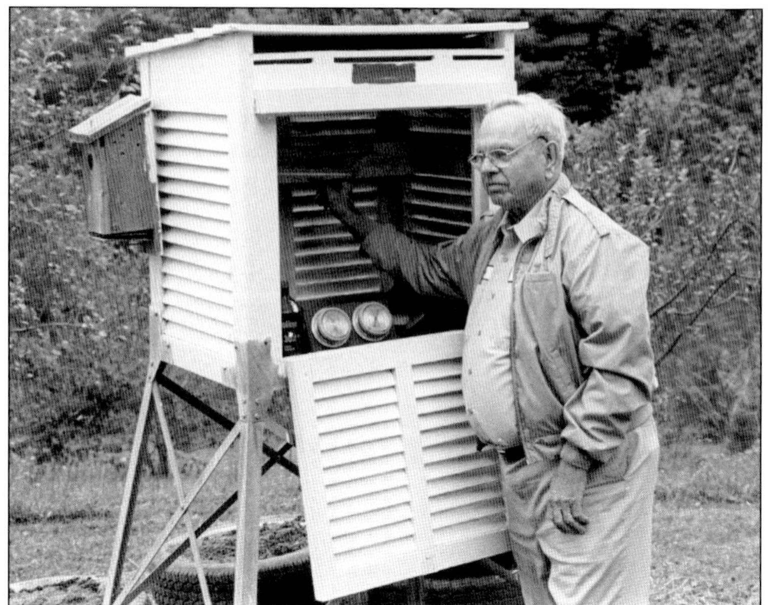

Before Ray's Weather, run by local politician and meteorologist Ray Russell (born 1957), Joe Cecil Minor (1920–2005) was the man with his eye to the sky. Minor worked for 20 years for the *Watauga Democrat*, taught at Watauga High School, founded Minor's Printing Company, and worked for the US Weather Bureau for 40 years. He is shown checking his data in October 1994. (George Flowers Collection.)

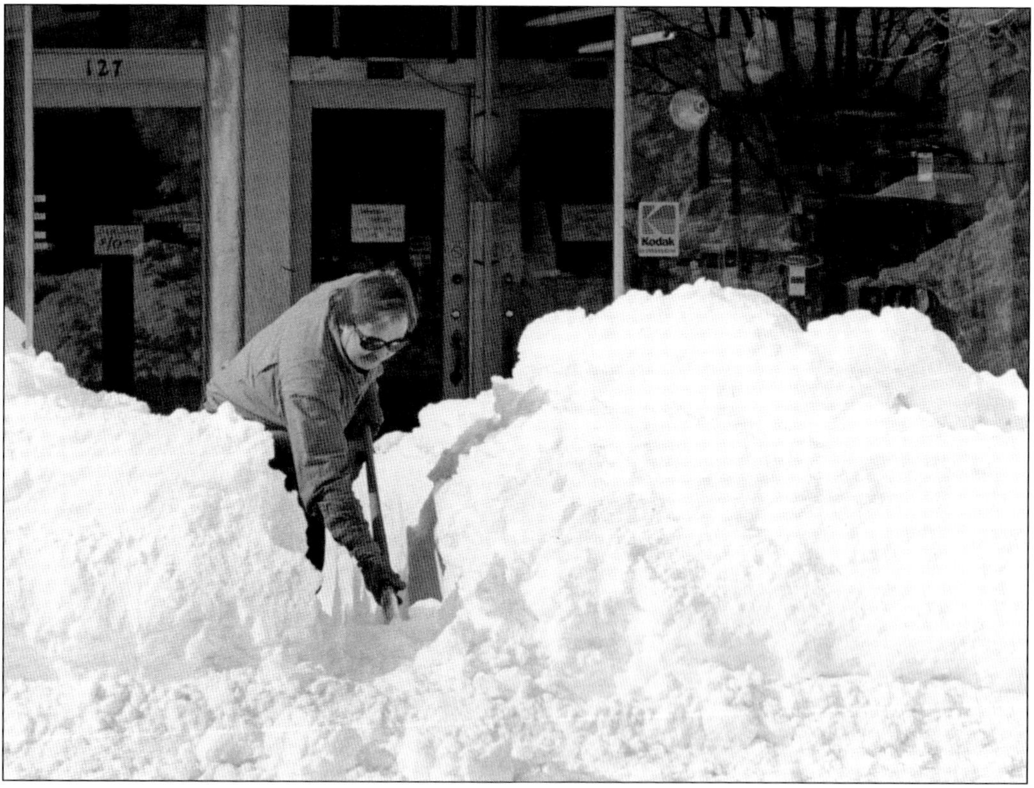

One wonders if Joe Minor knew what was coming in March 1993, when the Storm of the Century ravaged Boone with 30 inches of snow and plunged temperatures into the low teens. The powerful storm necessitated National Guard rescues, as with the March 1960 blizzard. Bob Powell, of the Kelly and Greene Camera Store in the Qualls Block, is pictured shoveling snow after the storm. (George Flowers Collection.)

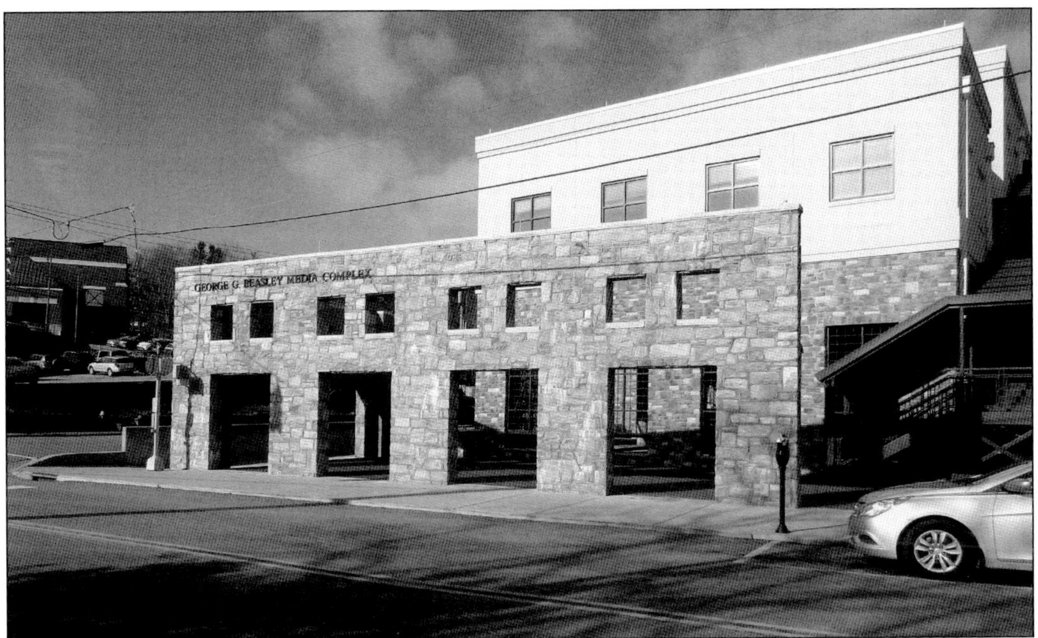

Appalachian State University encroached further on downtown Boone when it bought the former Boone Bus Terminal and demolished it in 2011. Despite promising to clean and reuse the original stones in the construction of a curtain wall for the Beasley Broadcasting Complex, the new wall failed to replicate the original piercings and uses stones of a different cut, suggesting they are not the originals. (Carolina Historical Consulting, LLC, Collection.)

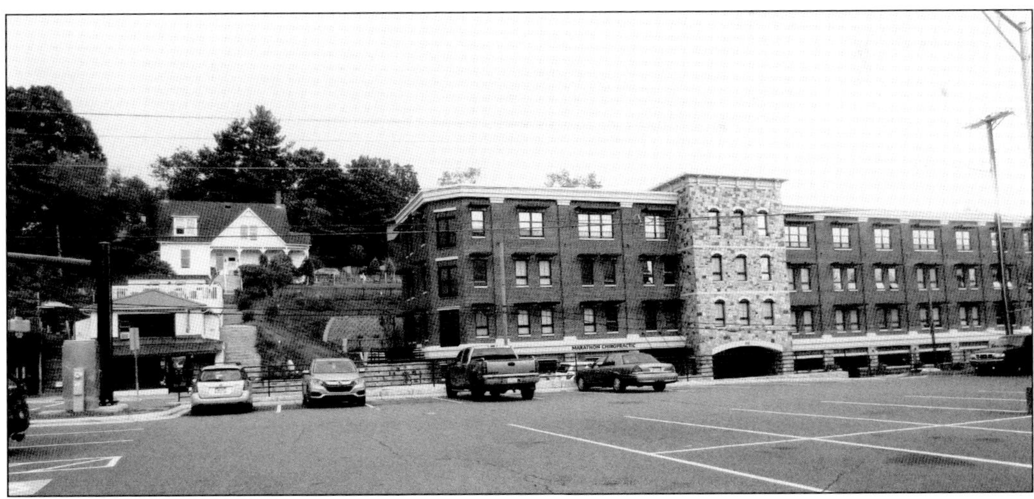

In the mid-2010s, Boone Town Council approved several out-of-scale, mixed-use housing complexes built to appeal to college students. This 2021 image shows the new King Street Flats building dwarfing the historic John W. Hodges Sr. House (1910) and its associated garage/office building (1930) on King Street near Church Street. Other complexes included the Standard and Rivers Walk, which both stretch well over 500 feet in length. (Eric Plaag Collection.)

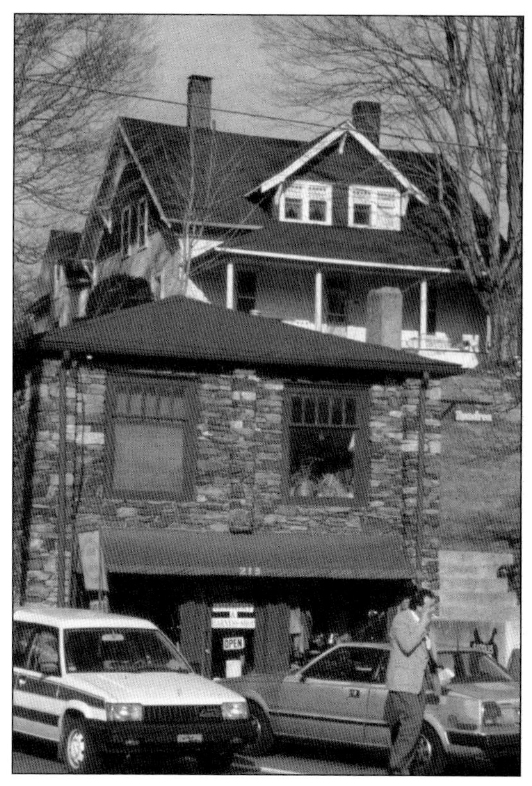

Ongoing threats to the town's historic resources prompted the Boone Historic Preservation Commission to conduct a comprehensive architectural survey of downtown Boone beginning in 2015. In 2017, the Boone Town Council, with owner consent, officially designated the Frank A. Linney House and the Linney Law Office, pictured around 1995, as local historic landmarks. The Boone post office was designated as a landmark in 2016. (Downtown Boone Development Association Collection.)

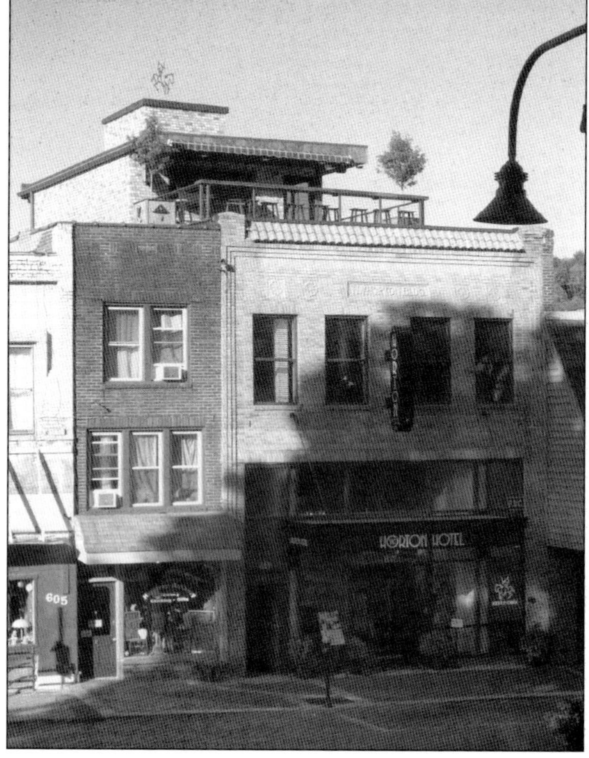

A strong desire for outdoor seating prompted several downtown building owners to pursue rooftop dining options during the 2010s. While some projects were carried out as part of general adaptive reuse and preservation efforts, the careful balance between preservation and adaptive reuse was not always achieved. Pictured here in August 2019 is the Horton Hotel, an adaptive reuse of the H.W. Horton Building. (Carolina Historical Consulting, LLC, Collection.)

John Cooper, chairman at the Mast General Store, poses at the Little Red Schoolhouse in Valle Crucis around 1990. He and his wife, Faye, reinvigorated Boone with their 1987 purchase and renovation of Hunt's Department Store for a new Mast location. In the 2010s, they facilitated the resurrection of the Appalachian Theatre. They received the Order of the Long Leaf Pine in 2017. (Historic Boone Collection.)

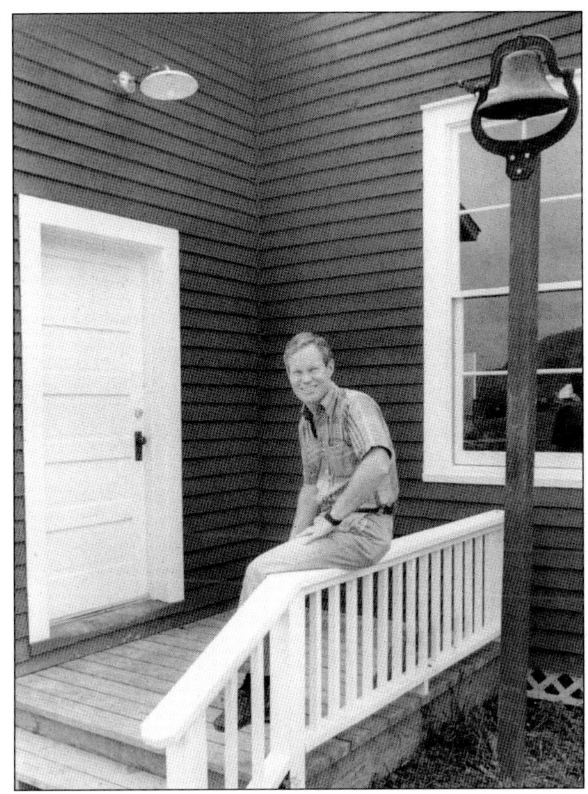

After the Appalachian Theatre closed in 2007, a developer purchased the property, gutted most of the building, and then lost the property to foreclosure during the Great Recession. The Town of Boone purchased the property, then worked with the Appalachian Theatre of the High Country—which now owns the site—to rehabilitate the theater into a modern performance venue. It reopened in October 2019. (Carolina Historical Consulting LLC Collection.)

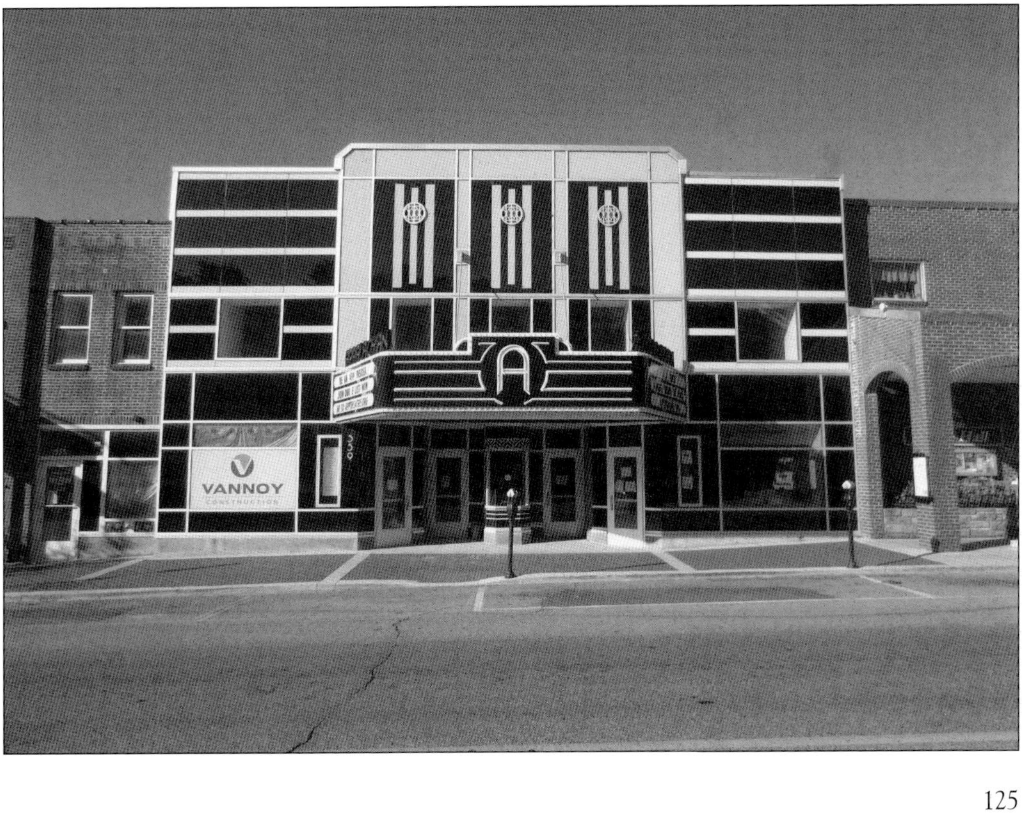

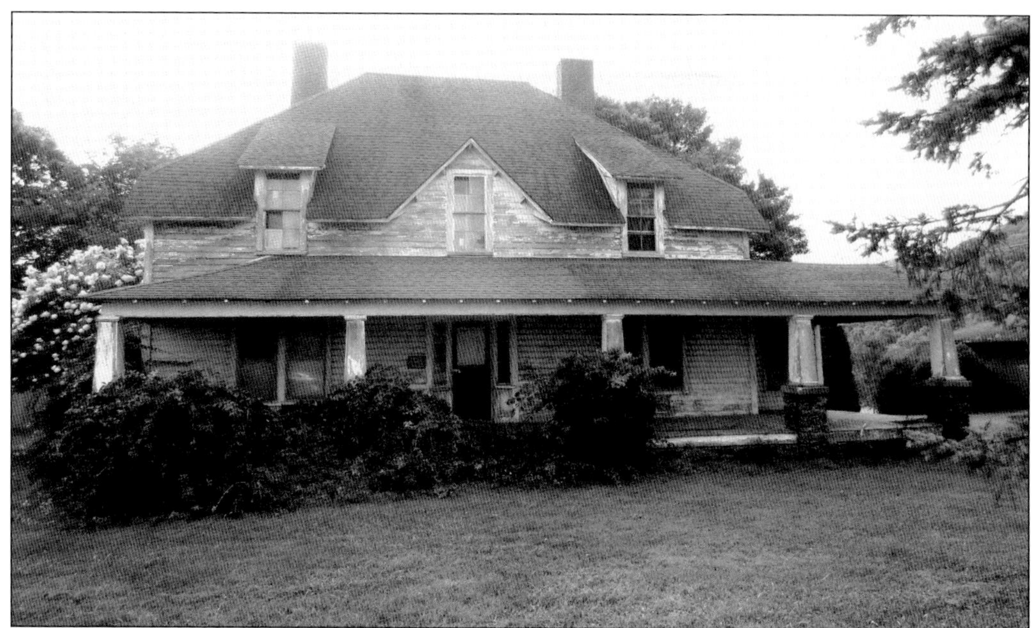

The William Wallace Dixon Edmisten House (1894), once located at the intersection of Deerfield and Blowing Rock Roads, was clad in German siding and featured a center-hall plan with an unusually steep hipped roof clad in tin. A 1930s barn was also on the site. The Watauga Medical Center acquired the National Register–eligible property in 2016, then demolished both buildings in 2020 for a construction staging area. (Eric Plaag Collection.)

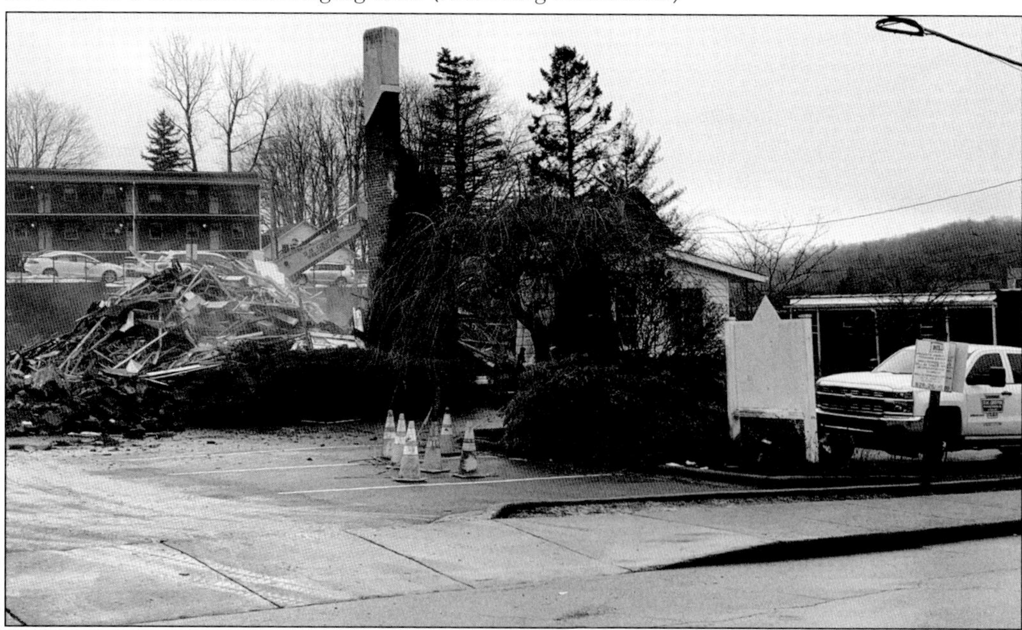

Eager to create a parking area closer to the courthouse, the Watauga County commissioners acquired the Hardin House in 2018 for use as a future parking deck site. Despite an agreement with the Town of Boone to explore an alternative location nearby, the commissioners voted suddenly—over public opposition—to demolish the house. The county bulldozed the house in January 2021, triggering outrage throughout the community. (Eric Plaag Collection.)

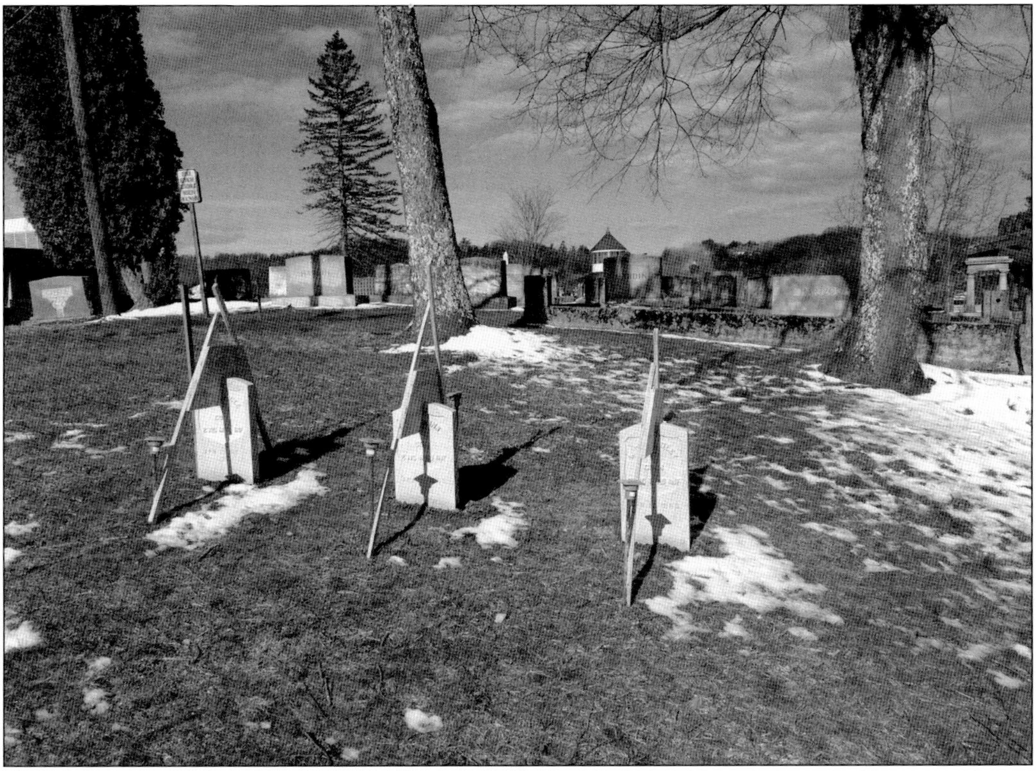

Following Stoneman's Raid in 1865, three Union soldiers died from disease and were buried in the Black section of the Boone Cemetery. Markers provided in the 1870s disappeared in the early 2000s. In 2018, the Town of Boone installed replacement stones with the assistance of the local Grand Army of the Republic chapter. This March 2018 image shows the newly installed stones just before their dedication. (Eric Plaag Collection.)

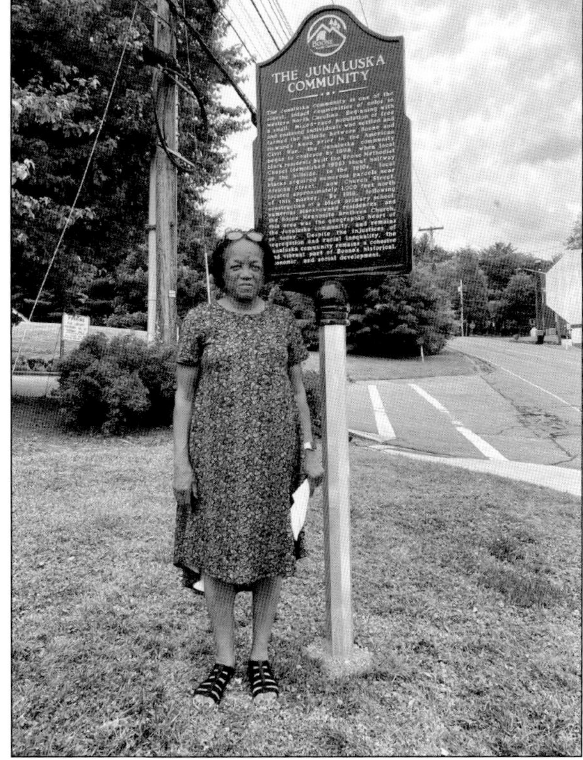

The Town of Boone has its own historical marker program, with a number of sites in the pipeline for recognition. In 2021, the Boone Historic Preservation Commission, the Town of Boone, and the Junaluska Historical Association worked together to create this marker honoring the history and resilience of the Junaluska community. Roberta Jackson, facilitator for the JHA, stands next to the marker in June 2021. (Sai Estep Collection.)

Consistent with our mission to preserve history on a local level, this book was printed in South Carolina on American-made paper and manufactured entirely in the United States. Products carrying the accredited Forest Stewardship Council (FSC) label are printed on 100 percent FSC-certified paper.

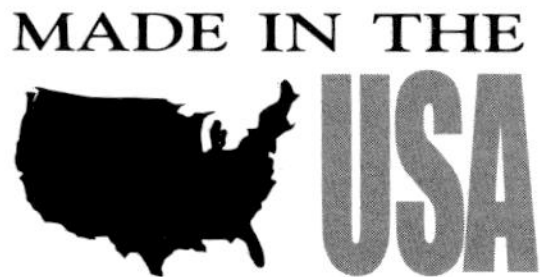